# Objectifying Measures

*The Dominance of High-Stakes
Testing and the Politics of Schooling*

Amanda Walker Johnson

TEMPLE UNIVERSITY PRESS
Philadelphia

Temple University Press
1601 North Broad Street
Philadelphia, PA 19122
www.temple.edu/tempress

♾ The paper used in this publication meets the requirements of the American
National Standard for Information Sciences—Permanence of Paper for Printed Library
Materials, ANSI Z39.48-1992

Library of Congress Cataloging-in-Publication Data

Johnson, Amanda Walker.
    Objectifying measures : the dominance of high-stakes testing and the politics of
schooling / Amanda Walker Johnson.
        p.   cm.
    Includes bibliographical references and index.
    ISBN 978-1-59213-905-7 (hardcover : alk. paper)—ISBN 978-1-59213-906-4 (pbk. : alk.
paper)  1. Educational tests and measurements—Texas.   2. Examinations—
Validity—Texas.   I. Title.
    LB3052.T4J64 2009
    371.2609764—dc22                                                    2008048719

2 4 6 8 9 7 5 3 1

# Contents

# Acknowledgments

This work was supported by funding from the National Science Foundation and the Ford Foundation, as well as resources from the University of Texas at Austin and from the University of Massachusetts Amherst.

First, I must thank the Honorable Representative Dora Olivo, whose unyielding commitment to quality educational experiences for all children was truly inspiring and transformational, and whose openness, kindness and mentorship made it possible for me to do this project. I also thank Vivian, Mary, and Angie, who also made this project possible, for providing me with invaluable knowledge, help, and camaraderie. I also thank those tireless activists who worked over the course of the 78th session of the Texas Legislature for equity in education, especially those that frequented Representative Olivo's office to offer help.

I am extremely grateful to the people who most helped and inspired me in the research and writing process: Edmund T. Gordon, Angela Valenzuela, Charles Hale, João Costa Vargas, and Asale Angel-Ajani. Thanks for teaching me not only what activist scholarship is, but also, by example, how it is done. I also thank Justine Dymond, who helped me refine my writing. I give special thanks to Katya Gibel Mevorach for her mentorship and invaluable wisdom, and to others who have shaped my thinking, including Richard Valencia, Kamala Visweswaran, Melbourne Tapper, Sheila Walker, Mary S. Black, and the late and wonderful teacher Enrique (Henry) Trueba.

To the Center for African and African American Studies at the University of Texas at Austin, thank you for providing me support and the space to develop my research. In particular, I hope that this work honors the memory of Vincent Woodard, a beautiful writer and poet whose encouragement keeps me going to this day. I would not have been able to complete this project without the peer mentors at the Center who helped me secure funding, find the courage to begin writing, and see how to balance activism and scholarship, especially Jemima Pierre, Stephen Ward, Keisha-Khan Perry, Shaka McGlotten, Whitney Battle-Baptiste, Lisa Moore, Paula Saunders, Kevin Foster, and B.C. Harrison.

I am indebted to Maria "Cuca" Robledo Montecel and Roy Johnson of the Intercultural Development Research Association and the entire IDRA staff, who provided me with tremendous warmth and support to be able to finish the initial writing stage.

I also wish to acknowledge the tremendous teachers I met over the course of this project, especially Ms. Smith, whose love for her students and passion for teaching have been inspiring. I must also thank all the students I tutored, who helped me remember why I was writing.

Thanks to Micah Kleit and Temple University Press for giving me this tremendous chance, and to the University of Massachusetts Amherst for giving me the opportunity to continue my work and develop as an engaged scholar, especially the faculty, staff, and students of the Anthropology Department.

Finally, I thank my parents Adonica and Lawrence Walker, and also Rowena and John Roby and James Phillip Johnson for showing so much support along the way, and my sisters Erika Williams, Angela Walker, and Tina Walker and my "other-sister" Rukiya Surles for their unending support, for listening to my ideas and frustrations and helping me to get through the rough patches. Also, I thank my great friend Nadia Heredia, who was always there to help me and provide moral support. To Nygel, Mayme, and Mason, thanks for helping me stay grounded, particularly after long hours of writing. I thank especially Phillip Johnson, who has been my rock and source of courage during this whole process and without whom this project would not have been possible.

# 1 / Introduction

In 1984, the Texas Legislature began constructing an educational system that would place higher and higher stakes on students' performance on standardized tests. More than twenty years later, students must pass state-mandated tests not only to graduate from high school, but also to move on to the fourth, sixth, and ninth grades. Ironically, the constant public surveillance, the constant dissemination of statistics, and the "continual alteration" and "doublethink," characteristics of the world imagined by George Orwell in *1984*, are all aspects of the system of high-stakes testing in Texas. Students are constantly being tested, not only by the state, but also by individual districts preparing students for the state exam. Test results for schools and districts are highly publicized in the media, painted across headlines in nearly every major Texas newspaper. Between 1984 and 2004, Texas had phased in three different assessment exams, and each new exam had increased in difficulty. In 2004, the score considered passing for the exams was higher than that of the previous year. This system of testing, which has been named "accountability," leaves students to bear the largest burden. High-stakes testing systems are only fueled by educational heroic myths such as the idealization of Joe Clark in *Lean on Me*, for which the real measure of pedagogical success is the unveiling of the envelope with the standardized test results.

Behind the statistics and the educational heroic myths are students like Jessica,[1] a bright young Latina high school student I tutored at a local Austin Public Library branch, whose mother drove across town in the dizzying maze of city traffic to bring her daughter to after-school tutoring in math. I could tell that Jessica was not receiving the kind of personal attention she needed in school, and I suspected that the school may have even mistaken the difficulty she had storing information in her long-term memory for a lack of motivation. I learned from the tutoring coordinator at the library that Jessica had failed her Texas Assessment of Academic Skills (TAAS) test twice, and the coordinator asked me to continue to tutor her over the summer. She was already a junior and needed to pass the test soon in order to graduate with her peers. When the summer came, the coordinator told me that Jessica was not coming, that she had already begun calling herself a failure and was ready to give up. I never saw or heard from Jessica again. The hope in her eyes that appeared whenever she solved a difficult problem and the self-recognition in her voice that appeared when she found that she *did* understand algebra were dashed by a data-processing corporation far removed from her reality, by a test that could not truly represent her achievement, by a system that imposed on her a label of "failure," by a single statistic empowered to function as a gatekeeper between graduates and dropouts. Indeed, one could even describe her as "becoming a statistic," a symbol of an impending invisibility that would ultimately be attributed to her own individual deficiency. This book is for students like Jessica, who become objectified and silenced by the measures of high-stakes testing regimes.

This ethnographic study interrogates the connections between the political struggles in Texas that both produce and resist high-stakes testing and forms of truth produced about students through high-stakes testing, particularly statistics. Several questions form the basis of my study: What are the historical and political contexts and social implications of reducing students, like Jessica, to their test scores, particularly in a state such as Texas, with its racialized histories of colonization, slavery, Jim Crow and de facto segregation, gender conservativism, and regional and local economic disparities? What forms of objectification, knowledge production, and silences work not just to reinforce such a system of testing, but also to provide openings for challenging the system?

The impetus for this study and for a growing body of literature on high-stakes testing is both the passage of President George W. Bush's No Child Left Behind Act, requiring states to increase the amount of testing, and several legal challenges to state testing systems in Texas, New York, Minnesota, Louisiana, California, and Massachusetts. As national and state legislators addressed No Child Left Behind, students, parents, and organizations across the country began protesting against high-stakes testing. In Massachusetts, nearly three hundred students boycotted their state-mandated test and organized an "anti-MCAS [Massachusetts Comprehensive Assessment System] movement called the Student Coalition for Alternative to MCAS, SCAM." One sophomore who joined SCAM objected to the fact that "education is starting to be reduced to 'what we can put on the test,'" and another student held a sign at a rally that read, "Don't confine our minds to bubbles. Stop the MCAS" (Shaw 2000: 42).

In September 2002, twelve English and social studies teachers from Curie Metropolitan High School in Chicago composed a letter "intending to refuse to administer the controversial CASE (Chicago Academic Standards Examinations)" (Schmidt 2002). Two years earlier in Illinois, about two hundred students purposely filled in wrong answers in protest against a new state exit exam (Shaw 2000). The inequalities of standardized testing led seniors in Los Angeles to boycott the Stanford Achievement Test—Ninth Edition (SAT-9), and subsequently sparked a movement by the Coalition for Educational Justice to lobby for parental notification of their right to waive testing for their children (Wat 2003). Both the Los Angeles and San Francisco school boards voted to study and develop alternative assessments to the state-mandated tests, promoted by then governor Gray Davis. In Wisconsin, parents and educators fought against the imposition of high school exit exams and promotion exams (Shaw 2000). In Louisiana, Virginia, and Texas, tests were challenged in the courts on the basis that they were racially discriminatory. In 2002, NCS Pearson, with whom Texas contracts for administering and scoring its mandated tests, agreed to a $7 million settlement after it incorrectly reported that eight thousand students in Minnesota had failed their exams (Pugmire 2002).

In Texas, the Mexican American Legal Defense and Education Fund (MALDEF) challenged the state testing system, then the TAAS, in the courts on the basis that the testing system disproportionately denied Black and Latino students their high school diplomas. The federal court ruled in 1999 that despite the statistical proof of the disparate impact of the tests, the testing system, implemented with no (proven) intention to discriminate on the basis of race, was justifiable on the grounds that it was educationally necessary and objective. Further, the trend of decreasing gaps between Whites and students of color indicated to the court that the testing system, instead of creating discrimination, exposed inequalities and was then a tool for alleviating inequalities—ultimately caused by individual factors, such as socioeconomic status, parental involvement, and student motivation (*GI Forum et al. v. Texas Education Agency et al.*, 87 F. Supp. 2d 667 [2000]; Saucedo 2000). During the case, the Texas Legislature, under the guidance of then governor George W. Bush, passed bills requiring third-, fifth-, and eighth-grade students to pass a state-mandated exam in order to be promoted to the next grade; expanding the testing subjects required for high school graduation; and replacing the TAAS with a more difficult assessment called the Texas Assessment of Knowledge and Skills (TAKS).

Urged on by MALDEF, Texas state representative Dora Olivo led an effort to pass bills that would decrease the stakes of testing, expanding the decisions to promote students beyond testing, which had essentially become the single criterion for passing (Valenzuela 2002). The alternative Representative Olivo promoted was "multiple criteria," in which portfolios, grades, and teacher evaluations could be weighed against failure on state assessments, and which gave parents more input into the decision to pass or retain their children in a particular grade. In 2001, in the 77th Texas legislative session, Representative Olivo authored two multiple-criteria bills concerning graduation and the promotion of third, fifth, and eighth graders to the next grade. Though the bills passed through the House Public Education Committee and the full House, they were held (and effectively killed) in a Senate committee. At the national level, Senator Paul Wellstone[2] in 2001 proposed a similar multiple-criteria bill (S 460) to coincide with No Child Left Behind. Citing the report by the National Research Council of the National Academy of Sciences, commissioned by Congress in 1997, the bill (S 460, § 1(a)(5)(C)) stated the following: "High stakes decisions such as tracking, promotion, and graduation, should not automatically be made on the basis of a single test score but should be buttressed by other relevant information about the student's knowledge and skill, such as grades, teacher recommendations, and extenuating circumstances" (S 460, 107th Cong., 1st sess. (March 6, 2001).[3] Though it garnered support from teacher organizations such as the National Education Association and the National Council of Teachers of Mathematics, Wellstone's bill also suffered defeat.

Despite these defeats, in the 2003, 78th legislative session, the Texas representative attempted to pass the multiple-criteria bills again, with the stakes raised higher, since in 2003, for the first time in Texas, third graders would be required to pass state assessments in reading (TAKS) in order to go on to the fourth grade. It is this movement behind the effort to pass these multiple-criteria bills in Texas that forms the heart of my study.

In Texas, in the face of the court rulings and new legislation, a body of literature critiquing high-stakes testing emerged from the experts testifying in that case on the side of MALDEF, particularly Linda McNeil, Angela Valenzuela, Richard Valencia, and Walt Haney. McNeil (2000a) presented the historical and political-economic context in which testing in Texas was implemented, linking it to a broader project of educational reform led by Ross Perot in 1984. Advocates of testing in Texas, Skrla, Scheurich, and Johnson (2000) argued that the system raises student and school accountability (and achievement) through public access to disaggregated testing data[4] and a shift from an "input-driven" to "results-driven" accountability model; thus, the system effectively closes the educational gap between Whites and minorities. However, critics of testing argue that the mandate to raise scores at any cost creates new inequities since, increasingly, Texas schools practice the following: (1) teaching to the test, (2) retaining at-risk students in nontesting grades, (3) tracking students of color and economically disadvantaged students in special education courses to prevent their scores from affecting accountability ratings, and (4) encouraging dropping out (Haney 2000; McNeil 2000a, 2000b; Valencia et al. 2001). In *Raising Standards or Raising Barriers?* (2001) edited by Orfield and Kornhaber, Valenzuela and McNeil contributed to essays that explored the impact on students of color of testing, particularly minimum-competency tests and other state-mandated exams required for high school graduation (and recently for grade promotion). In the volume, authors linked present testing regimes to historical uses of testing, addressing and questioning the hypothesis that high-stakes exams increase educational quality and student motivation for learning, the likelihood of college attendance and completion and, ultimately, postsecondary work productivity. While some of the authors confirmed such a hypothesis, others, including Valenzuela and McNeil, argued that high-stakes testing adversely affects teaching and learning for students of color, particularly students with limited English proficiency; that such testing tends to result in increased dropout rates for students of color; and that it exacerbates inequalities by draining funding from state and federal public education budgets. Valenzuela (2002) argued that these adverse effects stem from placing so many stakes for students, teachers, and school administrators solely on standardized tests (or test results) and that "multiple compensatory criteria in assessment" would both provide a more "reliable and valid measure" of student achievement levels and relieve students, teachers, and families of the pressure associated with test anxiety (106–108).

While this body of literature critiques the educational merits of testing, my study takes an anthropological view of the culture of measurement that places such emphasis on test results, specifically on the production of testing statistics.[5] Many scholars have contextualized the intensification of testing in Texas and across the country within broader neoliberal movements for privatization of public education through intimate corporate involvement, such as occurs with the testing industry, in the public schools (Saltman 2000; Sacks 1999; Apple 2001; Bartlett et al. 2002; Collins 2001). In her ethnography of the Chicago public schools, Lipman (2004) contextualized the high-stakes environment imposed on schools within the intersection of the city's racial and political history and the transformation of the city into a global economic center. For Bartlett et al. (2002), this movement not only transforms the structure of schools to reflect the structure of the free market and industry—through standardized testing, charter schools, vouchers, and other forms of corporate partnership—but also affects local policy through the deployment of "the 'school in the service of the economy.'" These structural and discursive transformations constitute the "marketization of education" (6, 7). McNeil (2000a) conceptualized the discourse of what Bartlett et al. called the "marketization of education" as the articulation of educational goals in the "language of cost accounting" (264). Drawing from the work of Gould (1996) in *Mismeasure of Man*, Sacks (1999) attributed the exponential growth of the testing industry to "the near magical power that quantification, standardization, and the measuring of minds continues to have over Americans" (7). Critics of the accountability system, in Kentucky, for example (Whitford and Jones 2000), have argued that education is being reduced to the measurable, yet, as Sacks commented, standardized testing represents "no more than a statistical sampling of specific skills that are supposedly covered in the curriculum" (1999, 114). Saltman (2000) also asserted that testing allows for the "affirm[ing of] disadvantage as a statistical variable," and "factor[ing] out those disadvantages suffered by poor and nonwhite students" (25). For elementary school teacher Selma Wasserman (2001), the obsession with standards, testing, and quantification stems from the "presumed certainty of numbers" and numbers' "sense of security," given that "with the use of statistics and probability, we measure things that we cannot even see" (30). The political landscape of testing debates tends to be a veritable statistical battleground, in which opposing sides seize statistical methods of proving or disproving either the effectiveness or adverse effects of testing, of which the *GI Forum* case and the bell curve debates (Fraser 1994) are prime examples. I argue that what allows the technique of mass standardized testing and its use as a mode of controlling student populations; the articulation of school purposes through the language of accounting; and the hegemonic certainty of testing systems' production of truth, but also the terrain for the struggle over that production of truth, is *statistics*. Furthermore, the hegemony of testing as part of the marketization of education is maintained through statistical discourse.

I am interested in connecting studies of statistics to education, particularly because educational theory views schools as contradictory sites of both social reproduction, or socialization, and struggles for (and resistance against) cultural hegemony (Althusser 1971; Bowles and Gintis 1976; Bourdieu and Passeron 1977; Morrow and Torres 1995; Freire 1970; Aronowitz and Giroux 1991; Apple and Weis 1983; Willis 1981; Spindler 1997). Standardized testing has an intimate connection to statistics given that educational psychology, via psychologist Charles Spearman, was born out of the Galtonian school of statistics (Desrosières 1998: 139, 145), and the school's statistical innovations (for instance, the bell curve and quartiles) then made possible mass educational testing by state governments and the military (Lemann 1999). Examining testing and the marketization of education through the hegemony of statistical discourse, I follow Kamin (1974), Rose and Rose (1976), Gould (1996), and Valencia (1997) in viewing testing and its racial politics in terms of a cultural critique or study of science. Cultural studies of science (Rouse 1992; Traweek 1993) question the production of facts and the construction of objectivity by scientific networks (Latour 1987) in ways that reinforce capitalism (Rose and Rose 1976), racialization (Baker 1998; Du Bow 1995; Gould 1996; Harding 1993; Menchaca 1997; Stocking 1993; Tapper 1999; Vaughan 1991), constructions of gender and sexism (Haraway 1988; Harding 1991; Hubbard 1990; Keller 1992; Stepan and Gilman 1993; Easlea 1990; Russett 1989), and cultural views of subjectivity, particularly in light of weapons industries (Gusterson 1996), computer technology (Helmreich 1998), and reproductive technologies (Davis-Floyd and Dumit 1998). In terms of statistics, scholars have studied the development of probability calculus from the seventeenth-century on (Stigler 1986; Feinberg 1992; Daston 1988; Hacking 1991;

Porter 1986; Desrosières 1998),[6] but also the development of administrative statistics or "science of the state" (Foucault 1991; Woolf 1989; Hacking 1991; Desrosières 1998), in terms of colonization (Appadurai 1993; Asad 1994), the history of the United States (Cohen 1982; Alonso and Starr 1987), the politics of eugenics in Britain (MacKenzie 1981), racialization and resistance (Nobles 2000), as well as the crafting of nationalistic subjectivities (Urla 1993). While many of these studies tend to focus on modern conceptions of statistics, Woodward's study (1999) discusses statistics, subjectivity, and the formation of "structures of feeling" in the global capitalist postmodern era.

I conceptualize statistics in the Foucauldian sense not only as a discourse that, as a discourse of truth, possesses its own political economy, but also as a technique of governmentality embedded in processes of racialization, commodification, truth production, and subjectivity formation. For Foucault, discourse is the nexus of power and knowledge, whose transmission of power and silences provides the conditions for the reinforcement of power, yet also the conditions for resistance against that reinforcement (1978: 100). What counts as truth is not simply arbitrary, but is formed within a particular political economy, based on the preeminent role of scientific discourse, its production by dominant political and economic institutions (such as the university, military, and media), as well as its "immense diffusion and consumption" through educational and informational systems that in turn make it an "issue of a whole political debate and social confrontation" (Foucault 1984a: 73). These methodological challenges to a singular notion of knowledge and truth have inspired many studies of statistics, along with his writings on the connections between statistics and government, or what he terms *governmentality*. Foucault (1988c, 1991) argued that statistics, as a *savoir* of the state," not only was "indispensable for correct government" (1988c: 77), but also tied "problems specific to the population" to economy, providing the conditions for the emergence of "political economy" (1991: 99, 100). Given that statistics also formed a "moral science" (Hacking 1991), the science of government merged political economy and the "art of self-government."[7] McNay (1992) argued that Foucault conceived of self-government as both "self-policing" and a mode of resisting the "government of individualization" (68). In her critique of Foucault, Spivak (1988) noted the significance of Foucault's insights for analyzing power within the contexts impacted by colonialism, imperialism, and globalization: "Sometimes it seems as if the very brilliance of Foucault's analysis of the centuries of European imperialism produces a miniature version of that heterogeneous phenomenon: management of space—but by doctors; development of administrations—but in asylums; considerations of the periphery—but in terms of the insane, prisoners, and children. The clinic, the asylum, the prison, the university—all seem to be screen-allegories that foreclose a reading of the broader narratives of imperialism" (291).

To understand the ways in which the formation of statistical discourses functions through (and alongside) government and self-government to produce and reproduce particular relations of power, particularly gendered, racial, and class oppression, I connect Foucault's conception of statistics to theories of hegemony by Antonio Gramsci. Like Foucault, Gramsci is concerned with "formations," struggles, contradictions, education, and self-government. Gramsci's status as a political prisoner provided him deep insight into relations of power, leading him to conceptualize hegemony as a form of dominance that operates through an ideological struggle to gain consent or consensus, or the constant articulation of goals of disparate social groups in order to attain self-identification (of those different groups) with a particular collective, "national-popular," or universal will or worldview, that in fact maintains the dominance of a particular class or historic bloc (Simon 1991 [1982]; Mouffe 1979). Like Foucault's political economy of truth, the formation of what is considered truth, or common sense, depends on a type of silence as the "uncritical and largely unconscious way in which a person perceives the world" (Simon 1991 [1982]: 64), and also occurs in the context of struggle and through the educating of consent by the "interventionist state": "The state is both political society and civil society, in other words, hegemony protected by the armour of coercion" (Gramsci 1971: 263). The notion of hegemony allows us to consider the ways in which statistical discourses become common sense through struggle, negotiation, and articulation, as well as provides insight into the ways that particular groups form a historic bloc and function through the state in projecting their worldview and in structuring their dominance.[8] According to Gramsci while hegemony is "ethico-political, it must also be economic" (quoted in Mouffe 1979: 183), and this allows for a Marxist interpretation of the commodification (commodity fetishism) of statistical discourses and an understanding of how the formation of the common sense of testing intersects with economic interests. Thus, while Sacks and Wasserman explained the intensification of testing as a product of an obsession with quantification, I explain it as a product of both the processes by which statistical discourse becomes the commonsensical way of both representing educational achievement and governing educational systems and the individuals and populations within them; and also the political economy of that statistical truth whereby a particular coalition educates this common sense via state interventions and economic consumption.

For Desrosières (1998), the importance of statistics as a technique "for inventing, constructing, and proving scientific facts, both in the natural and social sciences" (3), derives from the process of statistical objectification, or "making *things that hold*, either because they are predictable or because, if unpredictable, their unpredictability can be mastered to some extent, thanks to the calculation of probability" (9; italics in original). Statistical objectification forms "solid things on which the managing of the social world is based" by uniting the "mastering of uncertainty" and the "creation of administrative and political spaces of equivalence" (10). In other words, the materialization of social facts through statistical discourse makes possible the scientific management, engineering, or governance of individuals and populations (see Seltzer and Anderson 2001; Miller and O'Leary 1987; Porter 1995).[9] In this sense, statistics form a "discourse network," described by Tapper (1999) as the assemblage of devices that "articulate certain phenomena [and individuals/populations] as natural or unproblematic targets or instruments of specific practices" (6). My objective is to question how statistical materialization becomes common sense or truth while masking the relations of power that both objectify and commodify or exploit people and knowledge. To me, this project is key in understanding McNeil's (2000a) observation about the process of standardization involved in high-stakes testing, in that "standardization widens educational inequalities and masks historical and persistent inequities" (230).

## Methodology

My study addresses the need indicated by reflections on educational ethnographies for conducting ethnographies outside the classroom. In a genealogy of social theory approaches to education,[10] Morrow and Torres (1995) suggested that what tends to be missing from educational social theory is a theory of public policy formation as a mediation of "societal processes" and the "microanalysis of conflicts within educational systems" (343). In his seminal school ethnography, Willis (1981) suggested a need for studies that shift the gaze toward educational institutions, in order to demystify structure and cultural processes. Similarly,

Devine (1996) pointed to a tendency of school ethnographers to neither go beyond the classroom nor examine broader issues of power—which for him starts even in the school hallways. In a reflection on his own ethnographies of Black students, McDermott (1997) wrote that his focus on Black students for answers to their failure wound up individualizing what is a cultural and social production of failure. These calls for a shift in the anthropological gaze from the student, which can be individualizing (see also MacLeod 1995), to institutions mirror the call for shifting the anthropological gaze from groups of people inscribed by processes of colonization and imperialism as "premodern" and "primitive" to the sociocultural processes central to modernity, a call that produced the anthropology of science (Fischer 1991: 530). This shift in the anthropological gaze emerged from critiques in the post–World War II era of the role of science, particularly with the bombings of Nagasaki and Hiroshima (Rose and Rose 1976), and anthropology in colonialism and U.S. imperialism (Balandier 1966 [1951]; Gough 1968; Lewis 1973; Asad 1973; Willis 1969; Fabian 1983). According to Gusterson (1996), the anthropology of science is part of a "third wave" of anthropology whose subject is "the functioning of power and flux of identities within an integrated global system" (x). Framed as "studying up" (Nader 1972; Helmreich 1998), ethnographies of science "deconstruct . . . [media and scientific] discourses precisely by drawing attention to their presumptions, their particular groundings, or the social contexts from which they are staged" (Fischer 1991: 529).

Like Bartlett et al. (2002), who suggested that the "ethnographic study of policy formation" should take into account the historical context, political economy, and social struggle (or micropolitics) inherent in discourse production and public debates, my study examines the importance of scientific discourses in forging, maintaining, and struggling against the hegemony of certain educational policies. Bartlett et al. (2002) employed an ethnographic method they called "critical-discourse analysis,"[11] which involves conducting "public anthropology," which "engages in and informs public debates around issues of economic and political participation and exclusion" (8). Their ethnographic methods of textual analysis, participant observation, and interviews form the basis for "ethnographic studies of policy formation," an approach that, first, "historically contextualizes contemporary debates, tracking the emergence of (now orthodox) discourses, revealing the political and economic changes that made such discourses possible (and for some, desirable), and implicitly comparing the current moment to a time when people imagined other purposes for education" and, second, "situates the actors who take up discourses, examining the micropolitics of actors' identities and actions" (24). I interpret the method adopted by Bartlett et al. as combining Foucauldian archaeology[12] and genealogy[13] with Gramscian studies of resistance.

My interest in using the anthropology of science as a "cultural critique" (Marcus and Fischer 1986) of testing stems from a broader history of vindicationist literature by scholars writing against racism (Drake 1980, see also Stepan and Gilman 1993).[14] One of the major projects of African American vindicationist literature from the end of the nineteenth to the beginning of the twentieth century was the formation of a "'race uplift' historiographic tradition"—with authors such as William J. Williams, Alexander Crummell, Anna Julia Cooper, Ida B. Wells, W.E.B. DuBois, and Carter G. Woodson—in order to counter the conception that the "Negro . . . is without history" (Robinson (2000 [1983]: 187–192). With scholars such as DuBois, C.L.R. James, and Richard Wright, Black historiography became radicalized, largely through the appropriation and challenge of Marxist historical materialism (Robinson 2000: 207–208, 287–288). These scholars recognized—as Stoler (1995) distinguished as one of Foucault's insights in his writings on race—that historiography is "a political force" (62), as it was DuBois who said, in *Black Reconstruction* (1962 [1935]), that "history is 'lies agreed upon'" and that the "real frontal attack on Reconstruction . . . came from the universities, especially Columbia and Johns Hopkins" (714, 718). In fact, part of the appeal of Foucault is due to my intellectual genealogy, as a Black female scholar, being informed by the "Black radical tradition" (Robinson 2000) and its project of opposing racism through radical historiography, a tradition that has informed and been informed by activism. As Ella Baker argued:

> In order for us as poor and oppressed people to become part of a society that is meaningful, the system under which we now exist has to be radically changed. This means that we are going to have to learn to think in radical terms. I use the term *radical* in its original meaning—getting down to and understanding the root cause. It means facing a system that does not lend itself to your needs and devising a means to change that system. That is easier said than done. But one of the things that has to be faced is, in the process of wanting to change that system, how much have we got to do to find out who we are, where we have come

from and where we are going. . . . I am saying as you must say, too, that in order to see where we are going we not only must *remember* where we have been, but we must *understand* where we have been. (Quoted in Moses and Cobb 2001: 3)

Thus, part of my project, in conjunction with the "public anthropology" method of Bartlett et al., is reexamining, or in Baker's terms "remembering," the history of statistics in relation to racism and the "development of . . . racial capitalism"[15] in order to understand the power relations embedded in statistical discourses today. In his historical examination of the role of anthropology in shaping racial discourse and policy in the United States, Lee Baker (1998) argued that "during . . . racial realignment in the U.S., particular approaches for understanding race come to the fore and shape public opinion, policy, and laws" justifying that realignment (218). For Baker, this history not only contextualizes the racial realignment of the 1980s, but also serves as a tool for opposing the neoliberal politics of colorblindness that simply silences the experiences and the persistence of racism. Despite the politics of colorblindness, discourses of race are everywhere,[16] especially as statistical discourse. The statistical essentialization of race is one of the areas that scholars opposing race essentialisms, such as Miles (1993) and Gilroy (2000), have not addressed. For me, studying statistical discourses in terms of their history, objectification, and politics helps to shed light on the contradictions of race essentialism, that is, not just the limitations of appealing to racial statistics due to their subjectivizing and objectifying force, but also the necessity of using statistics in the politics of negotiation due to the centrality of statistics to modern and postmodern hegemony.

Often studies of discourse are critiqued by feminists in particular both for leaving out questions of subjectivity and specific experiences (Deveaux 1994) and for reinforcing the study of "great White men" that further silences the experiences of marginalization. For Scheper-Hughes (1995), "If anthropologists deny themselves the power (because it implies a privileged position) to identify an ill or a wrong . . . they collaborate with the relations of power and silence that allow the destruction to continue" (419). However, not everyone views anthropology as emancipatory (see also Visweswaran 1994: 9), and in fact, it has long been regarded by Black scholars as one of the prime forces of racialization. In his article "Skeletons in the Anthropological Closet," Willis (1969) cited DuBois as having "described the black man as the 'football of anthropology'" (126). Gwaltney (1980) introduced his monumental ethnography *Drylongso* with a quote from Othman Sullivan: "I think this anthropology is another way to call me nigger" (xix). Robin D.G. Kelley (1997) argued that "ghetto ethnography" has been a major force in constructing the concept of the "ghetto underclass," as it not only re-ifies Black culture as a set of behaviors, reducing it to a "set of coping mechanisms," but also erases Black women (19) (at the same time that it pathologizes Black culture because of its "matriarchy" [see Moynihan 1965]). While many scholars of color have responded by conducting "insider anthropology" (Lewis 1973), insider status does not always guarantee an escape from the pathologization of Black culture. For Scheper-Hughes (1995), "The answer to the critique of anthropology is not a retreat from ethnography but rather an ethnography that is per-sonally engaged and politically committed" (419). However, ethnogra-phy is inherently problematic, due to the power differentials between the observed and the writer-ethnographer, as well as to the awkward position enabling the ethnographer to obtain status and financial gains through observing the pain and struggle of others (Behar 1993; Enslin 1994; and Gordon 1993).[17] The question Foucault (1994 [1973]: 84) asked of the clinic surfaces for me as a question we should pose of ethnography:

> But to look in order to know, to show in order to teach, is not this a tacit form of violence, all the more abusive for its silence, upon a sick body that demands to be comforted, not displayed? Can pain be a spectacle? Not only can it be, but it must be, by virtue of a subtle right that resides in the fact that no one is alone, the poor man less so than others, since he can only ob-tain assistance through the mediation of the rich . . . what is benevolence towards the poor is transformed into knowledge that is applicable to the rich.[18]

"Giving voice," from any standpoint and even under the guise of politi-cal commitment, often hides intellectuals' complicity in reproducing the international capitalist system and the construction and assimila-tion of subaltern women as other (Spivak 1988). For Spivak, stories of experience must be counterbalanced by studies of "ideological forma-tion" and "measuring silences" (296). Thus, one way of resolving some of the problems of ethnography is to follow Freire (1993 [1970]), who argued that the research process should parallel dialogue, with the subject of study being ideological formations and the themes of domination and liberation. Furthermore, as Freire attested, the "danger lies in the risk of shifting the focus of the investigation from the meaningful themes, to the people themselves, thereby treating the people as objects of the investigation" (1993 [1970]: 99). It is Freire's model that has informed the development of "activist anthropology," whose basic methodological steps consist of choosing research questions, collecting data, interpreting results, disseminating results, and validating results through collective effort with a certain (activist) group of people (Hale 2001: 14). The goal of this project was to become politically involved, conducting as close to what would count as activist anthropology as I could, with my anthropological gaze on the processes or strategies and forms of resistance against statistical objectification, without losing sight of the politics of experience.[19] The public anthropology approach by Bartlett et al. (2002) provided a basis for me to study discourses and movements, while staying politically engaged. The basis of my fieldwork began with my secondary research on the GI Forum case and with my decision to tutor math at a predominantly minority Austin high school (for the spring semesters of 1999 and 2000) and at a local branch of the Austin Public Library (from the summer of 1999 to the fall of 2001). These experiences provided me with a historical and social context with which to begin an ethnography on statistical objectification processes related to the Texas accountability system. Over the course of the study, I conducted mostly informal and nontaped interviews with Austin teachers and school staff, members of civil rights organizations, and employees of the Texas Education Agency. My true participant observation began when I attended a rally held by Texans for Quality Assessment in January of 2003, in support of creating multiple criteria for students in Texas, particularly third graders, who for the first time would be required to pass the new, more difficult state assessment in order to be promoted to the fourth grade. At the rally, I met an aide for Representative Dora Olivo sponsoring bills that would institute multiple criteria for both grade promotion and high school graduation. She was one of the few Black people attending the rally, and I asked her why she thought there were so few Black people there. My question piqued her interest, and at that time she introduced me to Representative Olivo, who then invited my husband and me to her office. There, the Representative invited me to volunteer for the office since, as a graduate student, I would be able to help with research needed to gain support for the bills; thus began my study. I drove to Representative Olivo's Austin office from San Antonio two to three times a week over the duration of the regular 78th legislative session, usually working there from five to ten hours per day, particularly toward the latter portion of the session, when the office became short in staff and when the other volunteer interns from the University of Texas had final exams. I was limited to some extent by driving from San Antonio, since severe weather on some occasions forced me to stay in San Antonio and because I limited the amount of time I spent in Austin so I would not have to drive home by myself too late at night. Representative Olivo was gracious enough to pay for my gas and give me a pass for free parking near the Capitol. I soon discovered that legislative work proceeded far beyond regular working hours, and I left many a night wishing that the others could go home at the same time I did. Most of the work I did in the office consisted of attending and taking notes regarding House Public Education Committee meetings, usually scheduled every Tuesday at 2 P.M., as well as researching for talking points that would aid in gaining support for the bills. I was even recruited by the Representative to help write a speech on multiple criteria for a press conference. However, as the session progressed, the office became short staffed, and I was needed for answering phones, filing bills, making copies, and running documents for the Representative to the House floor. At times, the Representative needed to recruit her friends to volunteer for the administrative assistant work. Working in the Capitol took a physical and emotional toll on me, and at times, it became so stressful that I experienced chest pains. As I spent less time on ethnography and more on filing bills, I worried that my position was better suited for a study of employment or the workplace than for one of educational politics.[20] While working as an intern, I was given access to meetings, luncheons, and dinners held exclusively for legislators, and I was able to speak with and listen to many different groups of people, from civil rights organizations (League of United Latino American Citizens [LULAC], MALDEF, NAACP, National Council of La Raza, and Intercultural Development Research Association [IDRA]) to groups lobbying for teachers, midwives, interior decorators, and people with disabilities. I also participated in a lobby day for Representative Olivo's multiple-criteria bills in which we, representatives from groups supporting the bills, visited the offices of House representatives in order to speak in support of the bills. Working in legislative offices also provided me access to news updates and search databases not available to the public. In observing the House Public Education Committee meetings, I was able to take notes as would a fly-on-the-wall anthropologist, but in other situations, I largely took notes after holding conversations or even after I drove home to San Antonio. Technology, particularly RealPlayer, made it possible to view committee meetings and floor proceedings in real time and taped over the Internet, both while I was in the office and when I was at home. RealPlayer, however, was no substitute for being physically present in meetings, given not only the wider range of vision, but also an embodied ability to sense the emotions concerning particular bill debates.

In addition to interviewing and participant observation, I also conducted a media review, being fortunate enough to be on mailing lists concerning educational news, and having access, as a University of Texas graduate student and a legislative intern, to electronic newspaper databases. I conducted most of the historical research in this book, particularly the history of statistics, through secondary sources. I did analyze primary statistical texts released by the Texas Education Agency on its Web site, as well as "nonsecure" (paper) documents given to me by a TEA employee, particularly the Technical Digest of 1999–2000, which summarizes the manner in which tests are designed, scored, and reported. I visited Internet Web sites dedicated to testing issues, particularly that of Texans for Quality Assessment and its links. Also, I watched television broadcasts of educational issues, primarily news, newsmagazines, and congressional proceedings, official speeches, and conference proceedings on C-SPAN.

## Writing

As I employed a public anthropology approach as a way of conducting activist research, the methodology of writing I have chosen for this project is also embedded in the politics of using anthropology as cultural critique. While Denzin (1997) located the movement of ethnographic writing as a form of cultural critique as a moment in (and reflecting) the postmodern, "multinational . . . to transgressive" phase of capitalism, I tend to draw on Lewis (1973) and Willis (1969), locating this moment in the crisis in anthropology that developed out of broader anticolonial struggles in which the role and truth of anthropology were challenged by the objectified subjects of anthropology.[21] For Marcus (1998 [1994]), postmodernist questionings of "conventional forms" have produced experimental, reflexive ethnographic writing that he calls "messy texts." According to Marcus, "These authors [of messy texts] refuse to assimilate too easily or by foreclosure the object of study, thus resisting the kind of academic colonialism whereby the deep assumption permeating the work is that the interests of the ethnographer and those of her subjects are somehow aligned" (1998 [1994]: 188).

Messy texts are "*symptoms* of a struggle" to challenge commonsense perceptions of the world and anthropology, to "critically displace sets of representations that no longer seem to account for the worlds we thought we knew, or at least could name" (Marcus 1998 [1994]: 189). While my method of writing in this ethnography may be considered a "messy text," I prefer Visweswaran's (1994) conception of ethnography as an "interrogative text" that "emphasizes the subject split into both subject and object, as continually in the process of construction: a 'subject in process,'" and that rests and risks its authority on constantly posing questions (62). In this sense, my text as interrogative is born not purely out of a postmodern concern for challenging convention, but out of my lived struggle against racism; against a form of "academic colonialism" that does not simply impose its interests on those it is studying, but has aided in the colonization and imperialist assimilation of people of color, of whom I am a part; and against a form of "disciplinary colonialism" that silences the interventions and scholarship of us "natives" (McClaurin 2001: 59). Thus, in the tradition of Black feminist anthropologists, inspired by DuBois, Fanon, and U.S. Third World feminists, my reflexive, interrogative text practices autoethnography that not only questions the division of the observer/observed (Denzin 1997: 225) and subject/object (Visweswaran 1994: 62), but also critiques the elitist and imperial temporal and spatial distancing of the anthropologist from the object-as-subject (Fabian 1983; Peters 1997) through an "amalgamation of self and community" or self and society (McClaurin 2001: 67). Thus, my autoethnography emerges exactly from the "interest of . . . her subjects," exactly from the politics of the "community" [22] of which I am a part. It does require the messiness of acknowledging academic colonialism, against which Marcus cautions, and I question whether we can really decolonize anthropology. It also requires me to interrogate the ways in which I am a producer of and produced by the very processes of statistical objectification and subjectification about which I am theorizing and writing. Through autoethnography, I acknowledge my double consciousness, as a product of the university and discipline of anthropology, but also as a Black woman with a critical and experientially grounded perspective or "embodied theoretical standpoint" (McClaurin 2001: 56–63, 65); as a theorist employing the language, theories, and methods of hegemonic and exclusionary canons; yet as a theorist capable of what

Sandoval (2000) called "differential movement," or exercising the "middle voice,"

> wherein the activist attempts to exercise power upon *what* is
> conceived as an object (as in the active verb form), and unlike
> positions of social subordination such as those of "pet," "game,"
> or "wild," positions permitted the oppressed in which exterior
> powers exercise domination on the citizen-subject, who can
> only act in response (as in the passive verb form), . . . the middle
> voice represents the consciousness required to transform any of
> the previous modes of resistance out of their active-or-passive
> incarnations into what White calls a "reflexive," or differential
> form. That reflexive mode of consciousness self-consciously de-
> ploys subjectivity and calls up a *new* morality of form that inter-
> venes in social reality through deploying an action that re-
> creates the agent even as the agent is creating the action—in an
> ongoing, chiasmic loop of transformation. The differential ac-
> tivist is thus made by the ideological intervention that she is
> making: the only predictable final outcome is transformation
> itself. (156–157)

My text escapes (or goes beyond) neither the "empirical omniscience" (Denzin 1997: 210) nor the claims of rigor and validity characteristic of modernist (yearnings for) scientific anthropology. My uses of narrative, self-reflectivity, and experiential standpoint are attempts at blurring the lines between fact and fiction (see Denzin 1997: 126–162), but in the sense that they attempt to politicize the production of truth while maintaining authority (Clifford 1988)—not only to chart the racial and gendered political economy of truth, in other words, to problematize the ways in which the production of facts objectify and commodify and exploit people and their knowledge (through statistics), but also to argue that the lived experiences of objectification are facts,[23] or truths that need to be taken into account in order to oppose the marketization of education, which ultimately is the "de-democratization" of education (McNeil 2000a), or the retrenchment of the welfare state's policies of redressing inequities, implemented as a result of historic struggles for civil and human rights.

In this project, I interrogate statistics as a hegemonic discourse network, whose genealogy as a science of the state and as a probability calculus (or mathematical science) allows it to be a technique not only of objectifying subjects through governmentality and exploitation, but also of producing truth, materializing social facts, and providing measures of certainty, representativeness, and significance. I argue that the hegemony of the high-stakes regime as an element of the marketization of education is maintained through the operation of statistics as a discourse network, allowing the coalition of the Right to do the following: (1) conduct the conduct of students, teachers, administrators, and the public—despite the appearance of freedom; (2) commodify knowledge and exploit public education through a system of competition; and (3) produce the truth of testing through notions of progress, representativeness, standards, and validity. I also examine questions of subjectivity in both the production of and resistance against statistical discourse. On the one hand, self-identification with statistics and becoming a producer of statistics—that is, "statistical subjectivity" (Urla 1993)—reinforced statistical discourse and the regime of high-stakes testing, yet, on the other hand, formed the basis for constructing a statistical counterdiscourse that challenged high-stakes testing. However, it was exactly the politicization of experiential narrative as a *contre-histoire* to statistical discourse that became both central to the resistance against high-stakes testing and also diagnostic of the forms of power (objectification) through which high-stakes testing operated. Thus, I viewed this form of resistance as constituting what Foucault (1983) called the "struggle against the submission of subjectivity" (213). While this resistance did not articulate race or anti-racism as its raison d'être, it not only emerged from the opposition to the impact of high-stakes testing on students of color (led by MALDEF), but was also racialized in terms of its being led by a Latina Democratic representative. Given both the articulation of race through statistical discourse and the use of testing as a technique of segregation, I also examine the ways in which the statistical discourse of high-stakes testing racialized U.S. Mexican and Black students as embodiments of risk and as the markers of failure and inefficiency. I consider the ways in which the dual strategies of statistical counterdiscourse and experiential narrative as *contre-histoire* signify what Sandoval (2000) called "differential movement," part of the "methodology of the oppressed." Further, this differential movement is present within and echoes my combining of the anthropology of science and autoethnographic activist anthropology, what may be called "studying up" with a view "from below."[24]

In the following chapters, I contextualize the Texas testing system historically and examine three forms of statistical objectification (governmentality, commodification, and statistical truth production) that I contend maintain the hegemony of the testing system. Chapter 2 provides a historical context for my involvement in the movement to pass multiple-criteria bills in the wake of the *GI Forum* decision that denied that the Texas testing system was racially discriminatory and of the passing of the "no social promotion" bills. I examine the emergence of testing in Texas in the context of desegregation, as well as the racial realignment of the Republican Party in Texas. In Chapter 3, I describe the ways in which students, teachers, and the public become manipulated or governed through statistics. Resistance against standardized testing, particularly by students, revealed the way in which the discourse network of standardized testing statistics objectifies students. I also explore the ways in which statistics impose a structure of feeling, particularly what Woodward (1999) called "statistical panic." Third, I view the ways in which statistical production supports practices of making students of color invisible statistically, objectifying marginalization and invisibility. In Chapter 4, I discuss the ways in which statistics allow for the commodification of students and their knowledge via the informational economy. Second, I argue that the assimilation of students, teachers, school administrators, and the public into a system of competition works to maintain the hegemony of the testing system. Third, I argue that in the neoliberal imperative to combine profitability with governmentality, conservatives are deploying statistical discourses in order to attack the democratization of the public school, in their general attack on the welfare state. Examining Desrosières's concept of statistical objectification in terms of stabilizing objects and "taming" uncertainty (Hacking 1991), Chapter 5 discusses the ways in which statistical fact production operates to make certain truths hegemonic. First, I call into question the ways that the statistical objectification of minority failure has underscored the hegemony of the testing system. Second, I view the ways in which polls on testing serve as tools for educating consent by statistically constructing a collective will. Third, I examine the way in which the statistical constructs of *standard error of measurement* and *correlation* also operate to stabilize objects and serve as a form of ideological glue between different objects. Fourth, I examine statistical subjectivity, including in my own practice, as a way of understanding the ways in which statistical discourses become a terrain for negotiating politics as well as common sense. In Chapter 6, I elucidate the ways in which narratives of children's experiences with testing served as the major political tool in gaining support for the multiple-criteria bills, which I describe as opposing statistical objectification. In this chapter, I reflect on my own "romanticization of resistance" (Abu-Lughod 1990) and interrogate the ways in which the "subaltern cannot speak" (Spivak 1988). In the concluding chapter, I summarize the various modes of objectification occurring under high-stakes testing in Texas, as well as address the problematic of "studying up," public anthropology, activist anthropology, and autoethnography. I also interrogate the politics of my arguments and whether or not my product will be useful to activists, exploring the concept of providing or prescribing solutions. In order to consider solutions, that is, the future, we need to first examine the historical context and political economy of testing in Texas.

# 2 / Contextualizing Education within the Racial Politics of Texas

I n a speech before the American Enterprise Institute in January of 2004, Education Secretary Rod Paige compared opponents of the president's No Child Left Behind Act to 1950s-era segregationists. According to Paige, the No Child Left Behind Act represents a political equivalent to the *Brown* decision itself, and the fact that "the very critics and organizations that applauded Brown and worked to implement it" are opposing the law—what he contends is leaving "minority children behind"—could only be explained by these organizations' commitment to "special interests" (Archibald 2004). For Paige, "racism cannot end as long as there is an achievement gap" (Archibald 2004). Subtracted from Paige's equating of the alleviation of racism with the achievement of a statistical equality in standardized test scores (between a White and Black norm) is the impact of social and politico-economic factors that shape racial inequalities within schooling (see McNeil 2000b). Of particular importance is that the No Child Left Behind Act was in 2001 the latest reincarnation of the Elementary and Secondary Education Act of 1965, an act that established Title I, described by Cook (2005) as "the largest, most far-reaching federal K-12 program, with $13 billion sent annually to school districts to help educate children living in poverty" (24). Whereas the funding of schools under Title I was a central part of Lyndon Johnson's War on Poverty, meant to provide relief for poor schools,[1] the No Child Left Behind Act has attached a punitive dimension to the funding, as "schools that don't meet adequate yearly progress face sanctions, including takeover, and must allow students to transfer to another school of their choice" (Cook 2005: 26). Considering the volume of scholarship that documents the historical negative impact of standardized testing on students of color and racial equity (e.g., Miller 1974; Fraser 1994; Valencia and Guadarrama 1996) and acknowledgment that results of standardized testing correlate with socioeconomic status and parental educational background, why would increased standardized testing be regarded as the harbinger of equality? Paige's suggestion that opposition to increased state-mandated testing parallels support for segregated systems commits a form of thinking comparable to doublethink (Orwell 1984 [1949]) that Sandoval (2000) called "retranslation," particularly characteristic of neoliberal and neoconservative hegemony: "[T]he late-capitalist retranslation of difference allows hierarchical and material differences in power between people to be erased from consciousness, even while these same economic and social privileges are bolstered" (75).

In fact, the "'leave no child behind' mantra" represents the Bush administration's rearticulation of a discourse used by Marian Wright Edelman in articulating the goals of the Children's Defense Fund (Townsend 2002). Speaking against policies that would drastically reduce services for families and children, Edelman issued a response entitled, "Mr. President, We Want Our Slogan Back." In this chapter, I examine the ways in which the movement toward intensifying high-stakes testing in Texas, rather than redressing segregation, reproduces racial and class-based school segregation. Contrary to Paige's suggestion that critics of testing are segregationists, state-mandated testing in Texas is inextricably linked to racial politics in the state, particularly the realignment of the Republican Party as anti–New Deal and anti-*Brown*.

## Racial Politics in Texas History

The current state of racial politics in the Texas education system reflects and emerges from the dynamics of the history of Texas. The incorporation of the state of Texas into the United States in 1845 brought about a racial dynamic unlike that in the states of the Southeast. Texas was first colonized by Spain in 1690, largely through the establishment of missions by the Franciscans that required the formation of alliances with Texas and Coahuiltecan Indians (Ménchaca 2001: 101). According to Ménchaca, while the Spanish imported about two hundred thousand African slaves—mostly Malinke from Mali—to Mexico, the colonies in Texas had few African slaves (2001: 43, 112). In 1810, "mestizo, mulatto, black, and Indian masses" revolted against Spain in the Mexican War of Independence (Taylor 1998: 37). Gaining independence by 1821, the newly independent Mexican government instituted liberal racial reforms that naturalized all nonslaves as citizens and instituted the legal infrastructure to undermine slavery (Ménchaca 2001: 162, 163). According to Taylor, the liberal laws enticed fugitive slaves and freed men and women to migrate to Texas in the 1820s. In the same period, Anglos, largely from the Old South, migrated to Texas and the Southwest, bringing slaves, but also an ideology and institution of slavery that both differed sharply from the Spanish-Mexican one and violated the Mexican constitution (and the spirit of independence).[2] The increased immigration of Anglos to Texas and their illegal acts of enslavement clashed with the Mexican government, which in 1829, led by Vincent Guerrero, who was of African descent, abolished slavery. This conflict underlined the battles waged by Anglo Texans for secession from Mexico (Ménchaca 2001: 166). According to White (1974: 19–21), when Anglos rose against the government in 1839, the first grievance Anglos used to justify their declaration of war was "the failure of the Mexican government to provide public education in Texas," despite the fact that compulsory schooling was decreed by the Republic of Mexico in 1829. White suggested that the contention centered on the requirement of the Mexican government that instruction be conducted in Spanish (19).

After Anglo Texans fought to establish independence from Mexico and statehood in the United States, the new government instituted laws and practices—including the formation of the coercive police force, the Texas Rangers—that redistributed Mexican-owned land to Anglos, essentially colonizing Mexican people and their land in Texas (see Blauner 1987). The Texas Constitution denied political enfranchisement and citizenship rights to Black and Native people, as well as Mexicans of African and Indian descent, and forbade the residence of freed Blacks without the consent of the Texas Congress. Blacks were either declared slaves or deported to Mexico. After the Treaty of Guadalupe Hidalgo, the U.S. federal government established laws denying Black and American Native people citizenship rights, and forbade people of mixed European and Indian descent both the right to vote and the right of citizenship (Menchaca 2001).

During the Civil War, many of the Confederates transplanted their slaves from the eastern states to Texas. Texas was the last state of the Confederacy to fall to the Union, on June 19, 1865, making Black slaves in Texas the last to be emancipated under Lincoln's Emancipation

Proclamation. In terms of education, freed Black people, through churches and a system of double taxation, formed public schools, accompanied by the establishment of public schools by the Freedmen's Bureau and northern philanthropists (Anderson 1988). According to DuBois (1962 [1935]), the origin of the public school system in the Reconstruction South in particular can be traced to the efforts of freed slaves. Additionally, DuBois asserted that without schooling, "the Negro would . . . have been driven back into slavery" (667).

In 1877, the southern states accepted the presidency of William Taft in exchange for the withdrawal of northern troops, known as the Great Compromise, bringing to an end the Reconstruction Era. In the aftermath of the Reconstruction Era, racial violence became particularly brutal in Texas. By the mid-1930s, Texas ranked third among southern states in lynching.[3] Additionally, once Texas's vast lands became targeted for establishing agricultural industries, railroads, and settlements, the U.S. government waged war with American Indian nations, either wiping out populations or pushing them out of Texas into Mexico or Oklahoma reservations by the 1870s (Menchaca 2001: 230). In 1915, Mexicans led an uprising including Blacks, Japanese, and Indians called the Liberating Army for Races and People and united under the Plan de San Diego to create an independent republic in the Southwest. After several raids, Texas Rangers hunted down, executed, and lynched Mexicans daily, burning their homes and forcing them to move (Montejano 1986: 117–123). The U.S. military even established a regiment of Black soldiers responsible for guarding the border of Texas against Mexicans racialized as "bandits" and Native American warrior nations, inciting racial tensions not only between Blacks on the one hand and Mexicans and Native Americans on the other, but also with the former Confederates, who viewed the presence of Black soldiers as a sign of continuing military occupation by the North (Taylor 1998: 165–167).

In terms of post-Reconstruction political economy, colonization and enslavement manifested themselves as segregation. According to DuBois (1962 [1935]), segregation emerged from the post-Reconstruction alliance among the White labor class, the southern oligarchy, and northern capitalists.[4] According to DuBois (1962 [1935]: 351), the political enfranchisement of Black people through the Thirteenth, Fourteenth, and Fifteenth constitutional amendments never accompanied economic emancipation or economic enfranchisement. Simultaneously, the establishment of sharecropping, vagrancy laws, and apprenticeship laws trapped Black workers into cheap labor. In the South, the legitimation of Black codes retrenched the political enfranchisement granted by the above-mentioned constitutional amendments and ensured Blacks limited access to land, juries, and proper education. According to DuBois, the prison system became a new form of slavery, and Taylor asserted that Texas became "notorious" for its "convict leasing system" (1998: 107). In terms of education, former Confederate Democrats in control of Texas state government, who viewed the public school as a product of Black freedom and the imposition of the Republican Freedmen's Bureau, repealed the system of public schooling set up by Republicans (White 1974; Veninga 1984). Once public education was reestablished by 1883, de jure segregation was enforced for Blacks and de facto segregation for Mexicans (San Miguel 1987; Donato 1997). In cities such as Austin, Black schools were incorporated into city districts. According to Winegarten (1995), in 1881, "a law . . . turned control of . . . urban schools over to all-white trustees" (92). Despite the Treaty of Guadalupe Hidalgo, which guaranteed equal treatment under the law for Mexicans in the Southwest (San Miguel and Valencia 1998), segregation of Mexicans in Texas became particularly hardened by the 1920s upon the migration of northern capitalists into Texas. The transformation of the agricultural economy to an industrial one further displaced Mexicans from their land and property, while vagrancy laws and residential codes coerced them into becoming a "reservoir of cheap Mexican labor" (Montejano 1986: 178).[5] In the 1920s, segregation of Blacks in Texas also intensified. In Austin, for example, a city ordinance called the "Master Plan" was passed in 1929 to push Blacks to the east side of the city. This plan accompanied policies such as the withholding of public services, construction of highways such as Interstate 35 and the Mopac Expressway, closure of Black schools, zoning changes, and restrictive housing acts that forced Black communities spread throughout the city to falter and be reconstituted; some of the lands were taken by the University of Texas (Jackson 1979). According to McArthur (1998), one of the contradictions of racial segregation in Progressive Era Texas was that it provided support for the growing feminist movement, permitting White women to enter more public spaces: "Enlarging public space for respectable white women was inseparable from constricting that of the African-American male; segregation made socially dangerous spaces 'safe' for the New South's new women" (87). In Texas, those public spaces for women's activism were exactly the politics around schooling, as women fought for public schooling and the introduction of kindergarten (McArthur 1998).

From the 1930s to the 1950s, Mexican American and African American political organizations waged legal campaigns against segregation, particularly in education. Through the formation of the League of United Latin American Citizens (LULAC), Mexican Americans lawyers of Texas challenged the segregation of Mexican American students in Del Rio, Texas. In the landmark case *Del Rio v. Salvatierra* (1930, 1931), the segregation of Mexicans based on race was rendered unconstitutional given LULAC's contention that the Texas Constitution held that segregation must occur between Whites and "colored"—meaning Negro—people, and Mexicans were not Negro, but White. The court ruled, however, that segregation based on language was permissible (Blanton 2003). In the 1940s, Thurgood Marshall and the Legal Defense Fund of the National Association for the Advancement of Colored People (NAACP) also took on racial segregation in Texas, first, successfully challenging Texas's all-white Democratic primary in *Smith v. Allwright* (321 U.S. 649 (64 S. Ct. 757) [1944]) and, second, successfully challenging the actions taken by the University of Texas Law School to provide severely inferior education to Black students in *Sweatt v. Painter* (339 U.S. 629 (70 S. Ct. 848) [1949]). In terms of using the courts to overturn the *Plessy v. Ferguson* doctrine of "separate but equal," the first successful case occurred in California with *Mendez v. Westminster* (161 F.2d 774 [1947]),[6] in which a federal court for the first time ruled unconstitutional the de jure educational segregation of Mexicans on the basis of race (San Miguel and Valencia 1998). The *Mendez* case sparked more legal battles in Texas, as a similar ruling was handed down in *Delgado v. Bastrop* (1948), but it also arguably provided the groundwork for *Brown v. Board of Education* (347 U.S. 483 (74 S. Ct. 686) [1954]), which struck down the "separate but equal" doctrine and de jure racial segregation. Not only did the NAACP file an amicus brief in the case, but the governor of California at the time of decision was none other than Earl Warren, the chief justice of the Supreme Court in *Brown v. Board of Education*.

## Subterfuge, Testing, and the Racial Realignment of the Republican Party

*Brown v. Board of Education* (1954) failed in many cases to bring about the end of segregation despite the ruling in *Brown II* (349 U.S. 294 (75 S. Ct. 753) [1955]) that desegregation occur "with all deliberate speed." While behavioral, evolutionary, familial, and cultural models have been proposed to explain the failure of *Brown* and other related educational reforms, these models tend to disregard the historical, political, and economic contexts of education in the United States (Bowles and Gintis 1976). Particularly ignored has been the long-term impact of the strategies of resistance employed by states—both in the South and in the North—to the mandates of *Brown*.

In the award-winning tome *Simple Justice*, Kluger (1975) warned of the South's (and the North's) "skill at [constructing] legal barriers to slow desegregation" (725). San Miguel even described the historical moment following the *Brown* decision as the "era of subterfuge": "[I]t was during this period that a multitude of practices—for example, freedom of choice plans, selected transfer and transportation plans, and classification systems based on language or scholastic ability—were utilized by local school districts to maintain segregated schools" (quoted in San Miguel and Valencia 1998: 377). One of the major strategies of avoiding desegregation was White suburbanization, which became legitimated in the cases of *San Antonio Independent School District v. Rodriguez* (411 U.S. 1, 93 (S. Ct. 1278) [1973]) and *Milliken v. Bradley I* (418 U.S. 717, 94 (S. Ct. 3112) [1974]). The cases prevented the legal recognition of the intersectionality of race and class in segregation litigation.[7] In the former case, plaintiffs from the Edgewood Independent School District in San Antonio, sparked by student walkouts, used the equal protection clause to charge that finance inequity among districts was unconstitutional. The case went to the Supreme Court after a district court had ruled in 1971 that the resource inequalities were unconstitutional. In a 5–4 decision, the Court ruled that education was not a fundamental right under the Constitution, that Texas had provided each student with the funding necessary for minimal basic skills, and that Rodriguez's attorneys from MALDEF did not establish "a suspect class" or an identifiable group for whom equal protection was denied (Kluger 1975; Kozol 1991; Farr and Trachtenburg 1999). Kozol described the *Rodriguez* decision as "the ending of an era of progressive change . . . [that] set the tone for the subsequent two decades which have left us with the present-day reality of separate and unequal public schools" (1991: 219). Kluger (1975) contextualized the decision in a critique similar to that of Bowles and Gintis: "Lurking unspoken in the background was the profoundly unsettling question of how far government in a capitalist nation dared to venture toward wiping away the advantages of private wealth in order to provide truly equal public services" (770).

Another Supreme Court decision that affirmed the nation's limits in providing equality was *Milliken v. Bradley I*, in which the court ruled against a desegregation remedy that integrated Detroit suburbs with the inner city. According to Freeman (1995) and Orfield (1996), the combination of the *Rodriguez* and *Milliken I* decisions legitimated the concentration or isolating of students of color in school districts while denying these districts resource equalization.[8] Freeman further argued that the decisions created a legal condition worse than *Plessy v. Ferguson* since under the latter at least "separate but equal" was required. For Freeman, in *Milliken I* the Supreme Court "for the first time applied antidiscrimination law to rationalize a segregated result in a case where a constitutional violation had been found to exist" (1995: 41).

According to Baker (2001), southern states looked to intelligence testing and tracking in elementary and secondary schools, college admissions exams, and teacher competency exams as forms for evading the mandates of major desegregation cases, which *Brown* has come to symbolize. In fact, Baker cited correspondence by attorney David W. Robinson of Charleston, South Carolina, in which he stated in response to a desegregation order in 1963, "[W]e need to press for a state-wide I.Q. and Achievement test administered in all our schools. This difference in achievement between the two races may be our last line of defense" (quoted in Baker 2001: 333–334). In addition to K–12 testing, National Teacher Examinations and college admissions tests were marketed to southern states in response to challenges for equalization of teacher salaries across race and to court challenges to segregation in higher education. In selling the National Teacher Examinations, educational assessment developer and expert Ben D. Wood remarked to an attorney that "at least a few . . . will qualify . . . to show the absence of discrimination" (quoted in Baker 2002: 327). The use of intelligence testing to evade laws enforcing equal treatment under the law had already had extensive practice in Texas and the Southwest before *Brown* as justification for de facto segregation of Mexican Americans from 1920 to 1940 (Blanton 2003).

Following Baker's assertion that the timing of the implementation of testing following desegregation orders "suggests a racial motivation" (2001: 336), I argue that testing was another form of evading desegregation in Texas couched in a language of equal opportunity. Further, the racial realignment of the Republican Party accompanied a party commitment to testing that ran alongside a commitment to "dismantle desegregation" (Orfield 1996), starting with the fact that the first state-mandated testing system was established in 1979 with the election of William Clements as governor, the first Republican elected governor since Reconstruction. Nationally, the Republican Party was not alone in supporting testing. According to Newman (1987), President Bill Clinton was the governor of Arkansas when it became the first state to require competency testing for teachers (158). Clinton also supported accountability and no social promotion bills as president.

The election of William Clements was the culmination of the transformation of the Republican Party, both in Texas and in the broader United States. Before the 1960s, Texas had been a one-party Democratic state, as the Republican Party served less as its own entity and more as a political space of negotiating between battling factions of the Democratic Party (Davidson 1990). A deep rift formed in the Texas Democratic Party in the 1940s over the New Deal policies of Democratic president Franklin Delano Roosevelt between liberal Democrats in support of FDR and conservatives deeply opposed to the New Deal. While the liberal faction had small victories in the 1940s, conservative governor and strict segregationist Allan Shivers, elected in 1949, put policies in place to prevent liberal Democrats from becoming elected. According to Davidson, the "Shivers machine" crossed party lines in the presidential race to push for the election of Republican Eisenhower in 1952. The liberalization of the Texas Democratic Party, culminating in the rise of liberal Ralph Yarborough and moderate Democrat Lyndon Baines Johnson to the U.S. Senate—where each voted for the civil rights bill in 1957—pushed many of the radical Right to support third-party candidates in presidential elections such as Strom Thurmond's Dixiecrats and George Wallace's American Party. Like the Shivers machine, the "Radical Right," composed of billionaires, evangelical Christians, and anticommunists (or McCarthyites), employed the strategy of using the Republican Party to oppose the liberal Democrats. In 1961 this strategy proved successful, for when Lyndon Johnson left his Senate seat to become vice president under John F. Kennedy, John Tower won the election for U.S. Senate as a Republican. According to Davidson (1990), "The modern Texas Republican party was born with the election of John Tower to the U.S. Senate" (198). Tower had been famous for his support of segregation, and as a senator, he became nationally famous for preventing the adoption of a more liberal civil rights agenda in the national Republican Party platform at the Republican Party convention in 1964. While in the Senate, Tower opposed the Civil Rights Act of 1964 and the Voting Rights Act of 1965; pushed for a constitutional amendment designating "forced busing" as unconstitutional; and opposed the adoption of the Martin Luther King holiday. In opposition to the Civil Rights Act, Tower successfully proposed an amendment to the bill that would strengthen the use of employment tests, going against recent court decisions that found employment tests to be discriminatory (Rodriguez and Weingast 2003).[9]

In the 1960s, Tower represented for Republicans in Texas what Barry Goldwater, strongly supported by John Tower, represented for a newly forming southern Republican base. When Senator Barry Goldwater of Arizona ran for president in 1964 as a Republican, he formed a base of southern voters opposed in particular to Kennedy's policy of sending federal troops to Mississippi when student James Meredith faced a riot in attempting to desegregate the University of Mississippi. According to Davidson (1990), Goldwater was "the first major-party candidate since race became prominent after World War II to pursue a southern White-oriented strategy," deploying not an overtly racialized or racist discourse, but a discourse of "state's rights" (226, 227). As Goldwater ran for president, Strom Thurmond and George Wallace switched to the Republican Party. Despite Goldwater's defeat by Lyndon Johnson, a new Republican base formed in the South, particularly in Texas, from which many of Goldwater's most powerful supporters came, including John Tower. Davidson wrote that "one of the most vocal supporters" of Goldwater was governor of California Ronald Reagan, who led a campaign to defeat an open-housing law (227). As the Democratic Party absorbed Black and Latino voters, the Republican Party in Texas coalesced around opposition to the imposition of a "second Reconstruction on the South" (205), particularly civil rights bills and desegregation. In this context, the Republican Party in Texas produced such leaders as George H. W. Bush and James Baker. For Davidson, "Race, rather than class, turned out to be the driving force behind party realignment" (239). Davidson even quoted Congressman Mickey Leland, who in 1982 remarked, "Blacks supporting the Republican Party is like a bunch of chickens getting together to support Col. Sanders" (235).

Thus, in 1979, the election of William Clements as the first Republican governor since Reconstruction had significant racial overtones. According to Davidson, one of the platforms on which Republicans, including Clements, ran for office was a commitment to end busing precisely because at the time more than twenty districts, including Austin, Houston, and Fort Worth, faced desegregation suits (237). In the first year of Clements's tenure as governor, the Texas legislature passed the Equal Educational Opportunity Act, which established the first state-mandated testing system, the Texas Assessment of Basic Skills

(TABS) (Haney 2000). In 1980, a close friend of Governor Clements, Ronald Reagan, was elected to the U.S. presidency, instituting a policy of "dismantling desegregation" that included removing federal funding of desegregation plans, limiting funds to desegregation centers, calling on the courts to end busing, and even suggesting that the Department of Education be disbanded (Orfield 1996: 16). In 1983, the Reagan administration published A *Nation at Risk*, submitting "proof" from standardized test results that U.S. students were lagging behind their international counterparts. Texas was among many states that used the manifesto as an impetus for reform, particularly by mandating standardized minimum-competency exams. Although Democratic candidate Mark White was elected governor of Texas in 1983, the person he chose to spearhead his educational reform in the Select Committee on Public Education (SCOPE), intended to fulfill the campaign promise to raise teachers' salaries, was Texas billionaire Ross Perot, who had served on Reagan's Foreign Intelligence Advisory Board[10] and also served on Governor Clements's War on Drugs Committee. As McNeil (2000a) documented, SCOPE became dominated by corporate leaders selected by Perot and sought more widespread reforms packaged in House Bill (HB) 72, including teacher certification exams; a no-pass, no-play rule; and new state-mandated exams (Texas Educational Assessment of Minimum Skills) that at the high school level required passage for a diploma. According to Newman (1987), for SCOPE, increased teacher salaries and increased funding to public education were not possible at the time because of a downturn in the Texas economy and because the legislature was not going to continue funding at the same or greater levels without "changes in accountability *and* quality assurances that the money was spent appropriately" (212). Newman also reported that in 1982 Texas had a surplus of $5 billion.

Because HB 72 failed to properly remedy the problem of finance inequity among school districts, the plaintiffs from *Rodriguez* and the attorneys from MALDEF sued again for finance inequity, this time in state court, in *Edgewood Independent School District v. Kirby* (see Farr and Trachtenburg 1999). Teaming with the Equity Center, MALDEF (using a strategy of fighting the inequity of school funding resources as a way of attacking racial inequality[11]) successfully argued the case before the Texas Supreme Court, and in 1990, the Texas school finance system was deemed unconstitutional. The court ordered the legislature to come up with a finance bill that would successfully equalize adequate and efficient funding. As the legislature debated and passed finance equity bills, which would become labeled "Robin Hood," and as the bills were taken before the court, the State Board of Education approved a more difficult statewide testing system, the Texas Assessment of Academic Skills (TAAS). The approval came despite statewide poor performance on the 1989 Texas Educational Assessment of Minimum Skills and projections that on the new high school exit exams, "at least 73 percent of African Americans and 67 percent of Hispanics [versus 50 percent of Whites] would fail the math portion of the test; at least 53 percent of African Americans and 54 percent of Hispanics [versus 29 percent of Whites] would fail the reading section; and at least 62 percent of African Americans and 45 percent of Hispanics [versus 36 percent of Whites] would fail the writing section" (*GI Forum et al. v. Texas Education Agency et al.* 87 F. Supp. 2d 667, 673 [2000]).

When in 1995 the courts finally approved state legislation (Senate Bill [SB] 7) that improved finance equity among school districts in Texas, the bill contained the provision of an accountability system that centered on the state-mandated test, the TAAS, dropout statistics, and school attendance rates (Farr and Trachtenberg 1999). According to Palmaffy (1998), the accountability system was put in place "to ensure that redistributed funds would be spent well."[12] While the Perot reforms brought to Texas a high school exit exam, the accountability system impressed higher stakes for schools, teachers, and students, such as the threat of state control; the power of test scores to determine principal tenure and teacher salary and promotion; and students' high school graduation and grade promotion (McNeil 2000a). Just days after finance equalization and fifteen years after desegregation court orders swept Texas, the Texas Education Agency (TEA) was demanding that poor, resegregated districts and schools perform at the same level as historically wealthy districts and schools. As Black educator Ruth Davis Sauls conveyed in an interview with Huston-Tillotson sociology professor Dr. Rosalee Martin on the issue of the TAAS test: "[I]t's been said over and over again that the students in the black schools were behind the students in the Anglo schools or the other schools. If this be the case, then how in the world could you expect the black child to then take a test and come out equal if their teaching or training has been what has been called inferior? How in the world can it come out in balance with the other students who had superior or master teachers all along?" (Martin 2001).

The imposition of the TAAS high school graduation or exit test resulted in the disproportionate denial of Black and Mexican American students high school diplomas, initiating legal action by the NAACP and MALDEF. The NAACP filed a complaint with the Office of Civil Rights in 1995 and reached a settlement with TEA on the agreement that the agency would provide proper remediation for students who failed the TAAS. MALDEF filed a class-action suit in the case *GI Forum et al. v. Texas Education Agency et al.*, charging that the TAAS tests unconstitutionally discriminated against Hispanic and Black students. In this case, nine students (eight Latino, one Black), Image de Tejas (an advocacy group for increasing federal employment of Latinos), and GI Forum (a Latino advocacy group composed of former GIs) became plaintiffs in a suit against the TEA, charging that the disproportionate number of Hispanic and African American students failing the state-mandated test, the TAAS, constituted racial discrimination. MALDEF, the attorneys for the plaintiffs, argued that the TAAS high school exit exam prevented a large number of Hispanic and African American students from graduating at a rate so disproportionate to that of White students that it constituted a disparate impact under discrimination laws and litigation. MALDEF argued that this disparate impact was caused by a test that did not meet the standard of educational necessity, showing that (1) the establishment of a cutoff score for passing or failing was guided by political reasons instead of educational standards, (2) the choice of items of the test failed to pass psychometric standards for the ridding of (racial) bias, and (3) the testing system accompanied educational policies that contradicted the stated purposes of the test (such as severely limiting the curriculum, causing increased dropout rates, and retaining students in the pre-test grade [ninth grade]) (Saucedo 2000). According to the TEA, not only was the TAAS educationally necessary, but it also served as a system for discovering which districts and schools needed improvement. The TEA argued that the decreasing racial gaps in test scores evidenced that the test was not racist; rather, it was a tool for redressing racial inequalities throughout the state. In 1999, Reagan-appointed judge Edward Prado, himself a former student of the Edgewood School District, ruled that while MALDEF proved that the TAAS did produce a statistically significant disparate impact on Black and Mexican American students, this disproportionality was not caused by the actions or any racist intentions of the TEA, but by the individual failure of students of color to attain a legitimate educational goal: "In short, the Court finds, on the basis of the evidence presented at trial, that the disparities in test scores do not result from flaws in the test or in the way it is administered. Instead, as the Plaintiffs themselves have argued, some minority students have, for a myriad of reasons, failed to keep up (or catch up) with their majority counterparts. It may be, as the TEA argues, that the TAAS test is one weapon in the fight to remedy this problem" (*GI Forum et al. v. Texas Education Agency et al.* 87 F. Supp. 2d 667, 683 [2000]).

In that same year, despite the questions about racial disparities materialized by testing at the high school level, under the leadership of then Republican governor George W. Bush, the legislature passed both a "no social promotion" bill (SB 4) that would require third, fifth, and eighth graders to pass the state-mandated exam before being promoted to the next grade, and a bill implementing a more difficult state-mandated testing system, the TAKS (Texas Assessment of Knowledge and Skills), to replace the TAAS. The bill passed in spite of rising cases of statistics-reporting fraud in districts across Texas. That same year, the Austin Independent School District ended busing at the high school and middle school levels, returning to the neighborhood schools model, and removing some of the last vestiges of the 1970 desegregation plans. Once Governor George Bush was elected president in 2000, the administration pushed for the broad expansion of testing in every grade under the No Child Left Behind Act.

## The Context of Texas Racial Realignment and the 78th Legislature

> You know, if we had elected [Strom Thurmond] 30 years ago, we wouldn't be in the mess we are in today.
>
> —Trent Lott, December 5, 2002[13]

The 78th legislative session of 2003 marked a historic moment in Texas politics, as it was the first time since Reconstruction that Republicans dominated the Texas House as well as the governorship and Senate. The racial significance of the 78th session and Republican control of the state government was not lost on an *Austin American Statesman* journalist, Ken Herman (2003), who reported that "White Democrats . . . are vanishing from the Texas legislature" given the presence of "only three white Democratic Senators [out of 31 total senators and 12 Democratic senators] and 19 white Representatives [out of 150 total representatives and 62 Democratic representatives]" and *no* White women Democrats in the legislature. The author suggested that the disappearance of White Democrats resulted from "their GOP foes target[ing] them one by one, district by district." Democratic representative Garnet Coleman told Herman that "[i]t shows that somebody was really smart in drawing maps. They know how to eliminate, through gerrymandering, districts that would elect Anglo Democrats." Herman suggested that the disappearance of White Democrats translates into the diminishing of Democratic power in the House.[14] Of the 107 Republican legislators, only two were non-White: one Mexican American and the other Asian American.

During the 78th legislative session, Republican control of the governorship, House, and Senate initiated legal reforms that were part of a broader national "radical" Republican strategy. Elements of that effort included the war in Iraq and the discourse on the "irrelevant United Nations," the recall of Governor Gray Davis in California, and the redistricting bills passed in Texas and Denver. A *Houston Chronicle* article described the 78th legislative session as historic given the "GOP control of all points of power in the statehouse," creating a situation in which "the always-present business lobby will be more influential than ever, and long-dormant priorities of social conservatives will be boosted," such as limiting abortion rights, promoting school prayer, creating school vouchers, and banning same-sex marriages (Robison and Ratcliffe 2003). The article described the business lobby as being "hardly [able to] restrain their glee," quoting Bill Hammond, the president of the Texas Association of Business as saying, "The outlook for Texas business has never been better" (Robison and Ratcliffe 2003). One of the first battles in the House in the 78th legislative session centered on a Republican-sponsored bill on tort reform that would limit the amount awarded in malpractice suits to $250,000.[15] The debate over the bill reflected the Republican strategy and strength, as Democrats found their attempts to amend the bill defeated at every instance (see also Elliot and Ratcliffe 2003). Republican House Speaker Tom Craddick said of the debate, "It was the most passionate debate I've seen in the 35 years I've been in the House" (Elliot and Ratcliffe 2003). However, Representative Dunnam (D-Waco) called a point of order, revealing that the Republicans had held a meeting closed to the public that considered combining HB 3, which would cap awards from malpractice suits, and HB 4, which would limit awards from other civil lawsuits. Such an action violated the House rules that stipulated that all committee meetings must be open to the public. However, the new incarnation of HB 4 was speedily reintroduced and eventually passed by the House 94–46. Another major battle for Democrats centered on the state budget, and an editorial in the *Houston Chronicle* (2003a) called the state budget a "horror show":

> The state budget process, which Republican leaders said would lead to new efficiencies and a healthy transparency, is beginning to resemble something closer to a murky Dickensian novel in which ill health plays the central role.
>
> From children's health insurance to Medicaid availability to cuts in mental health care and other programs, the procession of hearings and testimony paints a grim picture for tens of thousands of disadvantaged Texans. And this is a state already known far and wide for its miserly ways.

The "murky Dickensian" aura that haunted state budget debates seemed to echo in the freedom with which Republican representative Debbie Riddle made the following comment during a debate in a Border and International Affairs Committee meeting on health care for undocumented workers: "Where did this idea come from that everybody deserves free education, free medical care, free whatever? It comes from Moscow, from Russia. It comes straight out of the pit of hell. . . . And it is cleverly disguised as having a tender heart. It's not a tender heart. It's ripping the heart out of this country" (quoted in Taylor 2003).

The racist overtones of her comment sparked members of the Mexican American Legislative Caucus to react symbolically, wearing badges that read, "I'm from the Pit of Hell." On April 29, after the House debated several bills late into the night, representatives felt free to mock the Black vernacular, as Representative Keffer, responding to another male representative's calling him "brother," pointed his fingers down awkwardly, mimicking a stereotypical "homeboy," saying "What it is?" The acceptance of Riddle's comments and Keffer's mimicry to me symbolized the true lack of representation and political power Latino and Black people had and still have in the legislature. By the end of the session, this lack of power expressed itself in the redistricting bill that was pushed quickly through the House under the pressure of U.S. House Majority Leader Tom Delay and Bush adviser Karl Rove. The bill would redraw district boundaries, giving Republicans more seats in the U.S. House of Representatives than Democrats, and radically decreasing the voting power of people of color. Given that Republicans would vote en masse, having the majority, Democrats protested by refusing to allow a quorum in the House necessary to pass the bill. Following a tactic used by senators in 1979, "the Killer Bees," Democrats fled the state in a protest that garnered national attention and, despite the defection of a few Democrats (such as Representatives Garnet Coleman and Harold Dutton), successfully thwarted the attempts to pass a redistricting bill in the regular session. While Democrats across the state praised the protest, calling the fleeing representatives "Killer D's," Republicans reacted harshly, sending state troopers and the Texas Rangers after the representatives. Headlines called the Democrats "AWOL," and Speaker of the House Tom Craddick labeled them "Chicken D's." The Texas Republican Party Web site (http://www.texasgop.org) even posted playing cards of the Democratic representatives,[16] mimicking the move by the U.S. Army in Iraq when it distributed playing cards whose faces were members and leaders of Saddam Hussein's administration. Despite the protest, the governor was able to pass the bill after calling a third special session.[17]

In terms of educational reforms, the major legislation facing the House was a bill to sunset the Robin Hood bill passed in 1995 in accordance with *Edgewood v. Kirby*. At the first House Public Education Committee hearing, Public Education Committee chairman, Representative Kent Grusendorf, presented his Robin Hood sunset bill, HB 604. Many of the legislators justified the sunset as taking a proactive stance in the face of an impending lawsuit by Orange County that threatened to render the current system unconstitutional since it could be argued that the redistributive finance system approached an illegal state property tax. As I discuss in Chapter 4, the provisions that would be eliminated by the passage of the sunset bill were those that provided for equity and that accounted for costs in education. Although the bill passed the House, it did not pass the Senate. After four special sessions called by Governor Rick Perry, the legislature still had not enacted a bill, leaving Robin Hood intact—for the time being. One of the more radical bills was HB 859 by Representative Jerry Madden, a bill that could strengthen a law implemented in 1995 to allow school districts to become home-rule school districts, also called "charter districts."[18] Under current law, a home-rule school district can be established by a school board if the following occurs: a district charter is requested by a petition signed by at least 5 percent of registered voters in the district, or two-thirds of the school board vote to commission a charter; and that charter is approved by a majority of voters in that district with a minimum voter turnout of 25 percent of registered voters on the first try and 20 percent on the second (TEC § 12(B)). Current law also contains stipulations that the charter must comply with federal regulations under which public school districts are bound, including nondiscrimination. At the Public Education Committee hearing on Tuesday March 4, 2003, Madden described HB 859 as relieving districts of "laborious" requirements, noting that not a single school district sought to establish a charter district. However, for civil rights advocates the bill raised alarm in the Capitol. Under HB 859, a home-rule district charter could be commissioned by a petition signed by a significantly lower number of voters, by 5 percent of the "number of votes received in the district by all candidates for governor in the most recent gubernatorial election" instead of 5 percent of registered voters. Likewise, a majority of a school board under HB 859 could commission a home-rule school district charter instead of the two-thirds required in current law. Radically, HB 859 would lift the following restrictions for the development of home-rule or charter school districts:

1. Discrimination against students with disabilities and on the basis of race, socioeconomic status, learning disability, or family support status
2. Educator certification
3. Interdistrict transfers
4. Class-size limits
5. High school graduation requirements
6. Special education programs
7. Bilingual programs—if the district does not offer them
8. Prekindergarten programs
9. Safety provisions relating to transportation
10. Charter commission reflecting the socioeconomic and racial makeup of the district
11. Determination of compliance with Voting Rights Act
12. Minimum voter turnout of 25 percent of registered voters on the first try and 20 percent on the second
13. Governance section on choosing of officers

While the question of resegregation was not raised at the committee hearing, my thoughts were that this is exactly what the bill intended to do. One of the ironies in the bill is the exemption of districts from high school graduation requirements, thus from the TAKS requirements. The ultimate surprise for me was the approval of the bill by the Public Education Committee with the support of Black representative Harold

Dutton from Houston. Representative Dutton also surprisingly supported HB 2465, a bill sponsored by Representative Grusendorf that would establish a pilot voucher program in the state.[19] Neither of the bills reached the House floor for a vote, as Representatives Madden and Grusendorf postponed consideration several times—which a legislative aide suggested to me meant that the bills lacked the sufficient support—before the Democratic protest against the redistricting bill ended further discussions of bills on the floor. Although these bills did not pass in the regular session, their approval by the Public Education Committee signified the direction the committee (and the selection of the committee) intended to pursue, a direction that would intensify racial and class inequalities. The historic seventy-eighth Republican-led state government intended to end the finance equity system that was the very justification for the establishment of the test-based accountability system in Texas. Given the force of the accountability movement and its Republican leadership, one strategy of Democrats in the U.S. Senate and Texas House became embodied in the movement for multiple criteria.

## Conclusion

Testing as a mode of educational reform must be looked at in the historical and politico-economic context of segregation (and desegregation and resegregation). In Texas, the political force of testing as a mode of educational reform is in part a product of the racial realignment of the Republican Party. As southern states evaded desegregation orders, standardized testing became one way of maintaining racial barriers without the appearance of intent to discriminate. In Texas, the Republican Party coalesced in part due to opposition to desegregation, and the emergence of testing coincides with the rise of the new party to power. Further, the emergence of the "new" Republican Party in opposition to Roosevelt's New Deal provides the context for the modern Texas Republican broader strategy of neoliberal privatization reforms such as charter districts and vouchers. Through my ethnography, I found that the movement for multiple criteria, while coming out of struggles against racism, articulated a broader struggle, one that I argue in the next chapter to be a struggle against objectification by testing and its statistical discourse.

# 3 / Statistical Objectification, Governmentality, and Race in High-Stakes Testing

On January 25, 2003, just before the start of the 78th session of the Texas legislature, a coalition formed by teachers, professors, and parents called Texans for Quality Assessment organized a rally in support of multiple-criteria bills. March 2003 would mark the first time that third graders were required to pass state assessments in reading (the Texas Assessment of Knowledge and Skills) in order to be promoted to the fourth grade. Under Texas law (TEC § 28.0211), students in the third, fifth, and eighth grades who fail testing requirements may still pass to the following grade if a committee composed of the student's parent, teacher, and principal, considering the students' complete academic record, unanimously decides to promote the student to the following grade. The law activates the committee only after the student retakes the test and fails twice more. Out of concern for the psychological effect that failing such a high-stakes test would have on young students, the multiple-criteria bill proposed that portfolios, grades, and teacher evaluations be used as multiple criteria after the first time a student failed a test. Additionally, the bill intended to empower parents by requiring that the committee deciding the student's fate unanimously vote to retain the student in the same grade. This would safeguard against the potential for principals to influence teachers' votes on the committees.

On that cold, drizzling Saturday afternoon, on the southwest side of the Capitol building in Austin, protestors circled a platform, which I estimated as having a radius of about ten to twelve people—some holding signs, some, including me, wearing Texans for Quality Assessment T-shirts. The crowd was mostly Hispanic and White and mostly women, with a few Black people.[1] There were contingents from Laredo (the largest, with about twenty to thirty students), El Paso, Edcouch-Elsa, Houston, Amarillo, Georgetown, and Austin. In the shadow of the intimidating Capitol building, I noticed a bronze general pointing his gun toward the East, which I thought was symbolic of the segregation pervading Austin, since the interstate divides the city into the Black and Latino east side and the mostly White west side. While one of the rallying points was the projection that forty-two thousand third graders could fail the TAKS in the following spring, I saw a different argument emerging, a critique of objectification by tests and their statistics, a critique symbolized by stories of children's personal experiences. There was a group of women wearing coats that on the back bore stories, such as the following worn by a White woman with graying hair: "I am marching for Peter. Peter is a first grader. His teacher told his mother (in September!) that she did not think he would do well on TAKS and needs a tutor. This is the child who writes in his journal such things as going on an excavation for fossils in his back-yard."[2]

A mother who had chosen to home-school her child and had been a prominent figure in the movement against high-stakes testing in Texas with her organization, Parents United Against TAAS, passed out miniature bubbles that afternoon. When it was time for her testimony at the microphone, she announced that the bubbles represented the bubbles on the test sheets. "Spread the word . . . collectively," she said; the Texas legislature has "sold out our schools to corporate test-makers." During the second half of the rally, a strategy session led by Representative Dora Olivo, the sponsor of the bills, we heard Susan Ohanian, a national speaker against the adverse affects of high-stakes testing. In her speech, she told us about a letter she received from a parent in a school with high-stakes testing: The parent's third-grade child didn't want to go to school, would vomit and break out in hives, and needed psychological help; all of this because the school had placed the child on the list as likely to fail a test. "We are harming children," she said.

Abu-Lughod (1990) suggested that resistance is really a "catalyst," a "*diagnostic* of power," and that moments of resistance can "tell us more about forms of power and how people are caught up in them" (42). Hearing the children's stories at the rally, I sensed that the movement for multiple criteria was engaging in what Foucault (1983) called the "struggle against the submission of subjectivity" (213).[3] For Foucault, this form of struggle opposes government (or "governmentality") that individualizes (by removing context and refusing collectivity), while suppressing individuality, thus also normalizing. The struggle calls into question the relationship between power and knowledge, centering on a "refusal of . . . abstractions, of economic and ideological state violence which ignore who we are individually, and also a refusal of a scientific or administrative inquisition which determines who one is" (212). The rally centered on such a struggle against the "submission of subjectivity" and objectification: calling attention to the specificity of children's experiences, refusing the knowledge that constructed and labeled students as "deficient," refusing the abstraction of education from the student via standardized tests (represented by the blowing of the bubbles), and presenting a case that the testing system imposed a system of violence on children. I argue that the submission of subjectivity imposed by the testing system is tied to the production of testing statistical discourse.

The tie between statistics and government is an intimate one, given the founding of statistics, literally "science of the state," as an administrative discipline (Desrosières 1998). According to Foucault (1988c, 1991), statistics—as a "*savoir* of the state"—became "indispensable for correct government" (1988c: 77) through the discursive construction of *population*. Whereas seventeenth-century (mercantilist) administrative statistics served as a description of the state, by the end of the nineteenth century, administrative statistics came to represent a tool for governmental intervention.[4] In the context of nation building, the notion of statistical *population* became an abstracted representation of the nation, constructing the purpose of government as "the welfare of the population" (Foucault 1991: 100). Statistics made possible the "birth of political economy," which merged two types of government: economy, as "the art of properly governing a family"; and politics, "the science of ruling a state" (Foucault 1991: 101).[5] Given that statistics also formed a moral science in the nineteenth century (Hacking 1991), the government of population merged political economy and the "art of self-government" (Foucault 1991: 91). Statistics, then, connect both to the sense of government as a mechanism for state rule but also to a broader sense of government, which Foucault argues is the "conduct of conduct," a means by which "to structure the possible field of actions of others" (Foucault 1983: 221). In this sense, statistics, as argued by Asad (1994), provide more than simply a "mode of understanding and representing populations," but function also "an instrument for regulating and transforming them" (76). In this sense, governmental statistics form the quintessential "discourse network," which Tapper (1999) defined as "the apparatuses of power, knowledge, storage, transmission, reproduction, training, surveillance, and discipline that make it possible to visualize certain objects, rendering them knowable, calculable, manipulable, and consequently, amenable to administration in the broadest sense of the word" (6).

In this chapter, I examine three ways in which testing statistics function as a discourse network in maintaining the hegemony of high-stakes testing in Texas. As the rally indicated, the testing system objectifies students, and I explore the ways in which the historical connection between statistics and standardized testing has provided the conditions for this objectification. Second, statistics not only objectify, but also govern through the conduct of conduct, and I discuss the way in which statistics, through what Woodward (1999) called "statistical panic," structured the ways in which people responded to the testing system. Third, I examine the racialized objectification of students, particularly the way in which testing statistics objectify—in Desrosières's (1998: 9) sense of "making *things that hold*"—the marginalization of students of color.

## "Trained Gorilla"

They [American industrialists] have understood that "trained gorilla" is just a phrase, that "unfortunately" the worker remains a man and even that during his work he thinks more, or at least has greater opportunities for thinking, once he has overcome the crisis of adaptation without being eliminated: and not only does the worker think, but the fact that he gets no immediate satisfaction from his work and realises that they are trying to reduce him to a trained gorilla, can lead him into a train of thought that is far from conformist. That the industrialists are concerned about such things is made clear from a whole series of cautionary measures and "educative" initiatives which are being brought out in Ford's books and the work of Phillip. (Gramsci 1988: 290)

Many scholars have likened the proliferation of standardized testing since the publication of *A Nation at Risk* to the Progressive Era use of the factory as the model for organizing school systems, largely influenced by Frederick Winslow Taylor's *Principles of Scientific Management* (1967 [1947]) (McNeil 2000a; Saltman 2000; Richards, Shore, and Sawicky 1996).[6] The American industrialists' characterization of workers as "trained gorilla[s]," to which Gramsci objected in the passage above, also originated from Taylor's *Principles*. For Gramsci, Taylor's trained gorilla represents the mechanization of the worker, which could be said to be a rearticulation itself of the eighteenth-century conception of "man-as-machine" and the "docile body" (Foucault 1995 [1978]). The link between schooling and the objectification of the worker as docile, automatous, and gorilla-like is two-fold: first, schools functioned as means for socializing children into their roles as workers (see Bowles and Gintis 1976) and second, the means for evaluating workers through quantification inspired means for evaluating students. Satirizing the use of statistics in *Hard Times*, (see Desrosières 1998: 174; Hacking 1991: 188), Charles Dickens comments both on the objectification of the worker and the objectification of students through statistics. The character of laborer Stephen Blackpool moved to a moment of resistance spoke of workers' grievances: "Most o' aw, rating 'em as so much Power, and reg'lating 'em as if they was figures in a soom, or machines: wi'out loves and likens, wi'out memories and inclinations, wi'out souls to weary and souls to hope" (Dickens (1996 [1907]): 143). At the same time, in a chapter titled "Murdering the Innocents," the schoolmaster Thomas Gradgrind referred to students as numbers ("Girl number twenty") and viewed students as "little pitchers . . . to be filled so full of facts" (6). Historicizing the quantification of workers and the conceptualization of "work" and "power" as linked within physics, Porter (1995) commented that "corporations began early to evaluate workers by quantity of production," and that such quantification not only supplied the basis for a "crucial kind of self-discipline," but also created the conditions in which "individuals are made governable" (44). The alienation of workers through the quantification of labor provided the basis for the "modern notion of intelligence" as a measurable, abstracted quantity (MacKenzie 1981: 34). Standardized tests have institutionalized a "Gradgrindian" vision of education as understood and governed by measure, "figures," and "arithmetic," particularly as testing serves as a mechanisms for both renaming students as numbers and treating students as if "vessels . . . ready to have imperial gallons of facts poured into them until they were full to the brim" (Dickens (1996 [1907]): 5). It was exactly students' resistance and narratives against standardized testing that "diagnosed" this form of power.

Over the duration of the 78th Texas legislative session, one student in particular, Kimberly Marciniak of San Antonio, became a famous symbol for her protest against testing. Her story was covered not only by several articles in the *San Antonio Express-News*, but also in newspapers across the state, in a television appearance on the local news, and in an interview on National Public Radio (Martinez 2003). The young student boycotted a field TAKS test after conducting a study on the TAAS (the previous test) in which she found that the state had implemented a program called the Texas Successful Schools Award program, granting schools rewards of between $500 and $5,000 for achieving high TAAS scores (Martinez 2003).[7] She wrote an essay objecting to the way in which the overemphasis on the test led her history class to become test preparation: "It was April, and going to Coach Bloomer's third-period history class had become a dreaded task. Since November, he had been systematically destroying my interest in what had once been my favorite subject" (quoted in Torres 2003). The young student had written to a reporter, "I don't want to be a statistic and I don't want to be a human guinea pig for the district" (quoted in Torres 2003). In this sentiment, the student equates the suppressing of learning and subjectivity by the testing system with being an object of an experiment and becoming a statistic.

On a link provided by Texans for Quality Assessment on their Web site, a study of college students' views of TAAS by Blalock and Haswell (2002) at the University of Texas A&M-Kingsville also exhibited students' feelings of being objectified, of the suppression of their subjectivity. The researchers asked students to send them e-mail message responses describing their views on the test. While the authors' content analysis revealed that 63 percent of the 402 comments about the TAAS were completely negative, and 15 percent largely negative, I found among the comments a feeling of the loss of agency. One college student lamented being known simply as a "name and a score" (13-252).[8] Another of the students in the college survey remarked that the TAAS tests "were so pointless that you could teach a chimpanzee to do these sort of problems" (01-002), revealing a feeling of being reduced to a trained gorilla. For one of the college students in the survey, "We became robots that were programmed to write in TAAS format and no other format" (03-041), and another student mentioned that for students' "whole lives they are pounded with information on how to take this test. They are like mini-robots ready to spit out the info" (05-084). Of the 402 responses, 127 remarked that the whole testing experience was either boring or a waste of time, and 179 remarked on how much teaching to the test went on. Students felt that their "opinions didn't matter" (10-001), that the school and testing systems were "not allowing us to think" (01-015). The students felt "TAAS-ed out" (01-016), subjected to "routine" (01-102), "drill" (10-193), "regurgitation" (14-236, 18-355), as if they "lived breathed and ate TAAS" (03-045), with the TAAS "crammed . . . down my throat" (16-303). One student called the time not spent on TAAS their "freedom time" (01-020). Students felt as if schools were only aiming for "recognition" (02-033), for "good statistics" (18-341), and one student even wrote that the testing system was "designed to give a bell curve for the state" (03-049).

In an article in the *Houston Chronicle*, school administrators expressed awareness of the way in which the pressure to produce statistical test results has objectified students. One Houston principal admitted that "[w]e have created TAAS robots," and another Houston principal remarked, "[I]f all we do is teach to the test, we will numb our kids to death" (Downing 2002). In *Savage Inequalities*, Kozol (1991) interviewed Principal Ruthie Green-Brown, who was dealing with the pressure of tests. She commented, "What is the result? We are preparing a generation of robots. Kids are learning exclusively through rote. . . . They do not learn to think, because their teachers are straitjacketed by tests that measure only isolated skills. . . . Is this what the country wants for its black children?" (143).

The students' experiences of alienation and the submission of subjectivity resulting from testing in Texas appear rooted in an existential objection to being governed by and as statistics. This resistance diagnoses a set of particular power relations embedded in the very system of schooling in the United States. How, then, are statistics, as an administrative science, connected to the ways in which testing "manifests the subjection of those who are perceived as objects and the objectification of those who are subjected" (Foucault 1995 [1975]: 184–185)?

According to Desrosières (1998), statistics involve two processes that combine administration and science: "the construction of a political space of equivalence and encoding and a mathematical processing often based on probability calculus" (13). The earliest form of administrative statistics, particularly in German statistics, was descriptions of the state in tabular form, and the table provided the spaces of equivalence that allowed the insertion of numbers (21). Foucault (1995 [1975]) described the table as a "technique of power and a procedure of knowledge" (148) that provided a means for the sorting and dividing practices through which school systems organized students, which was often based on class. Interestingly, Porter (1995) argued that the organization of educational systems "actually created the kinds of statistical populations that Galtonian psychology took as its basis" (210).

While the arrangement of students provided what Desrosières calls the "construction of political space of equivalence," the examination provided the means for the "mathematical processing" of students. For Foucault (1995 [1975]), the examination made possible the formation of knowledge (pedagogy) of an individual as "a describable, analysable object" at the same time that it operated as a normalizing "comparative system that made possible the measurement of overall phenomena, the description of groups, the characterization of collective facts, the calculation of the gaps between individuals, their distribution in a given 'population'" (190). Mass standardized testing in the United States emerged from the efforts to nationalize an American version of the IQ test, the Stanford-Binet (Lemann 1999), in which the test's founder, Lewis Terman, applied the Gaussian distribution or the bell curve to the IQ test (Gould 1996: 207). Testing also provided a means for scientifically rationalizing tracking (Porter 1995), a system of school organization developed out of the application of the factory model to schooling, particularly influenced by Taylor's scientific management (Oakes 1985). Embedded within the historical organization of schooling, examinations, and standardized testing is the use of statistics, in the form of the table or the distribution, as both a "procedure of knowledge" and a "technique of power" (Foucault 1995 [1975]: 148), as a discourse network regulating student bodies.

While proponents of the testing system push for data-driven improvement, this very process has objectified students. However, as Gramsci says of the trained gorilla, objectification never fully robs the student of agency. Hughes and Bailey (2002), interviewing high school students attending schools with exit exams in Indiana, found that students considered the tests, as a single determinant of their graduation, unfair, and that they were "suspicious of the scoring process" and concluded that "the test 'doesn't prove anything'" (75, 76). A student from San Antonio, Julie Rae Maldonado, wrote a satirical letter to the president, which appeared in the *San Antonio Express-News* in March 2003, thanking him "in the most sincere fashion for all you have done to the great state of Texas." With eloquence and creativity, her letter both recognized and refused the attempt to be normalized as a trained gorilla, a refusal that leads, as Gramsci suggested, to a "train of thought that is far from conformist":

> For weeks, children and teachers alike have been skipping joyously through the halls of my high school, with a happy cloud of failure looming over everything they do. But we don't worry about not graduating, because we are spending all of our time learning that TAKS test, subject by subject, question by question, diagram by diagram. We are no longer wasting our time with math or history!
>
> All of our educational needs have been condensed into one multiple choice and short answer test with a cheerful "No Pass, No Graduate!" label.
>
> When I am trained in English class how to form a Correct Opinion about a passage, I praise your name. When we go weeks on end in math class without a single homework problem, I am eternally grateful for your birth! Thank You for lightening our load, Mr. President! Now we only have to worry about not graduating, which isn't nearly as bad as worrying about getting educated. I personally am convinced that educating too much might cause instability and ultimately turn us all into American terrorists.

She even went on to say, "[T]he greatest thing about the TAKS test is that with its long life, and continued anti-education, we are assured to elect wonderful men like you, Mr. President, for the rest of this country's existence." Her letter recognizes testing as a "technique of power" that attempts to suppress subjectivity and literally "educate consent" (Gramsci 1971: 259), both to testing and to the uncritical support of President Bush, through "anti-education."

Using Abu-Lughod's (1990) conception of resistance as diagnostic, the struggle of students against the submission of subjectivity imposed by the testing system allows us to view the way in which the testing system objectifies students. The fact that the very protests against testing are articulated as objections to becoming a statistic, being just "a name and a score," and being used by schools to get "good statistics," reflects the centrality of statistics in the use of testing as a way of organizing and governing schooling.

## Statistical Panic and the Public Sphere

Governmentality works not only by inscribing students as governable objects, but also by the "conduct of conduct," or "structur[ing] the possible field of actions of others" (Foucault 1983: 221). One of the cornerstones of the test-based accountability system is the "constant and comparative public assessment" (Apple 2001: 72) through media reporting of school and district report cards. For Skrla, Scheurich, and Johnson (2000), the public dissemination of data within the Texas accountability system, particularly the disaggregation of data by race, evidences a "radical openness [that] is a major benefit to democracy itself and serves specific purposes in eliciting school and district transformations" (11). The equating of "publicity" with democracy is, for Habermas, a historical one, since "publicity, as the principle of public access to state decisions and of glasnost within social intercourse" (Peters 1997: 76), marks the transition from feudal states to modern democratic states. The state, "becom[ing] a *public thing*," enabled statistics, once considered "the mirror of the prince," to become the "mirror of the nation" (Desrosières 1998: 34), thus embedding statistics in the public sphere (324). However, in the context of postmodernity and late capitalism, the uncritical equating of democracy and publicity ignores the "deployment of a staged form of publicity" by organizations engaged in hegemonic projects (Habermas 1989: 236). For Woodward (1999), the omnipresence of statistics in the public sphere indicates not necessarily a sign of democracy, but a condition of postmodernity, an "expression of late capitalism" (179). In the form of probabilities, and produced in a "discourse of risk," statistics often create a "sense of foreboding and insecurity," a "structure of feeling" that Woodward has termed "statistical panic" (179–181): "The structure of feeling I have been calling statistical panic (and its oscillating partner, boredom) is a response to the social technology of statistics that has both contributed to the creation of the omnipresent discourse of risk and has produced a calculus to avoid that very risk, a prime contradiction of capitalist culture as we enter the third millennium" (196).

The "postmodern society of risk" has roots in the development of insurance technologies, which both constructed risk through probability calculus or predictive statistics and also established the means for ascribing value—as a "calculable" entity and as a form of capital—to risk (Ewald 1991). In the nineteenth century, insurance technologies merged with Western social and political economy through the governmental strategy of providing social insurance or social security—largely as a way of resolving the conflicts of capitalist (or industrial) society. By the end of the nineteenth century, according to Ewald (1991: 210), "[European] [s]ocieties envisage[d] themselves as a vast system of insurance." The success of insurance technologies, both private and governmental, depends on their ability to assuage fear of a catastrophic event (Ewald 1991: 208), indicating that moments of fear and panic are often deployed, or "staged" as Habermas might suggest, in corporate profit-seeking or governmental projects of hegemony. Despite a tendency for subjects in a postmodern society to reject the "depersonalizing force" of statistics (Woodward 1999: 186), not only are the statistical "objectification of possible experience" (Gordon 1991: 39) and the targeting of fear through the discourse of risk still hegemonic components of a wide range of political projects, but also the divide between statistical panic and boredom is guarded by a politics of statistical significance.[9]

In 2002, the Texas Education Agency's release of the projected scores on the new TAKS test caused widespread panic in Texas, and the statistical projections of the percentage of students at risk of failing became fodder not simply for a push for test preparation, but also for the political grounds for arguing for multiple criteria. In the spring, the TAKS would replace the TAAS, the state's previous system of testing. The replacement marked the taking effect of a key piece of legislation passed during and promoted by the administration of then governor George W. Bush, which enforced a "no social promotion" policy. In this first year of implementation, third graders would be the first class to have to pass the reading test in order to be promoted to the fourth grade. The number 42,000 emerged as the projected number of third graders expected to fail the third-grade TAKS reading test. Articles throughout Texas reflected the fear generated by this projection. An elementary school principal wrote in to the *Austin American-Statesman* that under the surface there was "fear running rampant throughout the system" (Kramer 2002). One mother said, "I've never seen so much high anxiety and stress in a third grade class. The kids are terrified" (Schmidt 2002). Another article called the projections "dismal and dispiriting" (Downing 2002). Assistant superintendent of curriculum and instruction for the Southwest School District in San Antonio said of the projections, "[I]t's staggering and it kind of takes your breath at first" (Gutierrez 2002). For a Houston mother, "It's like every student is in a suspense movie. Everybody knows something is going to happen, but nobody knows what" (Peabody 2003a). The pressure on young children is compounded by the fact that the stakes of these tests also determine schools' and districts' ratings, linked to a system of incentives and punishments (Valenzuela 2002). Additionally, stories circulated about children throwing up from all of the stress, elevating test anxiety to a whole new level, an occurrence happening not only in Texas, but also in North Carolina and Louisiana (Hardy 2003).

The number 42,000 stood also as a representation used by the organization Texans for Quality Assessment in rallies waged against the harmful effects of testing, embodied in the lobbying for multiple-criteria bills. The multiple-criteria bills proposed that portfolios, grades, and teacher evaluations be weighed against failure on state assessments, and that parents could have more input into the decision to pass or retain their children in a particular grade. According to Woodward (1999), "In part, the challenge for those who are activists is to convince others to understand the urgency implied in the tedious, quantitative language of the statistic. Boredom must be converted into concern, into a kind of panic" (185). While the collection of children's stories of experiences with testing were the most important part of the rallying points of the movement for the multiple-criteria bills, statistics were a significant part of the lobbying points: that forty-two thousand third graders were expected to fail; that disproportionately students of color would fail—20 percent of Hispanics and 25 percent of African Americans; and that the chances for a retained student to drop out of school later in his or her career were significant: 40 percent on one retention and 60 percent on the second, as stated in an "Organizer's Toolkit" designed and distributed by Representative Olivo. At a January 25 rally in 2003, Susan Ohanian stated the following about probability of failure: 50 percent of students retained once will not graduate high school, and that rate increases to 90 percent if a student is retained twice. The same sentiment was expressed by Arturo Almendarez, an assistant superintendent at Corpus Christi Independent School District, who cited a study showing that "a child who was retained one time in his or her schooling will be five times more likely to drop out than a classmate who has not repeated a grade. . . . [W]hen a child is held back twice, the student is practically guaranteed not to earn a diploma" (Eaton 2003).

According to Woodward, statistical panic is "usually fleeting. Based as it is on a number, it usually cannot be endured for long. Moreover, in virtually all cases it will surely be drowned out by another number" (1999: 185). Such a drowning out did occur over the session, and the statistical panic of the 42,000 third graders that TEA predicted would fail was replaced after the first administration of the test with the banality of 28,143 actual third graders who failed the English TAKS in addition to the 4,516 who failed the Spanish TAKS, and replaced by the third administration with the very boring statistic of 11,748 third graders failing the TAKS and in danger of being retained in the third grade (see Texas Education Agency 2003b–g). One supporter of the multiple-criteria bills dared to say in a strategy meeting before the test results came out, "[Y]ou almost wish the kids will fail this test in big numbers," revealing the sense that the support for multiple criteria necessitated a certain statistical panic. However, once the 28,413 drowned out the 42,000, newspapers such as the *Austin American-Statesman* reported jubilantly that "Students Rise to Challenge of Tougher Test in Reading: Third-Graders Breeze through State's New Assessment" (Blackwell 2003). By the third administration, 96 percent of third graders passed the TAKS, a fact on which Joe Bernal, a member of the State Board of Education commented, "I'm very happy; in fact, I'm ecstatic. . . . I didn't think we'd reach this level this soon" (Gutierrez 2003c). The good scores proved that passing the multiple-criteria bills would face major difficulty, exhibited by a *Houston Chronicle* editorial (2003) that reported only "a small percentage of children will be held back for failing TAKS. That's bad news only for those who favor social promotion over demonstrated academic mastery."

The good news of the third-grade TAKS passage rate even overshadowed the results of the tenth- and eleventh-grade TAKS high school exams, which, according to Gutierrez (2003b) of the *San Antonio Express-News*, "produce[d] massive failures." For high school students, the new, more difficult TAKS brought new graduation requirements. For students entering high school in the 2000–2001 school year, the state of Texas required them to pass three TAAS exams (reading, mathematics, and writing) deemed "exit-level exams" or pass three end-of-course exams (English II, Algebra I, and either Biology or U.S. History). Students took the exit-level exams in the tenth grade and upon failure given up to eight times to re-take each test. Under the new TAKS, the state required students entering high school beginning in 2001–2002 to pass four more difficult TAKS exams (English language arts, mathematics, social studies, and science) in order to graduate. Students took the exit-level exams in the eleventh grade and upon failure given up to five times to re-take each test. After the first administration of the TAKS in 2003, only 52 percent of all sophomores taking the test passed all of the exams (Texas Education Agency 2003h). These same students in the next year would have to pass all tests within five tries in order to graduate from high school. Only 35 percent of African American sophomores and 38 percent of Hispanic sophomores, compared to 66 percent of White students, passed all the tests (Texas Education Agency 2003h). It was a forewarning, as an *Austin American-Statesman* headline read, "Many 10th Graders on Way to Flunking, Test Data Show" (Martinez and Rodriguez 2003). The panic inherent in such numbers was tempered by the fact that the TAKS scores, as worrisome as they were, still exceeded the scores of the previous state test, the TAAS, in its first administration in 1990, according to Darlene Westbrook, Austin deputy superintendent for curriculum and instruction. She told reporters that she "was expecting that we would have a challenge" (Martinez and Rodriguez 2003), a comment very similar to a comment by Texas Education Commissioner Felipe Alanis that "[w]e expected high school to be our most challenging area" (Gutierrez 2003a). Although the legislative session ended before the TEA released the results of the high school exam, there was still a quieted panic that prompted a Republican legislative aide to tell a group of us lobbying for the multiple-criteria bills that because high school TAKS passing rates were projected to be so low, the multiple-criteria bill for high school would have a better chance than that for the third, fifth, and eighth grades. By the end of the session, however, neither bill had passed the House.

## Materializing Invisibility and "Pushing Out"

> A mental block is built over time in the Anglo mind that says we shouldn't count, hence we aren't seen and don't exist.
>
> — José Angel Gutiérrez (1998: 59)

> 'Cause I've been to ___ and ___ high school before, and it seems like they try to make you drop out instead of helping you. And I plan to send 'em an invitation to my graduation.
>
> — "Roy," Texas high school student[10]

The statistical panic surrounding test scores must be understood in the context of the sanctions-rewards system attached to test results. According to Valenzuela (2002), such a highly publicized, highly stressful system of sanctions produces "perverse incentives . . . to marginalize children through various mechanisms" (103). One such mechanism is the encouraging of students to drop out or the phenomenon of "pushing out," a component of what McNeil (2000b) called the practice of "artificially manipulating the testable student populations" (512) in order to produce a particular institutional score. According to Haney (2000), the increased retention rates of Hispanic and Black students in the ninth grade and increasing dropout rates of students of color since the implementation of the TAAS constituted a statistical anomaly.[11] In filing suit against the TEA for the disproportionate impact of the testing requirements on African American and Hispanic students, MALDEF wrote in its post-trial brief, "It is on behalf of these 'olvidados' and 'desaparecidos'—victims of an educational system harmful and arbitrary in its effect on students—that the Plaintiffs seek relief from the TAAS Exit requirements" (Kauffman, Morales, and Saucedo 1999: 1). The terms *olvidados* (the forgotten) and *desaparecidos* (the disappeared) call attention to not only the politics of silence in racializing and racial discourse (Trouillot 1995) and the mechanisms of forgetting within scientific discourse (Adorno and Horkheimer 1979 [1944]: 230), but also the practicing of a racialized, state-sanctioned violence.[12]

Arguably, racial bodies as *desaparecidos* is a key component in the U.S. racial history itself, given that genocide, land displacement, market displacement, and political displacement have been central to U.S. racialization and the establishment of U.S. hegemony globally (DuBois 1962 [1935]; Montejano 1986; Takaki 1979). Further, as Anzaldúa (1999) suggested, the violence of racial displacements is rooted in objectification (59).[13] While Stoler (1995) suggested, using Foucault, that state racism involves the right over life (biopower), Davis's (1983 [1981]) work suggests that state racism demands control of the right over life not simply as the right to kill, but as a right to containment. According to Davis, "one of racism's salient features [is] the assumption that white men— especially with economic power—possess an incontestable right of access to Black women's bodies," in other words, "assumed property rights over Black people" (175). For Collins (1998), the "politics of containment" operates by producing hypervisibility as it simultaneously produces invisibility (35). Such invisibility as a form of containment can be understood in terms of what Silva (2001) described as the construction (or deployment) of "blackness and brownness" as "always-already" outside of the transcendental domain of justice and legality (436). In such a deployment, racial injustice is not simply defined by exclusion from participation within the normalized processes, but by an "outsidedness" by which racial violence, such as police brutality, becomes legitimate and normalized. This outsidedness is surely not an inscription only of blackness, but that of racial other (see Takaki 1979),[14] and can also be inscribed in a particular racial population through statistics. In *The Dark Side of Numbers*, Seltzer and Anderson (2001) asserted, "As many commentators have indicated, particularly in the literature on the efforts of European colonialists to control populations in their far-flung empires . . . there is a darker side to the development of these systems. Population data systems also permit the identification of vulnerable subpopulations within the larger population, or even the definition of entire population as 'outcasts' and a threat to the overall health of the state" (482).

This darker side can be conceptualized in terms of racial governmentality. Tapper (1999) extended Foucault's concept of governmentality to describe the way in which a particular racialized population becomes identified as a target for government intervention. In education, the inscription of "at-risk" defines racial populations as threats to the overall productiveness of U.S. society. As a predictive concept (because it is a statistical-probabilistic concept) and as a technology of risk, the notion of "at-risk" allows for the targeting of these racial populations through governmental policies (Margonis 1992). In the Texas testing regime, Black and Latino bodies and populations become inscribed as "at-risk" and are targeted by school administrators. In many cases, students of color expected to fail the test are pushed out, or as Dan Rather (2004) reported in a *60 Minutes II* segment titled "The Texas Miracle," "literally subtracted," as if disposable statistical data:[15]

> DAN RATHER [narrating]: Houston schools also won national acclaim for raising average scores on a statewide achievement test given to tenth graders. Principals were judged on how well their students did on that test. So, in Houston's schools, Kimball [former assistant principal of Sharpstown] says principals taught addition by subtraction. They raised the average test scores by keeping low-performing kids from taking the test. In some cases, that meant the kids never got to the tenth grade at all.
>
> ROBERT KIMBALL: It's real easy to do.
>
> RATHER [interviewing]: It is?
>
> KIMBALL: What Sharpstown High School did, and many other schools did, they said, okay, you can not go to the tenth grade unless you pass all these courses.
>
> RATHER: In the ninth grade?
>
> KIMBALL: In the ninth grade.

RATHER: What's wrong with that? Some people might say, well, that's pretty healthy. Hold them back in the ninth grade until they've got those basics down, and then move 'em along.

KIMBALL: Because you didn't . . . you failed Algebra, you may be in the ninth grade three years until you pass that course. But that's not a social promotion if you just allow the student go to the tenth grade, just, you now, let them take Algebra again and work on it there.

RATHER [narrating]: That's just what happened to Perla Arredondo. She passed all of her classes in ninth grade, but was then told she had to repeat the same grade and the same courses.

RATHER [interviewing]: Why did you spend three years in the ninth grade?

ARREDONDO: Because I went to my counselor's office and I told her, I said, you're giving me the wrong courses because I already passed them. So, she said, "Don't worry about it. I know what I'm doing, that's my job."

RATHER [narrating]: Perla spent three years in the ninth grade. She did fail Algebra, but passed it in summer school. Finally, she was promoted . . . right past tenth grade and that important test, and into the eleventh. Without enough credits to graduate, Perla dropped out. But she was smart enough to work as a cashier, a secretary, and a waitress, where she learned an important lesson.

ARREDONDO: I know that I could get a good job without a high school diploma, you know, I can get it as a waitress, and I don't want to be doing that all my life.

RATHER [interviewing]: Why, do you have some reason for wanting a better job, other than just to do better?

ARREDONDO: For my dad and for my mom, you know, I want to give them . . . I want them to be proud of me. You know, that's another thing I want, for them, you know, I want them to be proud of what I am.

This portion of the "The Texas Miracle" segment provides an example of the phenomenon of pushing out that has been being uncovered in the press since the selection of Rod Paige, former Houston superintendent, as national secretary of education and the passage of the No Child Left Behind Act. In his last years of tenure as superintendent of the Houston Independent School District, Paige placed extreme pressure on his district to raise TAAS scores, lower dropout rates, and increase accountability ratings. According to Peabody, Mason, and Bernstein (2003), "Paige created a boiler-room, no excuses atmosphere that effectively forced employees to massage scores and statistics." The *60 Minutes II* segment reported that Paige gave principals one-year contracts based on their statistical production, providing large incentives to those who succeeded while threatening harsh sanctions to those who failed. Interestingly (or ironically), in the segment, the education secretary sat at his desk, upon which a plaque read, "The buck stops here." Teachers felt they had no choice but to cheat and falsify data, and in the summer of 2003, one particular high school, Sharpstown, faced with allegations of falsifying data, became the center of national controversy. Sharpstown Assistant Principal Kimball charged that the high school had been masking its dropout rate by coding students' reasons for leaving in ways that would not be counted officially as dropout, a practice that yielded a phenomenal 0 percent dropout rate.[16] Kimball took his findings to State Representative Rick Noriega, who then asked the TEA to issue an audit not only of Sharpstown, but also of other high schools in the Houston area. The TEA substantiated the claim, but an even more sinister plot was being uncovered: while the district was hiding its true dropout rates, it was in fact pushing out students at risk of failing the TAAS. As Peabody, Mason, and Bernstein (2003) wrote, "Teachers have said students who passed all their classes are sometimes held back to keep their low test scores from affecting accountability records in the next grade. Poor performers are also weeded out with disciplinary expulsion or alternative placement." In the *60 Minutes II* segment, Gilbert Moreno, director of the Association for the Advancement of Mexican Americans, said, "There are some horrible stories. . . . A youngster passed, say, five different subjects, passed the English, but wasn't given Algebra, and then was later told at the end of the year, well, you're not gonna pass to the tenth grade, you never passed Algebra, you never took Algebra. And the youngster goes, I never knew this. And it looks almost that there was an attempt to maybe identify some certain students and not give them the required curriculum" (Rather 2004).

Moreno even suggested that one school had retained up to 60 percent of its ninth graders. An official from the TEA found that retaining a student in ninth grade, then skipping that student past the tenth-grade test, as happened to Arredondo, was practiced not only in Houston, but across the state. Texas was apparently not the only state to engage in pushing out students at risk of lowering institutional scores. In July 2003,

Lewin and Medina (2003) of the *New York Times* reported that in New York City, students "who may tarnish the schools' statistics" were being pushed toward equivalency degree programs. Other cases of pushing out were reported in Birmingham and Miami (see also Ward 2003; *Washington Times* 2003). In an editorial column entitled "Leave No Child Behind Means Make 'Em Vanish," Bill Maher (2003) wrote, "[I]t does take a special kind of Texas-size nerve to then treat those children like cards in a gin rummy hand, where you get to ditch the two low ones, and where bodies just disappear like dissidents in Argentina."

Nichols and Berliner (2005) suggested that it is the high-stakes environment that has led to the distortion and corruption of both the educational process and the very indicators of accountability—not only through cheating, but also through "gaming the system" by encouraging students to drop out and subsequently misrepresenting dropout rates, teaching to the test, and manipulating test cutoff scores and pass-fail rates. Just three years after the implementation of the accountability system in 1993, the TEA established the Special Data Inquiry Unit (SDIU) to investigate claims of data manipulation. Scandals in several districts prompted the comptroller to form a Public Education Integrity Taskforce. In a teacher roundtable discussion held by the integrity taskforce, teachers revealed that the pressure of testing from both within and outside the district led to cases not only in which teachers cheated through prompting students, changing answers, and invalidating tests, but also in which administrators "ARDed out" students—that is, exempted students through special education—or suspended or expelled students before the test. According to one teacher, "In the Houston area, a high amount of Afro-American male students are put in special ed classes to get them exempted from TAAS [because it is] believed that they will not perform well" (Public Education Integrity Taskforce 2001). Another participant in the group reported that in the Rio Grande Valley in South Texas on the border of Mexico, with high enrollments of Latino students, there were "[s]o many special ed kids . . . , they were cited for it . . . 28% special ed in the Valley" (Public Education Integrity Taskforce 2001). Another teacher even suggested that "[s]ome districts swap students for testing" (Public Education Integrity Taskforce 2001). In 1999, the Austin Independent School District was indicted on charges of tampering with governmental records for manipulating test scores. I was informed by an Austin LULAC member that it was the tests of some Latino males in which names were changed to their social security numbers in order to disqualify their tests from being scored. According to Reyes (2001), placement in disciplinary alternative educational programs (DAEPs), "experiencing an explosive growth," may also serve as a mechanism for "subtracting" students in order to raise overall institutional scores. In a study of disciplinary placements from 1996 to 2000, Reyes found that "state juvenile laws and state discipline laws have merged to criminalize low student achievement. The data show that the new criminalization of school discipline has disproportionately targeted minority students and students who read below grade level or who may have other instructionally related problems" (555).

In a Public Education Committee hearing on a bill that would charge that districts better account for the true number of dropouts, Representative Harold Dutton argued that current systems of counting students are "designed so you don't appear to have a problem," and "students are lost in this statistical battle." The same can be said for the manner in which student bodies are manipulated for testing. Not only are students simply "lost," but their invisibility is materialized by practices of displacement from regular tracks and from schools. In the articles on Sharpstown and pushing out, and in the *60 Minutes II* segment, there is one clear omission in the discussion of push-outs: a discourse of race. However, Gilbert Moreno implied race in a very subtle way as he said, "[I]t looks almost that there was an attempt to maybe identify some *certain* students and not give them the required curriculum" (Rather 2004; my italics). Greg Palast (2004), author of *The Best Democracy Money Can Buy*, wrote in a letter to President George W. Bush, "And if I bring up the race of the kids with the low score, don't get all snippy with me, telling me your program is colorblind. We know the color of the kids left behind; and it's not the color of the kids you went to school with at Philips Andover Academy." He titled his commentary, "The New Educational Eugenics in George Bush's State of the Union."

## Conclusion

With increasing corporate intervention in public education, in Texas and across the country, market metaphors and cost-accounting models are increasingly being applied to public education, attaching extreme significance to quantitative measures (Saltman 2000; Sacks 1999; Apple 2001; Bartlett et al. 2002; Collins 2001; McNeil 2000a). The "truths" about testing are articulated through statistical discourses, produced in computerized data-management systems, test-based school and district ratings, and constant media publication of test results. In Texas, standardized test results are linked to accountability systems, which promise rewards for those who produce good statistics, such as monetary prizes for districts and bonuses for school officials. In contrast, the production of bad statistics, beyond being constantly visible in media reports, brings on grade retention or failure for students, possible firing of school officials, administrative takeover of schools, or even school closure. Thus, the testing process generates an extreme, and very public, anxiety, the stakes of which produce truly harmful effects on students.

One of the ways in which the testing system maintains its hegemony is by the use of statistics as a form of governance: turning students into governable objects, conducting the conduct of the public through statistical panic, and hiding the practice of pushing out, which marginalizes and attempts to literally subtract students of color. The resistance against high-stakes testing emerged as a struggle against the submission of subjectivity, signaling not only a tendency to overemphasize testing statistics, but also the very inscription of students as statistics. The students' objections to becoming a statistic, a "name and a score," reveal the use of statistics as a discourse network. The objectification of students (as a form of power) is buttressed by the constant public dissemination of their test performance, abstracted into a school's institutional score or an overall passing rate. While public assessment is considered a sign of democracy, it nevertheless also governs the public sphere by conducting conduct and constructing the structure of feeling of statistical panic. While this statistical panic may be used as a rallying point for politics, the state and media have the ability to temper that panic through an underlying perception of statistical significance. Thus, because the number of third-grade students who failed the TAKS was lower than that of the widely publicized prediction, administrators and newspapers could speak of how third graders exceeded expectations. Not only was the number of students who did fail by the end of the school year not "significant," but the political questioning of the state's policy of high-stakes testing itself became silenced. Also silenced are the mechanisms by which schools obtain their scores, particularly the targeting of students of color as at-risk and the objectification of at-risk students as disposable data through the literally subtractive process of pushing out. The simultaneity of being hypervisibly at risk and invisibly pushed out is symptomatic of a broader racializing politics of containment. The inscription as a governable object is only part of the story of standardized testing, since it is accompanied by another form of statistical objectification in the Marxist sense: exploitation. In the next chapter, I discuss issues of exploitation and the political economy of the statistical discourse of high-stakes testing.

# 4 / Commodification, Privatization, and Political Economy of Statistical Discourse

## Houston Story

At a House Public Education Committee meeting on February 27, 2001, I arrived to find that the meeting was standing room only. A large group of mostly Black parents crowded the room wearing green T-shirts reading "Children Equal Profit." When their time came to speak hours later, these parents, who have been characterized by education literature as apathetic, revealed that they had driven from Houston to speak about the commodification of their children. Testimony revealed that the parents created Children Equal Profit as a parody of CEP, Community Education Partners, in Houston, a for-profit company that provides alternative schooling or alternative placement for students who violate school rules on violence, part of a zero-tolerance policy. The parents told the committee that Rod Paige, as superintendent of the Houston Independent School District (HISD) signed an $18 million annual contract with CEP to guarantee that twenty-five hundred students would be placed in alternative placement for 180 days regardless of infraction, despite the district's own policy of alternative placement for 11 days up to the end of the school semester. While an NAACP representative provided statistics on the disproportionate alternative placement of students of color, the most moving testimony came from the stories of parents desperate to find better opportunities for their children. One parent told of her five-year-old child having bruises on his arms from being pinned by a teacher and of a teacher being asleep in the classroom set aside for autistic children, calling the alternative placement "not education, just a place to put students where they don't need to get education." Children were placed in isolation in a small area with a partition for hours at a time, said the mother, and she added, "What happens to children who are not able to explain?" Another mother stood up and explained that they tried to place her child in alternative placement allegedly because "he doesn't think before he acts and needs more severe punishment." She also said that the principal lacked concern for her child, waiting until the TAAS test to place him in a class. She quit her job in order to send her child to another school, a private school, for which she had to leave at 6:15 in the morning just to get her son to school on time. For her, this committee meeting was the only forum in which to voice her protest, and she posed the question to Representative Paul Sadler, the education committee chair, "What can you do?" He responded that unless she put her child back in the public school system, there was nothing he could do. Sadler, however, grew angry upon hearing about the contract and asked a board representative for HISD about the contract, saying, "I'm a little bit concerned with a contract that guarantees twenty-five hundred students to AP [alternative placement]. How could a board approve such a thing?" The board representative responded with a statistical discourse claiming that "schools were much safer" with the CEP alternative placement, and that there was a pattern of schools being slow to send students there.

In "Numbers Racket," Metcalf (2001) wrote that CEP was established by a group of Republicans from Tennessee with ties to former secretary of education in the senior Bush administration, Lamar Alexander. Metcalf argued that the alternative placement was a way to avoid high dropout rates, and found that chaos ruled. Parents were not receiving report cards, exams were not being graded due to understaffing, students were being placed in classes lower than their abilities, teachers were given classes of thirty to forty students, and fighting often erupted. According to one student, "It was like a jail" (Metcalf 2001: 24). A research specialist for the HISD Department of Research and Accountability, Thomas Kellow, found that while students' academic performance at CEP worsened over time, an Internet press release claimed that CEP achieved "an average growth in reading of 2.4 grade levels and an average growth in math of 2.2" (24). When Kellow e-mailed eighteen hundred statisticians about the data, he was reprimanded by the district, was "moved to a workstation without Internet access," and found that his computer had been tampered with (24). Metcalf ended his article with this poignant quote from a female employee at CEP: "Rod

Paige's scores in Houston look good on paper. But he sacrificed so many kids to get there" (quoted in Metcalf 2001: 24).

In February of 2003, the Channel 11 News Defenders in Houston found schools under pressure to change dropout rates, revealing loopholes in which school officials would cook the books by reporting students as transferring or receiving a GED instead of dropping out. According to Werner (2003), "Some of the school districts reward schools for keeping track of kids and keeping them in class because with high enough test scores and low drop-out rates, employees get bonuses—that means money for everyone from the janitor to the principal . . . unfortunately, some HISD schools seem more interested in cash than in the kids. And the kids are suffering."

The payoff for HISD was the Broad Prize in Education, worth $500,000. According to Brad Duggan of Just for the Kids, a research and policy organization in Texas, at a House Public Education Committee meeting on accountability on February 18, 2003, the selection of HISD for the prize revealed how the "accountability system [had] driven more effective change. All of this happened because of data . . . and efficiency in the system." It is no wonder that Linda McNeil, at the January rally for the multiple-criteria bills, compared the current system in Texas to Enron. An Austin high school teacher told me as she reflected on the TAAS that "someone is benefiting and it is not the kids. It must be about money."

While, in the previous chapter, I discussed objectification in the sense of manipulation, in this chapter, I consider the political economy of that objectification, exploring the term *objectification* in a Marxist sense, considering questions of exploitation and commodification. First, I discuss what Bartlett et al. (2002) called the "marketization of education," in order to contextualize testing in Texas within a broader national ideological movement (the accountability movement), which both rearticulates the goals of education in terms of the economy and exploits economic opportunities in or privatizes aspects of the public education system. Second, I discuss the centrality of statistics in the creation of those opportunities through making possible the commodification of knowledge. I also discuss more in depth the major economic players in the accountability movement in Texas and the incentive system with schools that operates to secure the hegemony of the testing system. Third, I discuss the ways in which the profitability of the testing movement is juxtaposed with a broader ideological attack on the welfare state and, in this case, on public schools. I argue that one of the main components of that ideological attack has been the recuperation of statistical discourses that have historically been used to oppose social security (in the broad sense, as state provisions for social welfare).

## The Marketization of Education

> Do America's schools need a "Dow Jones Index"?
>
> —James W. Guthrie (1994)

The actions of the HISD constitute what Bartlett et al. (2002) described as the "marketization of education." Characterized by the recuperation of 1920s scientific management of schools, the marketization of education includes the policy implementation of intensified standardized testing and tracking, investment in charter schools or schools of choice (and in the case of Texas, charter districts), and privatization of partial or entire public school operations. Accompanying these policies is a "cultural change in the perception of school's purpose" from a democratic perception to an economic one, laced with market metaphors and enhanced by the racialization of poverty and failure (Bartlett et al. 2002: 6). According to Bartlett et al. (2002), this movement for the marketization of public schools, becoming known as the "accountability movement," obtained its hegemony from the coalescing of the "New Right" (Apple 2001), which encompasses four groups: neoliberals, neoconservatives, authoritarian populists, and the managerial and professional middle class. According to Apple, neoliberals share a commitment to rearticulating politics into an economic paradigm stressing free markets, privatization, and individualism (individual responsibility), without government intervention—that is, unless government resources are employed to further the free market economy (17–20, 38–41). In the neoliberal formulation, democratic freedom equals free market and free competition. Neoconservatives, according to Apple, center their politics in the sense of return (to a nostalgic or romantic past), traditional values, and cultural order, discursively forming a notion of societal decline as a way of constructing "the Other" as a pollutant, contaminant, or pathology (20–22). According to Apple, neoconservatives favor a small, strong state centered on regulation, surveillance, and discipline (20–22, 47–53). By authoritarian populists, Apple was referring to the religious Right, formed out of the conservative evangelical movement or a form of Protestantism that stresses individualism, the need for salvation, and the naturalization of sociopolitical conditions as God's will (22–28). Finally, the managerial and professional middle class refers to a group of people who supply technical expertise to the state and corporations, particularly in management and efficiency (57–59). As products of suburbanization (thus segregation), the managerial and professional middle class expresses a commitment to meritocracy, and while their political views may be moderate or even liberal, they can exploit the job openings created by a "regulatory state" (57, 75). The loss of middle-management jobs, increased personal debt with simultaneous heavy credit marketing, and the outsourcing of manufacturing jobs overseas have caused a shrinking of the middle class (Bartlett et al. 2002: 9). Additionally, these economic misfortunes caused the middle class to break with the liberal democratic concept of redistributive justice, a concept characteristic of the welfare state (9). The joining of forces among neoliberals, neoconservatives, and the managerial middle class has produced the discourse of crisis in public education through the media and research organizations, a discourse in which corporate and conservative leaders invested heavily. Further, the New Right became prolific in forming powerful lobby organizations whose purpose was to "educate" legislators to implement policies in concert with privatization (Bartlett et al. 2002: 9–11).

The alignment of the New Right was also hastened in opposition to desegregation policies[1] and federal expenditures for such reform (Saltman 2000).[2] Demands for accountability and movements toward performance contracting (as a means of privatizing operations of public education) occurred following the passage of the Elementary and Secondary Education Act of 1965, which established the federally funded programs of Title I, Job Corps, and Head Start (Richards, Shore, and Sawicky 1996). For Mansbridge (1986), the glue between the middle class and the New Right was also formed by the opposition to the Equal Rights Amendment: "The battle against the ERA was one of the first in which the New Right used 'women's issues' to forge a coalition of the traditional Radical Right, religious activists, and that previously relatively apolitical segment of the noncosmopolitan working and middle classes that was deeply disturbed by the cultural changes—especially the changes in sexual mores—in the second half of the twentieth century" (16).

The opposition to equality in pay between men and women could also explain the opposition toward teacher unions. Apple (2001) argued that the broad-based approach of the New Right accommodates neoliberal interests in privatization and neoconservative interests in a strong state, returning to traditional education (back to basics) through the use of public assessment, which combines "marketized individualism and [constant] control" and surveillance (72). This need for public assessment, couched in terms of value and the language of salvation, appeals to the religious Right, for whom the Protestant ethic presumes individual responsibility for social positioning (infusing a market philosophy into Christianity) and the concept of moral decay in schools allows for a militant approach to public scrutiny of teachers. Public assessment also creates opportunities for the managerial class who populate the "evaluative state" and appeals to their commitment to patriarchal society and to meritocracy (75). The New Right's approach to education through public assessment allows "elites to profit from a once off-limits sector" (Saltman 2000: 8) while creating a discourse of failure that delegitimizes redistributive justice of the welfare state, particularly of public school systems.[3]

I argue that what provides the conditions for profitability and the discourse of failure (or profiting from failure) is in fact the "political economy"[4] of statistical discourse. First, statistical discourse creates the possibility for education to be articulated in economic terms, as Guthrie's joke about education having a Dow Jones index suggests. Second, statistics, as an administrative science, provides the measures of efficiency necessary for regulation, and necessitates professionals to collect, analyze, and report statistical data. Third, statistics has historically served as a terrain for articulating discourses of difference, for example racial discourses which establish White as norms and racial "Others" as deviants.

## Commodification of Statistical Knowledge

> Someone profits while the children fail.
>
> —Representative Harold Dutton[5]

The case of HISD exemplifies the political economy of statistical discourse, in that good statistics (or good statistical production) proved to be a hot commodity. For its good statistics, the district won the Broad Prize in Education, worth $500,000. Gluckman (2002) suggested that the "hard-data, number crunching world of the business roundtables . . . [is] now setting the education-reform agenda," and it is exactly the number-crunching companies, such as NCS Pearson, and other data-managing organizations, such as the National Center for Educational

Accountability, with their mantra of "data-driven assessment" that seem to benefit most from what Richards, Shore, and Sawicky (1996) called the "potentially vast education market" (54). According to Sacks (1999), "sales of standardized tests to public schools, in real dollars, more than doubled between 1960 and 1989 to $100 million a year" (6). A large portion of the cost of standardized tests comes from companies that process those tests, producing student scores and statistics. Arguably, the connection between test-score processing and computer development is an intimate and historical one, since according to Lemann (1999), one of IBM's original projects was to develop a machine to score tests. (Perhaps it is no wonder that one of the leaders of the national accountability movement is IBM CEO Louis Gerstner.) In the late twentieth and early twenty-first centuries, one of the largest companies in the United States processing test score data is NCS Pearson. NCS, or National Computer Systems, is a data-processing company acquired in 2000 by the Britain-based corporation Pearson, "an international media company with market leading businesses in education, strategic business information and consumer publishing" (Pearson 2002a). In 2002, the Pearson Education division included NCS as well as well-known educational textbook publishers such as Scott Foresman, Prentice Hall, Addison-Wesley, and Allyn & Bacon/Longman. On its Web site, Pearson Education proclaims, "There has never been a better time to be in the business of education." The Web site continues, "With federal and state governments [in the United States] wanting both to measure academic progress against clear standards and modernise their school systems, we are seeing faster rates of growth in demand for testing and the enterprise software that powers many schools. The acquisition of NCS . . . means we can meet this demand and work with schools to embed assessment as part of the daily curriculum and to tailor learning to the needs of each student" (Pearson 2002b).

According to Pearson Education, the market for educational publishing in the United States in 2002 was "valued at some $8bn . . . [and] is currently growing on average at around 8% per year" (Pearson 2002b). Furthermore, as the Web site notes, "The trends in the US are also playing out in developed countries around the world, [where] school rolls are growing even more rapidly . . . and, around the world, ownership of educational publishing and learning companies is often fragmented, creating major opportunities for consolidation and growth. As the world's most international education company, we are in a very good position to capitalise on these trends" (Pearson 2002b).

In 2000, the Texas Education Agency (TEA) signed a contract with NCS Pearson, giving them $233 million over five years, increasing from $19.5 million in 1995 to $68.6 million in 2001 (Gluckman 2002). According to the "2001 Comprehensive Report" by TEA (2001a), the agency expected to spend $69.14 million on accountability and assessment in the 2000–2001 fiscal year. In the 2002–2003 school year (fiscal year 2003), NCS received more than $53 million in contracts, and the Psychological Corporation of Harcourt, responsible for developing the TAAS test, received about $1.3 million, giving a sense of the extent to which data-processing, statistics-producing companies profit from testing (TEA 2003a). In addition, companies that promise to boost schools' statistical production, such as test-prep company Lightspan, also earn huge profits, and just in 2002, Austin Independent School District, despite massive budget cuts, signed a contract with Lightspan for $1 million.

The profitability of statistical production can be understood in the context of what Hardt and Negri (2000) have described as the "passage toward an informational economy" (289). Ecological limitations to industrial expansion coupled with a "computer and communication revolution of production" facilitated a shift from a global economy centered on industrial production to one centered on the traffic of information and communications (272, 291). However, the shift occurred also as a politico-economic response to movements in the 1960s and 1970s resisting against Fordist modes of production that centered on assembly-line mass production and Taylorist forms of discipline, or scientific management, that, as Gramsci argued, constructed workers as "trained gorillas" (see Chapter 3). For Hardt and Negri, these movements demanded democracy, flexibility, politics of difference, and a higher "social valu[ation] of cooperation and communication" (275). While communication technologies absorb and rearticulate the demands for democracy, flexibility, and difference, these technologies are, nevertheless, coming under more and more centralized control: "[T]oday we are witnessing a competition among transnational corporations to establish and consolidate quasi-monopolies over the new information infrastructure. The various telecommunication corporations, computer hardware and software manufacturers, and information and entertainment corporations are merging and expanding their operations, scrambling to partition and control the new continents of productive networks" (300).

This merging is clearly evident not only in the acquisition of NCS by Pearson, an international media company, but also in other companies involved in test production and textbook publication, such as Harcourt General (Harcourt, Brace, Jovanovich), which was acquired in 1991 by General Cinemas and then "purchased by British-Dutch scientific publisher Reed Elsevier" by the year 2002 (Gluckman 2002). According to Rosales (2000), Harcourt, Brace, Jovanovich has also owned Sea World (155). Gluckman (2002) referred to these acquisitions as "edutainment," using the word with which French media company Vivendi Universal SA described its acquisition of education publishing company Houghton Mifflin.

Within an informational economy, testing and its statistical production have become super-exploitative, serving both as a means of dividing core/professional and contingent workers and as a means of objectifying or commodifying knowledge and information. According to Persuad and Lusane (2000), the informational economy demarcates an economy based on high-skilled and low-skilled service work, divided between two types of flexible laborers: "core workers," "the upper rung of professionals [such as] consultants, executives, upper-level managers, medical, computer and informational specialists"; and "contingent workers," "those supplying unskilled personal services, taxi drivers, security personnel, food service workers, lawn care workers, office cleaners, retail sales, and so on" (26). High-stakes testing erects further barriers to high school completion, piled upon already-present systems of tracking and the racial and class dynamics of dropping out (Lipman 2004: 173; see also Oakes 1985; Fine 1991). In a study of Chicago, Lipman (2004) found that it is exactly the schools challenged by the dynamics of racism and poverty and legacies of state neglect that are under the most pressure to raise scores. Such schools are those most likely to limit their curriculum to test preparation, often forced to comply by their district, despite the fact that those basic-skills curricula rob students of the kind of critical-thinking skills and knowledge most valued in an informational economy (115).

In addition to exaggerating stratification of labor forces, high-stakes testing produces opportunities for the commodification of knowledge. Cicotti, Cini, and de Maria (1976) argued that the necessary conditions for the transformation of information into a nonmaterial commodity, that is, its objectification, are that "information [is] made quantitative and its consumption measurable" (43). Thus, at the heart of the informational economy and its globalization is the quantitative objectification of information.

Statistical objectification is particularly crucial in the production of social information as a commodity, being not only the extension (or application) of the language of capitalism and commerce to the social, but also a *"technologie assurentiel"* or tool of "social assurance," that is, a governmental science deemed necessary to "providing a stable social order" (Hacking 1991: 183). According to Porter (1995), the "language of quantification [has been] more important than English in the European campaign to create a unified business environment" (77). Central to this unification is the administrative science of statistics (and its discourse),[6] whose genealogy can be traced to the development of eighteenth-century political economies, in which the language of commerce (arithmetic) merged with the concerns of the state for the wealth and governance of its populations,[7] both metropole (Desrosières 1998: 250; see also Woolf 1989; Foucault 1991; Porter 1995; Cohen 1982) and colony (Appadurai 1993; Asad 1994). In the nineteenth century, the German word for a largely descriptive "science of the state," *Statistik* (in English, *statistics*, and in French, *statistique*), became essentially enumerative or quantitative (Desrosières 1998: 16–44; Woolf 1989: 590–592). By the mid-nineteenth century, the census and other governmental statistics transformed in their functions from providing the basis for taxation and comprehensive analyses to bodies of knowledge and tools for policy intervention (Appadurai 1993: 321; Desrosières 1998: 221; Nobles 2000). At the same time, in the midst of political and social upheaval, social scientists and social reformers fused administrative or government statistics and probability calculus into a "social physics," a "positivist . . . social construction of reality" (Woolf 1989: 592) or of "society": "The apparition of the new entity, *society*, objectified and seen from the outside, endowed with autonomous laws in relation to individuals characterizes the thought of all the founding fathers of sociology, a science taking shape precisely at this time. Comte, Marx, Le Play, Tocqueville, and Durkheim [and Quetelet]: despite their differences . . . all were confronted with the disorders and the breakdown of the old social fabric brought about by the political upheavals in France and the industrial revolution in England" (Desrosières 1998: 79).

According to Procacci (1991), statistics aided in the "task of governing poverty," by making sense of the "chaos of pauperism" (160, 164). Organizers of statistical congresses focused on "les misérables," as social reformers used statistics in order to "reorganize the 'boundary conditions'" (Hacking 1991: 188). For Donzelot (1991a), statistics were incorporated in the project of the welfare state in France as a means of resolving the contradiction between the "language of rights" and the inevitable inequality of industrialization. At the turn of the century,

Galton and Pearson headed the establishment of mathematical statistics as an autonomous discipline through the efforts of their English biometric school of eugenics (Desrosières 1998; Porter 2002), spawning disciplines such as educational psychology and econometrics, as well as innovations in sampling techniques. By the end of the world wars, welfare and social security legislation and regulation (particularly the New Deal in the United States); the development of national consumer markets and market studies; and national elections and campaign polls secured the professionalization of government statisticians (Desrosières 1998: 225; see also 176, 194). As statistics served a key role in the development of the welfare state in response to crises in industrial capitalism understanding, controlling, and governing the poor and "savages," it also played a key role in incorporating nation-states into an international system of competition, becoming hegemonic as "the language of the modern nation-state" (Urla 1993: 831).[8]

While Hardt and Negri (2000) have argued that labor in the informational economy "functions outside of measure" due to greater flexibility in work schedules and disruption of "all the other economic and/or political measures that have been imposed upon it [labor]" (357), in the context of an informational economy, the imposition of economic and/or political measures on labor introduces more opportunities for the creation of capital. The proliferation and expansion of standardized testing, particularly high-stakes examinations that determine grade promotion (or retention) and high school graduation, are a prime example of the intensifying imposition of measurement on (children's) labor; of the profitability of labor-related statistical information and knowledge; and of the use of measurement to reproduce (structure and justify) occupational divisions between the professional and the unskilled worker. Despite Foucault's (1994 [1971]) observation that modern human sciences tend to view the reduction to quantity as naive and thus signify a "retreat of mathesis" (or order and taxonomy) (349), the postmodern world is inundated with statistics (Woodward 1999), arguably representing the penetration of capital into every aspect of our lives, or the incorporation of every aspect of our lives into the capitalist sphere. For Porter (1995), "This is not because the world is inherently statistical. It is because quantifiers have made it statistical, the better to manage it" (213). I would add "the better to profit from it."

The combination of management and profitability is central to understanding the ways in which corporate leadership co-opts educational reform (see Bowles and Gintis 1976: 179). The profit motive becomes clearer when we examine the accountability movement of the 1980s to the present, a movement for which the 1983 report by the National Commission on Education, *A Nation at Risk*, provided the impetus and "instigated more than 300 state and national business reports and commissions assessing public schools" (Bartlett et al. 2002: 11). In 1989, the National Business Roundtable campaigned heavily for its chapters to influence state governors to reform (Bartlett et al. 2002: 11), and according to Metcalf (2002), one of the founding texts of the accountability movement was *Reinventing Education: Entrepreneurship in America's Public Schools*, by Louis Gerstner, chairman of IBM, a member of the National Business Roundtable. At the National Education Summit in 1996, Gerstner helped found Achieve, Inc., "a nonprofit organization created by governors and corporate leaders to help states and the private sector raise standards and performance in America's schools" (Achieve, Inc. 2002). The board and chairmanship for Achieve, Inc., has consisted of governors from California, Georgia, Michigan, Oklahoma, Ohio, and Washington and corporate leaders from Boeing, Intel, State Farm Insurance, Prudential, and Williams, signifying the coalition of governors and corporate leaders in educational reform. In Texas, *A Nation at Risk* initiated the study committee on education that then governor Mark White designated as the Select Committee on Public Education in 1984; billionaire Ross Perot was selected as the committee's leader. The reforms proposed by the study committee eclipsed the reforms for higher teacher salaries sought by the teacher organizations that helped elect White for the governorship (McNeil 2000a). Some even referred to the group gathered by Ross Perot to head the meetings as his "little group of dictators" (Newman 1987: 195). The business lobby Texas Business and Education Council, whose founding members included Tom Luce, one of Perot's advisers on the Select Committee on Public Education (Peterson and Wilder 2002), was so instrumental in the development of the Texas school accountability system that, according to Salinas and Reidel (2007), proceedings of a Texas Business and Education Council board meeting defined the very language of the bill that established the accountability system between 1993 and 1995 (48). In 2001, Charles Miller, Tom Luce, Representative Kent Grusendorf, and Sandy Kress founded another organization, the Texas Public Education Reform Foundation. Representative Grusendorf served as the chair of the House Public Education Committee during the 78th legislative session. In 2003, the agenda of Texas Public Education Reform Foundation read nearly as the Public Education Committee's agenda itself.

A 2007 report of the U.S. Senate Committee on Health, Education, and Welfare, led by Massachusetts senator Edward Kennedy, nationally raised questions about potential conflicts of interest for key figures present in governmental positions, who might have been employees of the very companies who profit from legislation (Kennedy 2007). The report focused on the Reading First Program, instituted by the No Child Left Behind Act, which, according to the report, is "a 6-year program that focuses on implementing scientifically-based reading research programs and practices in K–3 classrooms" (2). For example, the report highlighted Dr. Edward Kame'enui, who, as director of a Western Technical Assistance Center for the Reading First Program from 2003 to 2005 and then serving as commissioner for special education research for the U.S. Department of Education, received more than $675,000 in royalties and compensation from Pearson/Scott Foresman between 2003 and 2006 (5). The report also suggested that Dr. Kame'enui lobbied for the company. In 2005, key figures in Texas reform came under public scrutiny for such links. For example, Sandy Kress, a Democrat with close ties to President George W. Bush and architect of the president's No Child Left Behind Act (Peterson and Wilder 2002), was cited by *Texas Observer* columnist Emily Pyle (2005) as contracting as a lobbyist not only for textbook publisher McGraw-Hill, but also for Pearson, the very company whose contracts with the Texas Education Agency rose from approximately $53 million in fiscal year 2003 to approximately $88 million in fiscal year 2007 (TEA 2003a; TEA 2007).

In their document assessing the Texas assessment and accountability systems, Achieve, Inc. (2002) reported that "[i]n our view, business leaders must continue to play a strong role in anchoring public sentiment supporting high standards so that reforms can be sustained over time" (12). Part of anchoring public sentiment, or forming hegemony, has been the neoliberal combining of individualism and a regulatory state (Apple 2001) through the use of the rewards and sanctions system of public assessment—using testing statistics both to create opportunities for individual profit yet also manage educational differentiation. DuBois (1962 [1935]) recognized this strategy of corporations to combine strong government or regulatory state and marketized individualism in the spread of northern capitalist hegemony across the nation after the Civil War:

> Great corporations through their control of new capital, began to establish a super-government. On the one hand, they crushed

the robber-barons, the thieves and the grafters, and thus appeased those of the old school who demanded the old standards
of personal honesty. Secondly, they made treaty with the petty
bourgeoisie by guaranteeing them reasonable and certain income from their investments, while they gradually deprived
them of real control in industry. And finally, they made treaty
with labor by dealing with it as a powerful, determined unit and
dividing it up into skilled union labor, with which the new industry shared profit in the shape of a higher wage and other
privileges, and a great reservoir of common and foreign labor
which it kept at work at low wages with the threat of starvation
and with police control. (584)

In forming the hegemony of the accountability system, corporations,
through their influence on and connection to government, have used or
"recuperated"[9] this strategy of treaty making with different levels of the
educational system. The appeal of accountability is its promise to the
public and school boards to provide sanctions against the failing schools,
dysfunctional principals and school administrations, incompetent teachers, and socially promoted students. According to Bartlett et al. (2002),
this appeal allowed neoliberals to forge alliances with both neoconservatives, "appeased with promises of input in curriculum," and also "social evolutionists . . . placated with the promises of standardized testing" (10). Through governmental and state accountability regimes,
corporations have forged treaties with teaching professionals, principals,
and superintendents, like the petty bourgeoisie DuBois described, offering them better income and awards based on their statistical production. For instance, superintendents have been offered $25,000 bonuses
for raising scores (Kolker 1999). The legislature instituted a program
called the Texas Successful Schools Award Program, offering $500 to
$1,500 to schools with good scores on the TAAS (Martinez 2003).
Teachers in Texas could net "bonuses of up to $650" (Kolker 1999).
However, the promises of rewards are balanced by those of sanctions, in
which Texas superintendents' contracts contain clauses "that allow
them to be terminated should performance rates be low" (Kramer 2002).[10]
Principals and teachers are also threatened with reconstitution—in
which large masses of school faculty and administration are fired and
replacements hired—for low scores, particularly in schools whose majority of students are economically disadvantaged and Black or Latino
or both (Saltman 2000; Kozol 1991). I spoke to a teacher at such a high

school in Austin, who told me that due to the school's low accountability rating, in the following year the district was planning to fire and replace most of the teachers. Valenzuela (2002) wrote that:

> especially in poor, minority schools, logic dictates that when assessment gets tied to the threat of sanctions that teachers and administrators must bear if test scores drop or remain stagnant, perverse incentives exist to marginalize children through various mechanisms [such as] . . . relegating them to test-exempt status categories . . . ; "encouraging" the academically weak to remain so by retaining them at the ninth-grade level so that they do not become tenth-grade TAAS-test takers who lower school averages; and "pushing students out," such as by the practice of withdrawing students for lack of attendance. (103)

The Houston case of pushing out students and using privatized alternative education to lower dropout rates exemplifies Valenzuela's characterization. On the other side of the spectrum, schools often offer student laborers rewards for good scores beyond that of grade promotion. According to students in the survey conducted by Blalock and Haswell (2002), not only did schools receive monetary rewards for better scores (06-109, 12-224), but students received rewards mostly in the form of school trips (01-103) to Sea World (08-143) (owned by Harcourt General) and Schlitterbahn, a water theme park in New Braunfels, Texas (19-365).[11]

In addition to creating a rewards and sanctions system, the testing business has also created job opportunities within the Texas Education Agency, through the creation of the Accountability and Assessment divisions, as well as in the private corporations with whom the TEA contracts. For instance, in the summer, Harcourt Assessment—headquartered in San Antonio—posts several job announcements for test scorers, and many teachers and school librarians can supplement their income by scoring tests. There are also opportunities to earn money by writing test questions. Arguably, the professionalization of the accountability and testing systems makes resistance to the system more difficult because the fear of joblessness plaguing the United States constructs a protective defensiveness of all jobs. This situation is exacerbated by the production of a reservoir of highly skilled, highly educated laborers (Bowles and Gintis 1976), whereby large numbers of college graduates compete for scarce job opportunities within the informational economy and must often settle for contingent and temporary work without benefits. In addition to a protective defensiveness, fragmented and highly specialized jobs create a banalization (Trouillot 1995) that supports testing to become part of the habitus of educational practice. One Texas Education Agency employee in the Assessment division with whom I spoke described his job as "boring," and given the highly contested politics of testing, this sentiment indicated an alienation, a detached removal built into working conditions. The rewards and sanctions system is an example of the neoliberal use of statistics not only as a mechanism of incorporating students, teachers, and school administrators into an individualistic system of competition, but also as a mode of control, differentiation, and segregation.

## Efficiency and the Delegitimization of Public Education

For Valencia et al. (2001), results-driven accountability is too heavily focused on test scores, and through its refusal to acknowledge the historical and social context of educational inequality it both maintains racial inequalities and accommodates a discourse of "deficit thinking" that individualizes and racializes failure. Accountability discourse, constitutes a "late-capitalist retranslation of difference," by which the decontextualization, individualization, and erasure of inequalities accompany and support the very reinforcement of those inequalities (Sandoval 2000: 75). The "retranslation of difference" justifies privatization or "redistributing public resources to private high-tech, military, and carceral industries," by delegitimizing and dismantling the welfare state, particularly public education and the federal intervention systems aimed at class and race desegregation in public education (Saltman 2000: xiii). A key component of this strategy to delegitimize and dismantle social welfare and public education is statistical discourse, in particular, the recuperation of three important statistical discourses that relate population and economy: Malthusianism, eugenic meritocracy, and statistical quality control. Ironically, according to Desrosières (1998), it was Roosevelt's administration and its implementation of the New Deal that provided the conditions for the expansion of government statistics, an expansion for which former (Progressive Era) president Hoover could not obtain widespread support (194, 202).[12] Since the forming of the hegemonic conservative historic bloc in the 1980s, the opposition to the welfare state, particularly public education, has occurred through the resurrection of 1920s discourses of efficiency, Taylorist scientific management, and racial and gender conservativism characterized by neohereditarianism (Saltman 2000; McNeil 2000a; Valencia and Solórzano 1997). Part of the conservative strategy has been both the deconstruction of liberal statistical discourses of the welfare state and the recuperation of conservative statistical discourses historically deployed in opposition to social security, namely Malthusianism and eugenic meritocracy. These statistical discourses reinsert the Progressive Era concern for efficiency and Taylorism by applying the discourse of statistical quality control to social relationships.

## Malthusianism

According to Rothschild (1995), neoliberalism breaks with laissez-faire liberals of the eighteenth century, such as Adam Smith and Condorcet. While neoliberals view social security as "inimical to economic development" and "social equality as a form of luxury," laissez-faire liberals of the eighteenth century conceived of social security as a necessary "condition for the development of commerce" (Rothschild 1995: 711, 712). However, British political economist Thomas Robert Malthus inserted into political economy the political anxiety over the conflict between resources and population, proposing a law of population that stated that increased populousness is a detriment to future economic progress (versus the mercantilists' equating of increased populousness to the wealth of the nation). Further, Malthus opposed social security because it removes the "prudential check" on idleness by relieving the poor of the fear of poverty (Rothschild 1995: 728). According to Rothschild, in the 1990s a renewed Malthusianism arose with the anxiety over the shortage of natural resources,[13] a result of the tensions between "production and reproduction" (1995: 735).

Bowles and Gintis (1976) pointed to the contradiction between, on the one hand, the demand of technologies for white-collar workers and the need to create a reservoir of skilled white-collar laborers, and, on the other hand, the demand of the working-class and middle-class people of color and White women for affirmative action, that is, inclusion in the universities that produce white-collar workers. In the late 1960s and early 1970s, one of the strategies of the Carnegie Commission on Higher Education, an influential taskforce operated by the Carnegie Foundation to impact educational policy, according to the authors, was to "curb the rate of growth of the total postsecondary educational system to restrict

the size of the reserve army of white collar workers to politically accept-
able levels," at the same time advocating community college and vocational higher education (206). Clark (1961) called the function of the
community college system "cooling out," a way of resolving potential
conflict over the "dreams deferred" by the promise of higher education.
One of the ways of resolving the contradiction posed by affirmative action and its variants, such as the Ten Percent Plan,[14] is to restrict access
to high school diplomas. I heard a story from a mother whose son won a
scholarship to college but because he did not pass the TAAS exit exam
could not go to college and had to pursue a GED. For Bowles and Gintis (1976), one form of resolving the contradiction between accumulation and reproduction is the production of an "ideological perspective
which served to hide rather than clarify the sources of exploitation and
alienation of the capitalist order" (232). Renewed Malthusianism in the
accountability movement obscures and deflects the political anxiety
over the overpopulation of universities and an overpopulated reservoir
of skilled workers, particularly people of color—who find that educational opportunity does not automatically translate into economic
opportunity—through the ideology that the value of a high school diploma has decreased (see Hinds 2002) and that achieving accountability occurs through the deployment of fear[15]—the fear of failure in students, the fear of unemployment in teachers and administrators, and
the fear of school closure for communities.[16]

## Eugenic Meritocracy

As I write in Chapter 3, in the accountability system of Texas, high-
stakes testing and statistical projections are the mechanisms by which
fear or panic is deployed. According to MacKenzie (1981), "The building
of a system of education on the assumption that the extent to which a
child could benefit from education was determined by a single number
that was highly correlated with parental occupational position—the
children of professional and managerial parents 'having' the highest
average IQ—represented to a large degree the *institutionalisation* of the
eugenic model of society" (43). In the eugenic model of society, individuals' social or "civic worth," or inherited aptitude, in Galtonian terms, is
fixed and quantifiable, but also representable on a statistical scale that
follows the Gaussian distribution, or law of deviation, that contempora-
neously we know as the bell curve (Desrosières 1998: 112–127). Given

this view of society, proponents of eugenics opposed social security or social assistance because "these measures increased and strengthened the most [naturally] inept segments of the population" (262). In the view of eugenicists, the goal of state intervention should be to both minimize deviants or the naturally unfit, who cause "regression to mediocrity" (121–124), by actively decreasing their reproduction, either through sterilization or ceasing public assistance, and to also promote the reproduction of the well-to-do through the use of tax incentives for enlarging families, since "few manual workers paid income tax" (MacKenzie 1981: 21). With the invention of intelligence testing in the early twentieth century, eugenicists increasingly viewed civic worth as measured by the intelligence quotient, their IQ (MacKenzie 1981: 34; Gould 1996).[17] Sharing the pessimism of Malthusianism, eugenic meritocracy thus naturalized social inequality within a statistical discourse, reinforcing the trope of the inevitability of failure of liberal reforms inherent in Darwinian racial and sexual sciences of the nineteenth century.[18] DuBois (1962 [1935]) observed that Darwinian racial science was used to prove that post-Reconstruction reforms in the South were an impossibility (631). Russett (1989) traced the emergence of "sexual science" in the context of women's demands for suffrage, entrance into college, and economic independence (205).

In the 1960s and 1970s, social scientists resurrected this trope of statistically representing the (inevitability of the) failure of liberal reforms. Bowles and Gintis (1976) argued that "the barrage of statistical studies in the late 1960s and early 1970s—The Coleman Report, Jencks' study [*Inequality*], the evaluations of compensatory education and others—cleared the ground for a conservative counterattack" (6). The popularity of *The Bell Curve* by Hernstein and Murray in 1994 suggests the more recent acceptability of an overt rearticulation of eugenic meritocracy, while the propagation of testing since its publication suggests the covert application of its foundations. In a commentary on public financing and accountability, Heise (2002) argued that accountability systems and testing have "made it much easier for activists to appeal to the courts for more inputs . . . to define adequacy as that level of funding necessary for a school district and its students to meet state education standards," thus "enabl[ing] school districts to gain financially from their inability to perform at desired levels" (32). In Texas, however, school district funding equity was legitimated by the courts and legislature only when contingent upon an accountability system (see Chapter

2). Unlike Heise's contention that accountability systems enable the increasing of inputs, the reverse occurred in Texas. The increasing of inputs generated and justified the establishment of an accountability system. As mentioned in Chapter 2, according to Palmaffy (1998), the accountability system was put in place "to ensure that redistributed funds would be spent well."[19] Failure, then, does not tend to invite more money in Texas; rather, it tends to invite suspicion of corruption and justification for lower fund expenditure (see, e.g., Kozol 1991). The persistent failure of school districts and students, as shown in the *GI Forum* decision, is individualized, proof of the inevitability of the failure of social assistance since it is minorities' and poor districts' own "failure to catch up." Further, in Texas, the language of adequacy as "efficiency" in the face of massive cuts in federal and state budgets is increasingly being invoked to undermine the current system of equity.

## Efficiency, Taylorism, and Statistical Quality Control

As Saltman (2000) and McNeil (2000a) wrote, the use of efficiency in the accountability movement is a recuperation of the Taylorist scientific management model of educational reform promoted in the 1920s. Taylor's scientific management centered on promoting "national efficiency" by eliminating hidden wastes in human production through scientific management and the hierarchal reorganization of labor (Miller and O'Leary 1987: 251, 252). Taylorism is located within the historical intersection of physics with engineering and economics, a connection Porter (1995) stated first occurred in France during the Old Regime, when French engineers introduced into physics the concept of *work* (as an equation of force times distance) (55–60). This concept of work "made the labor of machines, animals, and men commensurable," but also provided a quantitative system by which human labor could be managed (55), creating the construct that O'Leary and Miller (1987) called "the governable person" (235). Taylorism invoked the physics of mechanical efficiency, later known as "quality control," dedicated to the problem of minimizing defective commodities in mass production, a science Shewhart (1986 [1939]) located historically in the introduction of interchangeable parts in 1787. By the 1920s, probability statistics was introduced into quality control, supplying to the engineer (in solving the problem of efficiency in mass production) both a "method of prediction that is subject to minimum error" and a "means of minimizing variability in the quality of a given product at a given cost of production" (9)—replacing a science of exactness with one of probability.[20]

Many authors have suggested that Taylorism is outdated in the late-capitalist era. According to Hardt and Negri (2000), social struggles for power and creativity in the 1960s and 1970s have rendered Taylorism unable to "control the dynamic of productive and social forces" (288). For Donzelot (1991b), late capitalism has progressed "beyond Taylorism" through the construction of "pleasure in work" (267–270). For Marshall (1999), within an informational and computerized economy, the absence of physical constraints signals a movement from a Foucauldian disciplinary society to one based on "busnopower," a form of power directed at choices. Similarly, Miller and O'Leary (1987) argued that as the Taylorist conception of "person as machine" gave way to the "motivationally-complex decision-maker" as early as the 1950s, a new form of power emerged that "operates through [the appearance of] freedom: a freedom for the individual to have an informal life within the organization, to deviate from criteria of rationality, to brood on personal problems, and to be influenced by the environment outside the firm" (263). In this case, the absence of visible controls and restrictions makes a worker feel free, while in reality maintaining forms of control (see Gordon 1991: 5). If these authors suggest that late capitalism has gone beyond Taylorism and discipline, why exactly do we see Taylorism and discipline in the reorganization of public education? Following Miller and O'Leary's (1987) contention that the "freedom as power" construct is in continuity with efficiency models of the 1920s, I argue that the reconstruction of the subject as one with variability, choices, decisions, and freedom is the extension of the probabilistic model of quality control to social organization. Castel (1991) observed that in computerized, advanced capitalist, particularly neoliberal states, new "preventive strategies of social administration" have displaced the notion of exactness, or "a particular precise danger embodied in a concrete individual or group," with that of risk, or "the effect of a combination of abstract *factors* which render more or less probable the occurrence of undesirable modes of behaviour" (287). For Castel, the new preventive strategies no longer center on individual subjects, but rather reduce and dissolve subjects into statistical risk factors, resulting in the subordination of the caretaking, intervening specialist to the autonomous policy- and decision-making manager. This probabilistic preventive social administration, then, constitutes a new mode of surveillance through "systematic predetection":

> The modern technologies of prevention are overarched by a grandiose technocractic rationalizing dream of absolute control of the accidental, understood as the irruption of the unpredictable. In the name of this myth of absolute eradication of risk, they construct a mass of new risks which constitute so many new targets for preventive intervention. . . . Thus, a vast hygienist utopia plays on the alternate registers of fear and security, including a delirium of rationality, an absolute reign of calculative reason and no less absolute prerogative of its agents, planners and technocrats, administrators of happiness for a life to which nothing happens. (Castel 1991: 289)

Like Taylorism, this preventive social administration is "obsessed with efficiency" (295). Castel's concept of the preventive social administration is similar to Hardt and Negri's (2000) notion of *omni-crisis*, which allows for continual intervention, but also repression and physical violence (as an extension of the police state) (35–38, 189).[21] This preventive social administration and omni-crisis, as an extension of statistical quality control, underlines discourses on public education. Continual intervention and portrayal of students in terms of statistical risk factors characterize the Texas accountability system and President Bush's No Child Left Behind, in which students in every grade are tested, and in theory, constant testing prevents incompetent students from receiving diplomas. Despite the heavy cost of testing, the economic discourse of efficiency is often invoked as the rationale and many times results in the scaling back of funding. The eugenic conception of a fixed quantum of intelligence is then corrected through a sort of postmodern multiplicity, replaced by the notion of a fixed achievement level at different grades.

## Delegitimizing Public School and Equity through Statistical Discourse

In observing the proceedings of the 78th legislative session, I became aware of dual strategies. On the one hand, testing intensified in terms of its consequences for students, its coverage of subjects, and its difficulty, and the accountability system was touted for markedly improving Texas schools. On the other hand, proposals for vouchers (renamed "freedom scholarships"), charter districts, and the repeal of equitable funding emerged, contradicting the discourse that testing was strengthening the Texas public school system. In the proposed charter districts and voucher schools, the intensified testing would not even be required. The *Texas Observer* (2003) claimed that the multiple-criteria bills "may also encounter opposition from proponents of vouchers. The more kids who flunk the test—and the worse the public schools look—the easier it will be to sell the public on a program that funnels students and state money into private, for-profit schools."

While measures for vouchers, charter districts, and repealing equitable funding did not pass in that regular session (in part due to the Democrats' protest against the redistricting bill, which prevented many bills from being heard before the full House), they still appeared to undermine the public school system, reminiscent of post–Reconstruction Era educational politics (see Chapter 2). For me, constituent in this attack on public schools was the deployment of a statistical discourse that combined Malthusianism, eugenic meritocracy, and statistical quality control, in which the following occurred: (1) the reduction of people to statistical factors in order to delegitimize public education as social security; (2) the exposition of the inefficiency of equity and the reconstruction of equality as just meritocracy and freedom as free market; (3) the naturalization of racial and socioeconomic inequity through the discourse of minimizing failure; and (4) the articulation of quality control as a form of gender conservatism.

## Statistical Reductionism in the Delegitimization of Public Education

The largest Public Education Committee meeting occurred March 18, 2003, convening on HB 2465, authored by Chairman Grusendorf—which was very similar to HB 658 by Representative Ron Wilson, an African American Democrat from Houston. The bill would establish a voucher pilot program in eleven districts with forty thousand students or more and with 50 percent or more of students receiving free or reduced-price lunch. The allocation, entitled "freedom scholarship," would cover the full cost of the private school. The meeting had been moved to the auditorium in anticipation of the crowds, and I had to find a seat in the spillover room and watch the event live on television until about halfway through the meeting. Grusendorf introduced his honored speaker, Milton Friedman, Nobel-prize winning economist and one of the architects of the neoliberal movement, who began his speech

asking, "Why [is there] so little progress" in public schools? After stating
that in reading, math, and literature, students are "way behind," he contended that public schooling, "like every socialist industry, is low quality and high cost." The findings of the *Nation at Risk* document of 1983,
he suggested, are "more true of this generation. SAT scores forty years ago
are higher than they are today. The dropout rate is increasing. The quality is going down, while the cost is going up." In the suburbs, public
schools approximated private schools, but in the low-income areas, because there was "no choice," there was "no reason for teachers and administrators to pay attention." For him, you "get at the real root of the
problem by competition." He even proclaimed with the fervor of a min-
ister looking for an "amen," "I don't like to call 'em public schools, but
'government schools.'" The government school should be in fear of "losing its customers." In critique of Friedman's statistics, Representative
Bob Griggs asked him whether or not historical conditions complicate
comparisons between public education now and that of forty years ago.
Such a critique echoed that of Malthus by Ensor that "to 'talk of population as of abstract numbers . . . led him to misjudge the causes of
economic successes'" (Rothschild 1995). Friedman's rhetoric followed
the characterization by Collins (1998) that "the public becomes recon-
figured as anything of poor quality," often in which social assistance is
associated with socialism in order to evoke McCarthyism (34). Accompanying such devaluation of the public are attempts to underfund social
services (33, 34). One of the criticisms of the No Child Left Behind Act
by congressional Democrats and by organizations such as the National
Education Association was that it was an unfunded mandate. In Texas,
the experimental site for the No Child Left Behind Act, the very year
that third graders would be forced to pass the new and more difficult
TAKS test in order to be promoted to the fourth grade, the legislature
scaled back funding. In a meeting on school finance, Representative
Rene Oliveira referred to the proceedings of the Appropriations Sub-
committee as "Saturday night's raid on public education," sparking
Chairman Grusendorf to interrupt, "Now, wait a minute." After a heated
debate, the chairman asked Representative Dan Branch, who sat on
that committee, whether there was a raid on public education, to which
Branch answered, "The net effect is to expand public education, [but
also] to find as many *efficiencies* as possible" (my italics). While lobbying for the multiple-criteria bills, a group of us met with a Republican
legislative aide to discuss the bills. The legislative aide, speaking to a
group of nearly all women of color, spelled out to us the reluctance of

the committee to hear and pass the multiple-criteria bills. I asked him why the chairman could not support the multiple-criteria bills, yet sponsored the voucher bill, which would allow students to attend private school and not be required to take the TAKS. He answered that, frankly, in his opinion, the chairman did not believe in public education, that private schools were simply better schools. In that office, sitting across from this legislative aide, it became as transparent as the glass walls and windows enclosing the meeting space that perhaps there was more to what Representative Oliveira let on in the meeting for HB 5; perhaps there was a raid on public education.

## The Inefficiency of Equity

> [The] notion of social or redistributive justice, insofar as it is invoked to justify intervention by the state, is one of the favourite targets of the neo-liberals.
>
> —Laclau and Mouffe (1985: 172)

For Republicans on the Public Education Committee, one of the biggest goals of the session was to repeal the finance equity system, referred to as the Robin Hood law, which recaptured money from the wealthier districts and distributed it to the poorer districts. I was shocked that the very first Public Education Committee meeting of the 78th session raised HB 604, the sunset bill that committee member Representative Branch called the "death sentence for Robin Hood." Just from studying about the Edgewood cases that led to the current law, I felt a sense of foreboding—that in this single number, 604, thirty years' worth of fighting for equity led by MALDEF and the families of Edgewood could be wiped out. Countering MALDEF, a Latina witness, representing Texas Hispanics Educating on Law and Politics (Texas HELP) even said that we should "put a stake through the heart of Robin Hood." Ironically, Chairman Grusendorf's own uncle, Bill Grusendorf, representing rural districts, officially testified "on" the bill, while really opposing the bill. He joked that he "would disappoint his mother" by testifying against Grusendorf's first bill as chair of the Public Education Committee.

Many witnesses contended that there was a need to conduct a study on what constituted an adequate education and scale back what committee member Representative Jerry Madden called "inefficient spending by districts." When committee member Oliveira responded that if districts could be equally poor, then "everybody could be equally stupid," I realized that adequate education could be defined in such a way as to provide an equitable system on the surface but leave money only for the basics. For districts that could not raise money outside the state budget, this posed particular problems. For example, a teacher at a predominantly minority high school in Austin told me that, sure, schools can be given equal amounts of money by the state, but her school might require that the money go into building repairs instead of providing more resources, while a school on the richer west side might be able to raise enough money in fund-raisers to cover the costs of building repairs. The librarian at the same minority school told me to take the libraries as an example. As we stood in their library, lined with half-empty bookshelves and at the time housing only two computers and one printer, he said that the library of a high school on the west side received enough private donations to have more than one *floor*. Later, looking on the west side school's Web site, I found that the school also sponsored annual summer trips to Hawaii. Additionally, an adequacy study might define education in such a way as to deny resources for courses beyond the basics, particularly art, music, and extracurricular activities. One witness even suggested that an adequate education is one that shapes students into "productive citizens in the economy." Although the bill passed the committee that night, with only Democratic representatives Scott Hochberg and Rene Oliveira voting against it (Representative Harold Dutton was absent), HB 604 did not make it past the House floor. However, Grusendorf attached the bill as a substitute to another of his bills, HB 5, whose intention he articulated as giving districts "monetary relief" of an extra $300 per student. After attending the meetings, I realized that the bill tried to dispel with the adjustments in the distribution of money, namely by giving districts money based purely on average daily attendance, instead of on a weighted average daily attendance and cost of education index that took into account the economic differentials in each city. For example, Laredo Independent School District, according to one witness, with its 99 percent Hispanic and 93 percent economically disadvantaged population, depended heavily upon the adjustments. Additionally, Chairman Grusendorf's uncle, Bill Grusendorf, speaking for rural schools, noted that the elimination of small school adjustments would hurt rural schools. For MALDEF lawyer Leticia Saucedo, the repealing of the equity provision of the finance structure "signals [the intent] to eliminate the equity principle." After posing several questions to Saucedo, Representative Madden, raising his voice, insisted, "[W]e have Supreme Court guidelines, do we not [that uphold the equity principle]?" Madden's question did not take into account the mood of the meeting: a mood of confidence expressed by the committee that the Texas Supreme Court would rule the current Robin Hood system, which relied on the principle of redistributive justice, unconstitutional. When Representative Griggs then asked, "Does adequacy trump equity?" I felt as did David Kennedy, superintendent of Gregory Portland in South Texas, who testified that to attach HB 604 to a bill that was meant to provide relief to districts in this year of federal budget cuts was "dishonest," a "red herring." I began to feel that all the talk of caps, inefficiency, crisis, and the "absolute failure" of Robin Hood, as one witness put it—a discourse filled with technical language of abbreviations and statistics—was a way to repeal, as Saucedo said in her testimony, "what Edgewood was all about." Madden ended the discussion on HB 5 with the following comment: "Don't you agree that the witnesses [against the bill] are like patriots who wouldn't throw out the Articles of Confederation?" As the committee postponed the vote until the room was cleared of all the discontents, and subsequently voted 7 (including Representative Dutton of Houston, the only Black representative on the committee) to 2 (Oliveira and Hochberg) to send it to the full House, I had an almost apocalyptic feeling of the coming of a new era of post-Reconstruction, much like the era that repealed the gains of the radical Republicans.

## The Naturalization of Inequality

According to Rothschild (1995), what proved so momentous for Malthus's "Essay on Population" was "his extension to social policy of the rhetoric of natural forces" (734). Similarly, the laws of physics contained in Quetelet's "average man" and Charles Booth's social categories, both of which were biologized by Galton and the eugenicists, provided a language with which reformers could articulate social policy (Desrosières 1998; MacKenzie 1981). Contained within the current neoliberal discourse is the naturalization of social inequalities, particularly in what I call the "discourse of the gap." Such a naturalizing discourse masks structures of inequality, an inequality supported by the bourgeoisie. According to MacKenzie, "[T]he eugenic theory of society corresponded in its main features to certain important aspects of the social interests and typical social experience of the professional middle class" (31).[22] Similarly, the theory of a "just meritocracy" (see LaClau and Mouffe 1985), founded on the ideal of Galton and Pearson, naturalizes inequality. In the committee meetings, discussion of the TAKS by a member of the Charles A. Dana Center at the University of Texas at Austin exemplified the naturalization of inequality. At the Public Education Committee meeting on accountability, the Dana Center expert commented, "You're going to have gaps with higher standard tests. It might take five or six years to get the gaps . . . close to zero." I had been warned by MALDEF attorney Leticia Saucedo that the argument by TEA in the *GI Forum* case—that the closing of "the gap" not only revealed the nondiscriminatory nature of the TAAS, but also signaled the improvement in education for students of color generated by the TAAS—would be exposed as false, since a new test would produce even larger gaps.

The statistical projections of the impact that the new TAKS test would have in 2003 did, in fact, show large gaps between the scores of White students and those of students of color. One test of this impact, used by MALDEF experts in the *GI Forum* case, is a statistical significance test created by the EEOC, termed the 80 percent rule. For example, according to the 80 percent rule, if the number of people in one group passing a test is less than 80 percent of the number of another group passing a test, then this shows a disparate impact. While there are many more tests of statistical significance required in order to prove the existence of racial discrimination (as well as proof of either intent or unnecessary impact) in U.S. courts, it nevertheless serves as a primary indicator of disparate impact in discrimination cases. According to the projections, in the grades at which passing the TAKS test determines promotion (third, fifth, and eighth) and graduation (eleventh), the passing rate of Black students was less than 80 percent of the passing rate of White students on the fifth-, eighth-, and eleventh-grade mathematics test; on the fifth- and eighth-grade reading tests and eleventh-grade English language arts test; and on the eleventh-grade science test. For Hispanic students, the 80 percent rule shows disparate impact in the eighth-grade and eleventh-grade mathematics test, and the eleventh-grade English language arts test. These projections ran counter to the argument made in the *GI Forum* case that the testing system was effectively "closing the gap." If the projections materialize, the comment that "you're going to have gaps with higher standard tests" appears as an attempt to resolve this contradiction by naturalizing and individualizing these differences, much in the same way as did Judge Prado, as he said the gaps might be caused by the failure of minority students to "catch up with their counterparts."

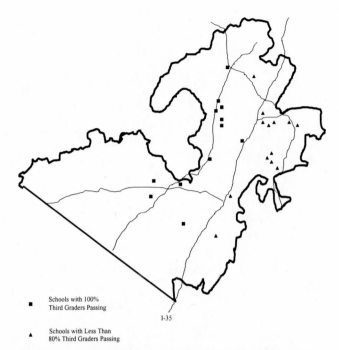

Schools with 100%
Third Graders Passing

I-35

Schools with Less Than
80% Third Graders Passing

**Figure 4.1    Austin Independent School District Highest and
Lowest Passing Rates: Third-Grade TAKS (First Administration)**

*Source: Austin American Statesman (2003) "Search Central Texas School Test
Scores and Ratings," http://www.statesman.com/metrostate/content/metro/
schools/index.html (accessed March 26, 2003).*

On the night the multiple-criteria bills were scheduled for a hearing before the House Public Education Committee, I showed the projections to an NAACP representative, who, thinking of the potential materialization of the results (as well as the full impact of the potential rejection of the multiple-criteria bills), said "they are creating an underclass." For her, as for me, it was clear that the testing system represented a form of economic "containment" (Saltman 2000: xvii; see also Collins 1998). One of the ways in which this occurs is the use of school testing statistics by real estate markets. The city of Austin, for example, is heavily segregated, with the line marking that segregation being Interstate 35, and I have heard some refer to it as "the color line." Figure 4.1 shows the schools with third graders with the highest passing rates and those with the highest failing rates in Austin. Figure 4.2 shows the concentration of wealth as a measure of median home prices, which I obtained from a

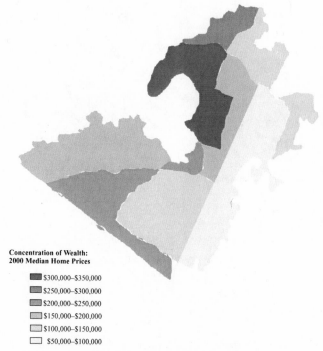

Concentration of Wealth:
2000 Median Home Prices

- $300,000–$350,000
- $250,000–$300,000
- $200,000–$250,000
- $150,000–$200,000
- $100,000–$150,000
- $50,000–$100,000

Figure 4.2   Austin: Concentration of Wealth

*Source: Jim McDonald (2002), "Area Map for Austin, TX," http://www.jimmac .com/areamap.cfm (accessed April 23, 2002).*

Realtor's Web site (McDonald 2002), and compared to a map of Austin Independent School District (TEA 2002b). The map was also inspired by an article in the *Austin Chronicle* (2002) called "AISD's Haves and Have Nots."

At the same time that the committee decided that maintaining the equitable funding system was inefficient and funding for public education in general was in jeopardy, a proposal to fund a program for career and technology education made "fiscal sense for the state," preventing students from becoming "a tax-burden for us tax-payers." Just who constituted this tax burden was answered by Representative Gene Seaman sponsoring the bill, who, earlier in the meeting, stated the "facts": "Fifty percent of male Hispanics are dropouts." He also reminded the audience of the "cliché [that dropping out] leads to the three P's: pregnant, prison, and parole." I was reminded of a racist comment made by the librarian of the predominantly minority school about Latino males. Arguing that his school should be provided with more programs in vocational education, he stated, confident in his knowledge of the racial geography, "they [Hispanic males] like autobody better than sex." At the meeting, this racialization of Latino boys, and by default the "willing" Latina girls as overly sexed beings, who drain state money by populating welfare rolls and prison cells, sketched the backdrop with which to accept the provisions of the bill, one of which would allow districts to contract with other districts, "using Chapter 41 money to help 42 districts [in a] skills-training program or apprenticeship." When Representative Griggs asked if this bill could create career and technology education magnet schools or "clustering" of schools, I couldn't help asking myself if this would constitute tracking a whole independent school district. The opposition to the bill came, ironically, not from the teacher organizations or civil rights organizations in attendance, but from the Texas Eagle Forum, a religious Right organization. The representative from the organization, who stood opposed to the committee's reforms for most of the session, argued that the bills promoted "lifetime tracking," "training instead of education," and the replacement of the diploma with the certificate for completion allowed by the career and technology education program. While for her the school-to-work program was reminiscent of socialist Germany, for me it sounded like a form of industrial education that Spivey (1978) called a "new slavery" in his book *Schooling for the New Slavery: Black Industrial Education, 1868–1915*.

## Quality Control and Gender Conservatism

> Just so you know; I do have a voice.
> —Representative Glenda Dawson[23]

Underlying the discursive attack on public education is an attack on the teaching profession as a predominantly female occupation. In Texas, more than 77 percent of teachers are women (TEA, Division of Performance Reporting 2003). At the meeting on HB 5, when Oliveira criticized the Appropriations Committee with committing a "raid on public education," one of his main concerns was that support for giving "relief" money to districts would have an adverse impact on teachers' health insurance. Texas teachers' fight for occupational protection without the benefit of collective bargaining in the state of Texas can be traced to the very origins of the accountability system itself. Teachers' own call for educational reform and higher salaries became co-opted and rearticulated through the Perot reforms, the rhetoric of which was dominated by a discourse of the "incompetent teacher," buttressed by statistics on the poor performance of Texas students (see McNeil 2000a). For McNeil, "The cost issue shifted the discussion of *teacher quality* into *quality control*" (2000a: 166; italics in original).

Apple (2001) suggested that since the "majority of teachers . . . are women," the attacks on teachers and teacher unions (as done by Milton Friedman in the committee hearing on vouchers) should be read in a broader context, as "part of a longer history of attacks on women's labor" (39). As Bowles and Gintis (1976) suggested, a major reform by Horace Mann in the Progressive Era was to replace male elementary teachers with females because they could be given lower pay: "The fact that female teachers were much cheaper to hire than males may have provided the main impetus for the feminization of the teaching staff" (171). The current accountability reform movement discursively produces the feminization of teaching as a deficiency and a *risk* in need of better (more masculine) management. For example, in "2002 Carnegie Challenge: Teaching as a Clinical Profession: A New Challenge for Education," Hinds (2002) of the Carnegie Corporation argued for the transformation of the teaching profession from its "long . . . treat[ment] as an art, craft, or second-rate occupation" and its "long and lingering reputation as a low-status job for women [that] continues to sabotage efforts to strengthen the profession" to a profession modeled after clinical medical school training (1). According to Newman (1987: 93), "intentionally omitted [from the Perot-led Select Committee on Public Education] were employed public school teachers or administrators," an omission argued to make the reform process more objective. The focus on objectivity and statistical data by the accountability movement—as evidenced in Brad Duggan's statement that "without data, you're just another person with an opinion"—may be a recuperation of the historical association of data with masculinity and opinions with femininity, as the English mathematician Arbuthnot in 1701 "promised a 'manly vigour of the mind' to all who studied mathematics, and condemned the 'weakness and effeminacy' of all those who preferred witty opinions over closely reasoned quantitative arguments" (Cohen 1982: 139). On October 20, 2002, *60 Minutes* aired a segment on girls' outperforming of boys on standardized tests, despite there being "statistically more boy geniuses than girls" (Stahl 2002). Appearing as an expert on the show, conservative Christina Hoff Summers blamed feminists and the "culture of women" for letting boys fall behind, a result of teachers' view that boys are "toxic." Lesley Stahl reported that at a predominantly Black single-sex school for boys with male teachers, "test scores for boys have jumped dramatically." The story thus recuperated Progressive Era fears of "emasculation" by female teachers and coeducation as expressed by psychologist G. Stanley Hall (see Russett 1989: 62). According to Feldstein (2000: 60), Hall's conception of women as bad mothers, or "mother-blaming," became hegemonic in 1950s and 1960s liberalism, evident, for example, in Moynihan's document on the Black American family, which rooted the Black family's cultural "pathology" in its "matriarchal" structure. For Maher (2002), the rearticulation of mother blaming as "teacher blaming" is a major component in the high-stakes testing movement: "this mostly White and female teaching force is being widely blamed, almost as if they are bad mothers, specifically for failing to educate student populations whose chronic poverty and inability to advance is laid either on themselves or the schools rather than on deeper social structural barriers" (7).

The structure of reforms in Texas, in which curricula are often described as "teacher-proof," treats teachers as mere executants (see Mc-Neil 2000a: 192–200),[24] suggesting that Castel's (1991) formulation of the preventive social administration—based on statistical quality control—that subordinates the care-taking specialist to the managerial administrator is inherently gendered.

## Conclusion

In this chapter, I discuss the ways in which statistical discourse underlies the marketization of education. The Houston case, in which the district signed a contract guaranteeing a number of students to an alternative placement school and in which statistical production won the district a $500,000 prize, exhibits the profitability of statistics within accountability reforms at which high-stakes testing is the center. The historic bloc through which the marketization of education has achieved hegemony is made up of neoliberal and neoconservative corporate leaders and governmental leaders, namely legislators and governors, but also members of the managerial class, who benefit from statistical expertise, and of the religious Right, who value (Protestant) individualism. The marketization of education includes, first, the articulation of the goals of education in terms of the market, which tends to be articulated within statistical discourse—as when Guthrie asked if education needs a Dow Jones index. Second, the marketization of education includes the privatization of educational realms, and I argue that the objectification (in the Marxist sense) or commodification of knowledge (both of and about students) is made possible through statistical discourse, a condition of the postmodern informational economy. High-stakes testing and its statistical discourse are thus super-exploitative, not only allowing corporations to profit from the production of testing statistics, but also creating a means by which to divide contingent and core laborers. Third, the creation of a rewards-sanctions system based on statistical production incorporates students, teachers, administrators, and the public into a system of competition that further sediments the hegemony of the testing regimes. The agenda of privatizing (and thus exploiting) public education is supported by the recuperation of conservative Malthusian and eugenic-meritocratic statistical discourses that deploy fear, the trope of efficiency, and the naturalization of inequality to delegitimize equity and redistributive justice. Further, the coalition of corporations and the state creates a preventive social administration that, through a discourse network of statistical quality control, both treats students as statistical risk factors and subordinates teachers (a largely female occupation) through a gendered discourse of deficiency. As the marketization of education depends on the production of statistical truth or objectification, in the next chapter, I discuss the means by which that truth is negotiated and objectified (in Desrosières's sense of "making hold") through statistical discourse.

# 5 / Statistical Objectification, Truth, and Hegemony

> Truth will not make us free, but taking control of the
> production of truth will.
>
> —Hardt and Negri (2000: 156)

While statistical discourse on testing allows for two types of objectification, in terms of treating students as manipulable objects and in terms of commodifying their knowledge and social information, a third mode of statistical objectification operates in reproducing the hegemony of the testing system. According to Desrosières (1998), "statistical objectification" is a way of stabilizing objects and providing forms for describing the relationship between them: "making *things that hold*, either because they are predictable or because, if unpredictable, their unpredictability can be mastered to some extent, thanks to the calculation of probability" (9). Embedded in the politics of networks and disciplinary expertise (Latour 1987; Fischer 1990), statistical objectification, as the production of scientific truth claims, can be better understood as *discourse*, as a terrain upon which occurs the struggle for truth (Urla 1993). Grounding statistics in this sense not only refuses an oversimplification of the science as a "*monstre froid*" (see Foucault 1991: 103) that operates separate from real, material, and human relations of power, but also allows space for considering the ways in which statistics are employed in contradictory and oppositional ways, as "tools in the crafting of modern subjectivity and social reality" (Urla 1993: 820).

Many commentators have attributed the hegemonic status of testing to the mystifying appeal of numbers. For example, Sacks (1999) attributed the "obsession" with testing in the United States to the "magical power" of statistics (7). Statistical objectification is central to understanding the hegemony of the testing system in Texas, evidenced partially in a ubiquity of statistics in debates on testing. In this chapter, I discuss the way in which the statistical objectification of failure is based on the popular religion of statistics as a language of progress and serves to naturalize minority failure. Second, I discuss the use of poll data to project a collective or national-popular will, in which the representativeness of Texans functions as a form of representation and interpellation. Third, I discuss statistical theories of standard error of measurement and correlation as they relate to what Desrosières called the two main objectives of statistics (to stabilize objects and construct relationships between those objects) to examine the ways in which the testing system is both legitimated and validated in the context of social struggles. Fourth, in each of these cases, I present cases of statistical subjectivity as modes of resistance.

## On Progress

In a commentary on the testing system in Texas and proposed changes by the multiple-criteria bills, Governor Rick Perry remarked, "We are not going to turn back the clock on progress.... We will ask our children to meet certain standards, and we will ask them from time to time to clear a higher hurdle" (quoted in Joyce 2003). The discourse of statistical progress proved to be a formidable barrier to gaining political support for the multiple-criteria bills, particularly in the context of proposals for voucher pilot programs in Texas. Although an Austin high school teacher expressed to me her opinion that all teachers were against the TAAS, two of the major teacher organizations lobbying in the Capitol, the Texas Federation of Teachers and the Association of Texas Professional Educators, did not support the multiple-criteria bills. Observing the House Public Education Committee meeting on vouchers on March 18, 2003, I wondered if the need to use testing to prove the progress of public schools explained in part the sentiment that Association of Texas Professional Educators representative Broch Gregg made to the *Texas Observer* (2003) in saying, "There may be some members who do support [the multiple-criteria bills]. . . . But this is not a good issue for us right now." In the voucher meeting, JoHannah Whitsett, testifying on behalf of the Association of Texas Professional Educators, argued that public schools did work, that the accountability system worked, and that since 1994, test scores were increasing. Lindsay Gustafson from the

Texas Classroom Teachers Association repeated this argument, stating that the accountability system works. Her testimony directly followed the impassioned testimony of a Black reverend, wearing a black T-shirt with the letters BAEO (Black Alliance for Educational Options) on it, that the "tests do not guarantee anything," particularly closing the "achievement gap," because he knew of a high school graduate "who could not read a Coke can." The reverend testified that if students were "placed in the right group, [they] don't have to take the TAAS [to graduate]." Committee member Representative Scott Hochberg asked the suit-clad Texas Classroom Teachers Association representative about this "conflicting testimony. Would you speak to this disparity?" Representative Jerry Madden also chimed in with a story that community college professors told him that there were high school graduates from Plano Independent School District, which at the time was one of the richest districts in Texas, who "couldn't write sentences." Even groups that did support the multiple-criteria bills, like Texas Freedom Network, a progressive advocacy organization used the statistical discourse of progress to defend public schools. Handing the committee statistical charts and graphs, Samantha Smoot of Texas Freedom Network compared voucher schools with charters, "low-performing schools" in which she said that students were "trapped." Texas Association of School Boards president Rick Ogden (whose organization opposed the multiple-criteria bills) used the proof of the recently released third-grade TAKS scores to show that schools were succeeding. Even committee member Representative Dan Branch interrupted the meeting to publicly document that his daughter passed the third-grade TAKS exam and that the whole third grade of his daughter's school passed. The appeal to the statistical discourse of progress at the meeting, even as contradictory testimony threatened the commonsense notion that testing was the panacea for public schools' ills, indicated a type of symbolic violence (Bourdieu 1977). By supporting the discourse of progress in testing as a real evaluation of teacher effectiveness, despite findings that the Texas accountability system in effect "de-skills" teachers (McNeil 2000a), the teacher organizations were in fact strengthening the very ideological attack on teachers inherent in the high-stakes testing movement. In the case of the teacher organizations, I see a delicate balance of self-government (see McNay 1992: 68) between the symbolic violence of accepting hegemonic discourses that in turn de-skill many in the teaching profession and the "war of position" (see Simon 1991 [1982]) in using that very hegemonic discourse to defend the existence of public school teachers.[1]

Ironically, earlier in the session, the Public Education Committee held a hearing on the accountability system in which experts for the state of Texas made virtually the same arguments as those made by teacher associations in the voucher hearing; further, the committee seemed to fully accept evidence that the test-based accountability system produced progress in the state. At the accountability hearing, the committee and audience seemed most compelled by the testimony provided by the Charles Dana Center at the University of Texas at Austin, which provided statistical data on what really defined the success of Texas testing: that the average score for African American students on the National Assessment of Education Progress in Texas was higher than that for White students in Louisiana, Mississippi, Missouri, Utah, West Virginia, Arkansas, and Hawaii. Additionally, the expert presented more charts, explaining that Texas was making progress, because African Americans who had taken Advanced Placement (AP) courses in high school scored higher GPAs in public higher education than "White kids" who had not taken AP courses in high school. While it was common sense to me that students who had taken AP courses, as I had, would be better prepared than those who had not enrolled in AP classes, I realized that my own conceptions battled a broader Gramscian common sense that equated Blackness with expected failure. My own reaction, seemingly isolated in the crowd of nodding heads and the occasional whispers of "hmm" and "wow," was that it seemed more than a little precarious to argue that because our *Blacks* do better than other states' *Whites*, we, the state of Texas, have progressed, proving the "testing system really worked." The argument seemed to equate progress with the moment that our expected failure has done better than their expected success. Further, I experienced the charts, coming from this well-meaning White expert with ties to civil rights organizations, as a reduction of Blackness to nothing more than a comparative device (Fanon 1967).

## Representativeness and the Collective Will

Over the course of the 78th legislative session, the struggle over the hegemony of testing was contested not only in the use and production of testing statistics themselves, but also through poll data. Legislators and their aides were invited to a press conference on testing by the organization Texas Public Education Reform Foundation (TPERF). The then commissioner of education was a guest speaker at the conference, and the chairman of the House Public Education Committee served as the TPERF spokesperson. The meeting centered on a recent poll conducted by the organization, from which they concluded, "Texans are saying, 'Don't mess with testing.'" One of the contradictions was that the chairman of the Public Education Committee also sponsored a bill for vouchers, or, what he called a more accurate term, "freedom scholarships," which would not require students using state assistance to take the TAKS. I, along with other participants who attended the conference, received a folder with the key findings of the poll, as well as other information related to the organization. Table 5.1 represents the document "Statewide Texas Education Survey" (TPERF 2002b), also presented at the conference on an overhead projector.

Another document in the folder given at the conference stated that the survey participants consisted of 808 randomly selected Texas adults and that the survey was conducted from August 4 through 6, with "a

TABLE 5.1   RESULTS OF "STATEWIDE TEXAS EDUCATION SURVEY" BY TPERF

| Page | Result | % Favor/ Agree | % Oppose/ Disagree | % Undecided/ Unsure |
|---|---|---|---|---|
| 2 | Texas adults overwhelmingly favor standardized testing. | 64 | 30 | 6 |
| 3 | Texas adults want schools to identify problems and points of strength early on. | 92 | 7 | 1 |
| 4 | Texas adults support a standardized testing program that is based on knowledge and skills instead of just memorization. | 78 | 14 | 7 |
| 5 | Texas adults support continuing testing and accountability using the TAKS test. | 79 | 15 | 6 |
| 6 | Texans support ending social promotion. | 82 | 16 | 2 |
| 7 | Texans say it is smart to use test[s to] measure school and hold schools accountable. | 77 | 20 | 2 |
| 9 | Standardized testing helps schools improve. | 53 | 34 | 12 |
| 10 | Seen, read, or heard anything recently about the new TAKS test? | 49 | 51 | |

margin of error of plus or minus 3.5 percent" (TPERF 2002a). In that same document, which I believe was a press release, the chairman of TPERF, Vidal Martinez, made the following remark: "The survey results validate the Texas public education reform movement . . . [and show] that we need to continue moving forward to make Texas schools and students the best in the nation" (TPERF 2002a). Because of the emphasis in the survey on the connection linking standardized tests, promotion, early diagnosis, and the eschewing of "teaching to the test," I read the survey as a response to the multiple-criteria bills or any proposals to alter the current accountability system. What the survey could attempt to prove is that the bills were not in accordance with Texan voters, and that Representative Dora Olivo did not represent her constituency by bringing up the bills. The production of the truth presupposes that there exists a quantifiable Texan habitus and uses this presupposition to then project a Texan collectivity in order to persuade others to accept standardized testing and "validate the reform movement," particularly in the face of troubling projections about the number of students who could fail the TAKS.

Despite the oft-quoted notion of statistics as "damned lies" that pervades perceptions of polls, political polls are nevertheless omnipresent in the U.S. media. Polls, then, perhaps more than other forms of statistical truth production, reveal what Desrosières suggested about statistics, that embedded in the "routine use of statistics . . . [is] in part a criticism of its own realism" (204). What could explain, then, the continuing persistence of polls? In the United States, broad public acceptance of polling and the statistical technique of sampling are rooted historically in the success of Gallup in predicting the reelection of Roosevelt in 1936 (Desrosières 1998: 205–206). At the same time, in the twentieth century, the function of statistics transforms from a tool of comprehensive analysis to one of intervention, particularly with the emergence of the welfare state. Poll results form a "visualization technology" (Helmreich 1998: 101) for revealing hidden essences, an abstract universal opinion hidden in the population and quantifiable within statistics, or exactly what Williams (1977) called a "structure of feeling." Statistical science, in its earliest senses, was named "social physics" by Adolphe Quetelet, aiding in (yet not fully encompassing) the formation of modern "human sciences" as that which could render visible invisible or "hidden forces" (Foucault 1994 [1971]: 364). Perhaps it is the "statistical magic" (Desrosières 1998: 71) of revealing hidden forces that facilitates the deployment of statistics in a way that "interpel-lates" or "hails" (Althusser 1971: 174) people into a projected "collective will" (Mouffe 1979).[2] According to Popkewitz (2000), polling and sur-veys constitute "performances of participation," which resolve tensions within governmental policy making that seems increasingly distanced and abstracted from the public, by "enabl[ing] people to believe that they were being consulted" (26). The reproduction of polls also limits criti-cisms to questioning the (comparative) quality of polls, rather than episte-mological questioning of the construction of knowledge by polls, such as that which characterized intradisciplinary debates on sampling (Des-rosières 1998). For example, in one committee hearing, when a witness challenged a poll on epistemological grounds, she was met with the re-sponse, "You don't believe in polls?" by a committee member. This re-sponse forced her to shift from a critique to an all-or-nothing, defensive stance on polls, which overshadowed the substance of her testimony.

In response to the TPERF press conference (and impacted by the "You don't believe in polls" moment), I took it as my own initiative, with the permission and support of Representative Olivo's then chief of staff, to research alternate poll data. Feeling that alternate statistics might be more convincing as a counter than my own internal critique of statis-tics, I conjured my own "statistical magic" (Desrosières 1998: 71), even citing poll results from sites and articles that might be considered ideo-logically opposed to multiple criteria. For example, from an article en-titled "Majority Agree with Bush's Position" on ending social promo-tion, I cited *Houston Chronicle / Dallas Morning* poll results that 76 percent "would rather leave the promotion decision up to the teacher based on the student's overall performance and 20 percent would base the decision on the results of a single state-wide test" (Walt 1998). I cre-ated a document in which I placed this poll's statistics opposite the TPERF survey result that "82% of Texans support no social promotion." From the Web page of Public Agenda, a nonprofit organization which publishes public opinion data and which at the time claimed there was no national backlash against testing, I cited the result that "78% think it's wrong to use the results of just one test to decide whether a student gets promoted or graduates" (Public Agenda et al. 2000). I even cited a survey from the Business Roundtable, one of the most prominent pro-ponents of accountability (see Chapter 4), that reported, "[T]he public is well aware of some of the limitations of [statewide] tests and recog-nizes the value of *measures in addition to tests*—primarily grades and teacher evaluations—in deciding whether to promote or to graduate students" (Public Agenda et al. 2000). In the document, I placed these poll statistics in opposition to the TPERF statistic on the support for "no social promotion." I also used poll results from groups that were ideologically similar to the multiple-criteria movement, particularly a Texas poll conducted by Harstad Strategic Research in 2002 and posted on the Texas State Teachers Association (2002) Web site, which included the following: "71% think a combination of grades, homework, and standardized tests should be used to determine student achievement"; "55% believe that testing is too excessive"; "57% believe too much emphasis is put on standardized testing"; and "59% believe that testing discourages innovation and creativity in the classroom." Although Representative Olivo's chief of staff thought that my charts were "terrific," later I felt as if I had betrayed what I considered to be the very heart of what this struggle represented: the use of narrative to oppose the statistical objectification of students by the imposition of unfair testing (see Chapter 6). Despite my inner feelings of betrayal, Representative Olivo did ultimately use the poll data within "talking points"—which function exactly like the "image fragment" into which "full-narrative is compacted," as Woodward (1999) described of postmodern language—handed out on the day she offered the multiple-criteria bills as committee substitutes to a bill that she might otherwise have opposed. A MALDEF attorney advised me that the bill might promote tracking of students of color. I learned that, given the short schedule of the Texas legislative session, often the only way to get a bill passed was as a substitute. While the House did vote in her substitutes to the bill, they were ultimately tabled by a Senate-House committee headed by none other than TPERF leader Representative Grusendorf. I watched Representative Olivo's "tactical subjectivity" (Sandoval 2000: 59), as herself a person in the contradictory state, fighting until the end, and re-viewed my statistical subjectivity in terms of a politics of *reappropriation*.

## Standard Error of Measurement and Making Objects Hold

For not only is there great potential for mismeasurement, but the human and technological factors that enter into the construction, administration, and scoring of these tests give us much reason to suspend our beliefs about their significance and their accuracy. We talk about students' test scores with the arrogance of the self-assured;

we are certain when we should, at the very least, be suspending
judgment.

—Selma Wasserman (2001: 35)

In November of 2002, the State Board of Education held a series of
public meetings addressing the setting of the standards for the new
TAKS test. Surrounding the hearings was the panic over projections
made by the Texas Education Agency in a document summarizing the
"projected impact" of the new TAKS (TEA 2002a). Because the state of
Texas empowered the TAKS reading exam to determine the promotion
of third graders to the fourth grade, the central panic centered on the
potential failure of thousands of students at so young an age. According
to the *Austin American-Statesman*, "Nearly one in four third-graders are
projected to fail. . . . More than three-fourths of those failing would be
black or Hispanic" (Suydam 2002). With the outcry of professionals and
the prospect of failing so many third-grade students, as discussed in
Chapter 3, the education commissioner and the State Board of Education responded by "lowering standards" for passing the set of tests to 2
SEM (standard error of measurement) below the panel recommendations. The State Board of Education decided that the recommended
standards would be phased in by raising the passing standard for students over a number of years. According to Haney (1999), "A common
practice in setting passing scores is to reduce an empirically established
passing score by one or two standard errors" (21). In the case of the new
test in Texas, this common practice of lowering the passing standard
served to politically buffer the test from potential challenges. As Bernstein (2002) commented in the *Texas Observer*, "A massive failure could
threaten the credibility of the new system just as it becomes established." The statistical tool of standard error of measurement, framed as
phasing in standards over time, provided a means for resolving tensions
caused by the prospect of accepting a test that would produce the failure of so many young students, for "suspending disbelief," as Wasserman stated. The tool of SEM aided in stabilizing not only the test, but
also, as the comment from Bernstein indicates, an entire network of
"technocratic" governance (Fischer 1990: 15) over public schools represented under the umbrella of the accountability system.

The "standard error of measurement" is defined in the Texas Education Agency Technical Digest of 1999–2000 (TEA, Student Assessment Division 2000) as "the amount of variance in a score resulting
from factors other than achievement" (46). The digest explains that the

standard error of measurement "can be helpful for quantifying the margin of error that occurs on every test," particularly in a situation in which "chance error" or "differential testing conditions" could impact the students' "observed score" or "the score actually achieved on a test." Such conditions could possibly cause differential movement from the "true score," which is defined as "the true ability of the student." According to the digest, "a standard error of measurement band placed around the [student's] observed score would result in a range of values that would most likely contain the student's *true score*" (46; my italics). A key assumption is that there exists an object a priori as a "true score," which represents the "true ability of the student." As Desrosières (1998) argued, "[T]he very choice of the expression 'error of measurement' implies a realistic epistemology, according to which objects preexist—at least in theory—the work of identification, definition, and delimitation" (307). The ability to take as assumptions that a score on a particular test can capture true ability and even that true ability is reducible to a number depends on a disciplinary sheltering (Kuhn 1996 [1962]) from the ongoing, vast, and contentious debates over knowledge and testing that call these assumptions into question. According to Danziger (1997), the sense of identity and the source of expertise for the community of psychologists working on intelligence testing derives from faith both in the notions of intelligence and ability as "real natural objects" and in the machinery that materialized and evidenced those objects into being (80). This faithful commitment is paralleled by the dogged faith that anthropologists place in ethnography and informants to reveal the hidden truths, often despite knowledge that the practice is implicated in relations of colonialism and imperialism (Fabian 1983; Lewis 1973; Said 1989).

The very notion of probability calculus as applicable to human beings or social sciences is historically linked to the attempt by Adolphe Quetelet to develop a "social physics" (Desrosières 1998). Quetelet borrowed heavily from error theory, a theory of probability used by physical scientists to attain precision (Porter 1995: 201). Quetelet was influenced by the work of Gauss, who proposed the curve $f(x) = e^{-x^2}$ as the distribution of elementary errors, and Pierre-Simone de Laplace, who "showed that even if the distribution of errors did not follow [this] law, the distribution of their *mean* generally inclined toward such a law, when the number of observations increased indefinitely" (Desrosières 1998: 64–65). In 1835, Quetelet conceived of the Gaussian distribution, known contemporarily as the bell curve, as the distribution of human attributes around an average ideal, which he called the "average man." Founder of eugenics Sir Francis Galton, in the late nineteenth century, rearticulated "probable error" as "standard deviation" (Desrosières 1998: 116), and Galton's work on heredity has deeply influenced, if not provided the foundations for, current considerations of "human aptitudes" to be measurable and comparable (Desrosières 1998: 113). The social conditions that facilitated the broad acceptability of notions of intelligence and ability as innate entities measurable with accuracy through the technologies of testing in the United States were, according to Danziger (1997), "hereditarianism, xenophobia, racism, and Social Darwinism" (81).

The TEA's technical digest indicates both a "taming" (Hacking 1991) of uncertainty through statistical tools of error and a sense of faith in "true ability" as an object. In the section on standard error of measurement, the digest explains that a "student's true score . . . is assumed to fall within one standard error of measurement of the observed score 68 percent of the time" (TEA, Student Assessment Division 2000: 46). Additionally, in a section that discusses the exit exam, the digest reads, "[A] student with a true achievement level at the passing standard would be likely to pass the test on the first attempt only 50% of the time. This is the definition of what it means . . . to be 'on the bubble'" (37). In order to resolve these uncertainties, the digest explained that students are given eight times to take the test, since the probability that a student "on the bubble" would pass the test increases to 99.6 percent after eight attempts at taking the test (37). As Haney (1999) argued in the *GI Forum* trial, "The reason this calculation seems to me erroneous, or at least potentially badly misleading, is because the authors have presented absolutely no evidence to show the probability that a student who fails the TAAS will continue to take the test seven more times" (16). Relying on "an extension of basic probability theory regarding the likelihood of passing subsequent administrations" (TEA, Student Assessment Division 2000: 36), the digest's authors dehumanize students' situated experiences of testing, reflecting a tendency, as Castel (1991) argued, for late-capitalist social administrations to refigure individual subjects as "a combinatory of statistical factors" (281) within a "calculus of probabilities" (288).

Missing from the calculation of probability is the weight of the accountability system. In the years 2001 and 2002, for example, students' performance on the spring administration of the TAAS counted toward schools' accountability ratings. For students in the tenth grade, who needed to retake tests, opportunities to retest took place in the subsequent summer, fall, and spring semesters. For those students held back in the tenth grade who needed to retake the test in the spring, their scores would also count toward accountability ratings (Texas Education Agency, Department of Accountability Reporting and Research 2001, 2002). The weight of accountability measures produces a stressful environment that differentiates the experience of taking a test in the summer and fall. However, the weight of accountability is invisible in the probability calculus discussed above. The accountability system that aggregates students' test scores into overall passing rates, particularly in the forms disseminated to the public, including researchers, suppresses the expert knowledge that given scores exist as approximations of an assumed true ability. Aggregates—even when represented as passing rates instead of norms—render invisible the "tamed" uncertainty of the formation of students' scores, just as much as they render invisible the individuality of students, the complexity of their academic careers, and the conditions in which they take tests. The double invisibility of error in the accountability ratings and public reports of passing rates, on the one hand, and of the weight of the accountability system on students' scores, on the other, is reflected in the differentiation of departments and sites of knowledge between "assessment" and "accountability" in the Texas Education Agency itself. This differentiation manifests itself not only abstractly on the agency's Web site on different Web pages, but also physically in the city of Austin. When I visited the Assessment Division in 2001, I was surprised to find that it was located miles away from the central agency office in downtown Austin.

This commentary is not meant to dismiss or demean the labor of hardworking and well-meaning professionals. What *is* of concern is the way in which we—professionals and academics—become involved in an apparatus of knowledge production that produces serious material implications for those children and adolescents who become the abstracted and objectified subjects of our knowledge. The "arrogance of self-assured[ness]" (Wasserman 1991) with which policy makers attach increasingly high stakes to tests depends to a large extent on the taming of errors and decontextualization through statistical tools, as well as on the absence of this taming in the most public ways in which data about passing rates are disseminated. As Dumit and Sensiper (1998) wrote, "[S]mall gaps in dissemination [of information] are enough to produce violent effects" (231).

# Race, Correlation, and the Struggle for Validity

The public debate in November of 2002 over the issue of standard error of measurement in setting the standards for the new TAKS test questioned not only the legitimacy of the testing system, but also its validity. In "Recommendations to the Texas State Board of Education on the Setting of the TAKS Standards," Confrey, Valenzuela, and Ortiz (2002) called into question the extent to which TEA properly established the validity of the test, an ethical standard of educational measurement that should precede the imposition of a testing system to which the stake of grade promotion or retention is attached.[3] Validity, according to the TEA's technical digest, is "a process of collecting evidence to support inferences from the use of the resulting scores from an assessment" (TEA, Student Assessment Division 2000: 49). Stated in another way, validity measures the relationship between test performance and achievement, mastery of objectives, or learning. According to Desrosières (1998), statistics "play a double role": they not only "stabilize objects"—such as test performance and achievement or mastery—but they also "provide forms for describing the *relationship* between objects thus constructed, and for testing the consistency of these links" (61). The most widely used statistical concept that performs the task of relating two objects is correlation. According to Suen and French (2003: 17), early conceptions of validity for testing were defined by correlation, as an early psychometrician in 1946 "stated that a test is valid for anything with which it correlates" (17). I view correlation as mirroring hegemony in the fact that it can "act as cement," or ideological glue (see Simon 1991 [1982]: 61) by binding together "otherwise incommensurable elements" (Asad 1994).

In the case of the testing system in Texas, *correlation* and related concepts of *regression* and *factor analysis* (see Desrosières 1998: 103) served as a terrain on which the validity of the two tests (the TAAS and the TAKS) were contested.

## The Struggle over Validity

For the TEA, sufficient validation of the TAAS consisted of establishing a correlation between test performance and another measure of performance, or *criterion validity*, and properly aligning or correlating test items with the state curriculum to ensure that the tests measures what it claims to measure, or *content validity* (49–50). In the case of criterion

validity, the other measure used to establish criterion validity is ironically students' performance in their courses—their grades. The technical digest gives several studies on which the criterion validity of the
TAAS (1999–2000) is based: (1) the correlation of 1992–1993 exit-level
TAAS mathematics scores with math grades in the same year; (2) two
studies correlating the 1994–1995 reading and writing exit-level tests with
pass/fail performance in English II courses; (3) the correlation of 1995–
1996 eighth-grade TAAS math tests with math grades for two large urban districts and one large suburban district; (4) the correlation of
1996–1997 eighth-grade social studies tests with grades in a large urban
district, a small urban district, a rural district, and two large suburban
districts; (5) the correlation of 1997–1998 third-grade TAAS reading
tests with pass/fail performance in the test takers' reading course; and
(6) the correlation of 1998–1999 Algebra I end-of-course tests with the
Algebra I course grade. According to the digest, "Since the tests assess
the Texas state mandated curriculum, which is required to be taught to
all students, the tests are not more or less valid for use with one subpopulation over another subpopulation" (TEA, Student Assessment Division 2000: 50, 51).

In the *GI Forum* case, Haney (1999) challenged the validity of the
tests, using data from a correlation study done in 1994–1995 on exit-
level reading. Haney found that the correlation between the reading
test and the English II grades was 0.34, and between the writing test and
English II grades was 0.32. While describing these as statistically significant because of the sample size, Haney questioned the strength of the
correlation since correlation coefficients range from −1 to 1, (−1 being
absolute negative statistical dependence, 0 being independence, and 1
being absolute positive dependence). He then presented a chart of differential passing rates for Black, Hispanic, and White students, finding
that while 28 percent of Black students and 27 percent of Hispanic students passed the English course but failed the reading exit test, 10.1
percent of Whites passed the course and failed the test. For the writing
test, 17.8 percent of Black students and 16.6 percent of Hispanics passed
the course but failed the test; the same occurred for 9.2 percent of
Whites. In this argument, Haney was establishing not only that the correlation of test performance to grades, that is, the criterion validity, is
weak, but also that testing and grades appear to correlate more for
White students than for Black and Hispanic students. However, Judge
Prado found this not to invalidate the TAAS, stating that in his opinion,
despite these disparities,

TEA has argued that a student's classroom grade cannot be equated to TAAS performance, as grades can measure a variety of factors, ranging from effort and improvement to objective mastery. The TAAS is a solely objective measurement of mastery. The Court finds that, based on the evidence, presented at trial, the test accomplishes what it sets out to accomplish, which is to provide an objective assessment of whether students have mastered a discrete set of skills and knowledge. (*GI Forum et al. v. Texas Education Agency et al.* 87 F. Supp. 2d 667, 680 [2000])

The validation of the testing system not only occurs through the correlation of test performance with grades, but also in the alignment of the actual items on the tests with the state-mandated curriculum (TEKS). While this process is not purely a statistical one, the challenge of this validation process from MALDEF in the *GI Forum* case did employ the statistical techniques of correlation and the related concept of factor analysis. For the TEA, content validity was sufficiently established through the formation of "committees consisting of educators from school districts across the state . . . for each subject area at each grade level" (TEA, Student Assessment Division 2000: 49). Additionally, that test items are written by independent contractors "provides for a system of checks and balances for item development and review that reduces single source bias" (49). I learned from a TEA employee that I could write a question for the TAAS and contract with Harcourt. I also spoke to a TEA employee who screens those questions, who said that occasionally he sees ridiculous, racially offensive questions. After screening, the questions go before a committee, and this process, according to TEA, rids the test of bias. When I told an NAACP member how surprised I was that I could write a question, she revealed to me that she was involved in the screening of questions but felt that without more educational psychologists or testing professionals, the process was simply an illusion for ridding the questions of bias. Likewise, in "Recommendations to the Texas State Board of Education on the Setting of the TAKS Standards," Confrey, Valenzuela, and Ortiz (2002) argued that the absence of content experts in the process of item selection compromised the test (7). In the *GI Forum* case, Ernesto Bernal (1999) made a similar argument, using factor analysis to suggest that the item-selection process was based more on establishing "face validity" and testing objectives "were set *logically* and then not checked for psychological consistency" (7). For Bernal, factor analysis showed not only that the "TAAS measures different factors for the different ethnic groups," but also that *"the TAAS measurement indicates such inconsistency that one cannot say whether any given youngster (or group of high school students) knows or does not know a certain skill, cannot say whether he/she has mastered or failed to master a given learning outcome, or even what the learning outcomes are!"* (8).

In fact, another TEA employee told me that the selection of test items depended on the committee's determination of whether the racial difference had represented bias or whether it could be attributed to "the gap." This sentiment was echoed in the testimony in the *GI Forum* case by consultant to the TEA Dr. Susan Phillips, who argued that "an equally plausible explanation for the differential performance is a true difference in average achievement levels for the two groups" (quoted in Gomez, Kastley, and Holleman 2000: 211), suggesting that implicit in test item selection is the inscription of Black and Latino bodies as less educable and lower achievers. Another expert for MALDEF, Martin Shapiro (1998) testified that in the reading, math, and writing portions of the 1994 and 1997 exit TAAS test, test items with the largest White-Black difference in percentage correct and with the largest White-Hispanic difference in percentage correct had the largest point-biserial correlations with performance on the remainder of the test, and those with the smallest differences in percentage correct had the smallest point-biserial correlations. In other words, the test items with the strongest correlation to overall performance on the test were the very items for which the score difference between Whites and Hispanics and between Whites and Black students was the greatest. The items with the least score difference between White students and either Black or Hispanic students correlated least with overall performance. Summarized by the MALDEF post-trial brief, "test construction procedure results in greater rather than less negative impact on minorities" (Kauffman et al. 1999: 36). Together, the testimonies of Bernal and Shapiro attempted to deconstruct the TEA's contention that the item selection process both establishes content validity and sufficiently guards against bias. However, in response to the testimony, particularly that of Shapiro, Judge Prado argued,

> The Court cannot quarrel with this evidence. However, the court finds that the Plaintiffs have not been able to demonstrate that the test, as validated and equated, does not best serve the State's goals of identifying and remediating educational problems. Be-

cause one of the goals of the TAAS test is to identify and remedy
problems in the State's educational system, no matter their
source, then it would be reasonable for the State to validate and
equate test items on some basis other than their disparate impact on certain groups. In addition, the State need not equate
its test on the basis of standards it rejects, such as subjective
teacher evaluations. (*GI Forum et al. v. Texas Education Agency
et al.* 87 F. Supp. 2d 667, 683 [2000])

The responses by the court to the challenges of test validity by experts
on the MALDEF side indicate, as we will see, both the deconstruction
of statistical proofs of discrimination and the retranslation of differences as deficiencies.

## Deconstructing Statistical Proofs of Discrimination

In the early 1970s, the courts legitimated statistical proofs of discrimination in the *disparate impact* doctrine. According to this doctrine, facially
neutral policies that created racially disproportionate effects, proved
with statistical tests, were in fact deemed racially discriminatory.[4] According to Freeman (1995), the era "managed to offer to black people
expectations of proportional racial political power, a working system of
equality of opportunity, if not actual jobs, and integrated schools" (41).
From the late 1970s, however, as the opposition to desegregation and
antidiscrimination claims gained steam, the courts narrowed the appli-
cability of the civil rights litigation and legislation. For Freeman, the
decision of *Washington v. Davis* (426 U.S. 229, 96 [S. Ct. 2040] 1976) set
a precedent for undoing the gains made in the arena of civil rights by
ruling that racially disproportionate effects did not by themselves constitute racial discrimination but required proof of intent. Greene (1995)
argued that in the 1989 *Wards Cove Packing Co. v. Atonio* (490 U.S.
642, 109 [S. Ct. 2115]) decision, the Supreme Court ruled through "a
surreal analysis of statistics," overturning a lower court decision on the
basis that "too much weight [had been given] to statistics that had demonstrated segregat[ion]" (292–293). In addition to litigation, law review
articles also began deconstructing statistical proofs of discrimination.
One notable example is Kingsley Browne (1993), who published a law
review entitled "Statistical Proof of Discrimination: Beyond 'Damned
Lies.'" In the article, he argued that "statistical evidence of intentional

discrimination should be abandoned as a primary method of proof" (477). According to Browne—who also believed that women's inability to crack the glass ceiling was due not to sexism, but to women's "natural preferences" (see Ward 1997)—the disparate impact doctrine is based on two false assumptions: (1) the "statistical fallacy" that statistically significant differences in employment are due not to chance, but to discrimination; and (2) the "central assumption" that "equal interest" and "qualifications are randomly distributed by race and sex within the qualified labor force" (482–484). This argument mirrors that made by Phillips in her *GI Forum* testimony, mentioned above, that perhaps differences in scores were due not to discrimination, but to "true difference in average achievement levels for the two groups." The simultaneity of the deconstruction of statistical proofs of discrimination yet also an upholding of a quantitatively reductive conception of meritocracy and a push for testing[5] evidences that deconstruction in and of itself is not simply equivalent to leftist/radical democratic or feminist politics, nor does it necessarily challenge all uses of statistics.

## Retranslating Differences into Deficiencies

> In short, the Court finds, on the basis of the evidence presented at trial, that the disparities in test scores do not result from flaws in the test or in the way it is administered. Instead, as the Plaintiffs themselves have argued, some minority students have, for a myriad of reasons, failed to keep up (or catch up) with their majority counterparts. It may be, as the TEA argues, that the TAAS test is one weapon in the fight to remedy this problem.
>
> —Judge Edward Prado (*GI Forum et al. v. Texas Education Agency et al.*, 87 F. Supp. 2d 667, 683 [2000])

Despite finding that MALDEF had met the criteria for showing disparate impact, Judge Prado nevertheless ruled that the impact was attributable to the failure of students themselves. The judge even retranslated a testing system, which had materialized such a disparate impact, as a remedy, indicating that forms of discrimination have increasingly become shielded from legal redress (Greene 1995: 292).[6] The ruling also reflects a tendency, as Freeman (1995) argued, "to 'declare the war is over,' to make the problem of racial discrimination go away by announcing that it has been solved," whereby social structures of inequality become rationalized (41). In litigation over the use of standardized testing for graduation decisions, the precedent for "declaring the war over" was set in the aftermath of court cases in Florida. In the *Debra P. v. Turlington* case of 1979, the Eleventh Circuit Court ruled that the implementation of minimum-competency tests as a requirement for graduation in Florida created an unlawful disparate impact because students forced to pass the exam had attended segregated schools (Elul 1999). In later cases, the court ruled that the tests could be implemented beginning with the first class that attended under the desegregation order. However, as Elul wrote, in the 1985 case of *Georgia State Conference Branches of NAACP v. Georgia*, "the Eleventh Circuit found that a school grouping system that disproportionately placed black students in lower groups did not perpetuate past discrimination because none of the students in question had ever attended school in a racially segregated system. Such a result is typical as courts come to view racial segregation in schools as a thing of the past" (513).[7]

In the *GI Forum* case, Judge Prado issued an order, siding with the state, that limited the amount of historical evidence presentable in the case to what he called a "snapshot," which would show that "educational inequalities existed at the time the TAAS test was implemented and that those inequalities render the test unfair" (quoted in Saucedo 2000: 416). While acknowledging the use of testing in Texas's past as a form of racial discrimination,[8] the judge ruled that MALDEF had not proven the existence of racial discrimination or inequalities at the time of the TAAS, dismissing the invoking of finance inequities proven by *Edgewood v. Kirby*. Similar to Elul, Saucedo asserted that "[t]he order severely curtailed the plaintiffs' ability to portray the effects of the TAAS exit test in light of the State's past use of standardized tests to discriminate against minorities and the resulting unequal educational opportunities for students. The court was not inclined to relate the history of discrimination in the public schools in Texas to disparity in TAAS exit scores" (2000: 416). Instead, the court legitimated the TEA's argument that the difference in test results were due to "socioeconomic factors, single-parent families, the need to work while in school, teen pregnancy, and similar reasons" (420). The ruling effectively argues that the testing system reflects *individual* failure, while the closure of gaps reflects *institutional* success. The simplification and denial of a history of past discrimination allowed for a different kind of historicizing about students through a racialized deficit model of failure, single parenthood, and teen pregnancy.[9] Reportedly, TEA expert witness Phillips, in consulting with NCS Pearson when the company faced lawsuits for mistakenly failing students on a Minnesota exit exam, advised employees of the company to avoid any settlements and to take the following action regarding those who failed to graduate: "We need to profile these kids. . . . Such things as their course grades, courses taken, attendance, discipline problems, trouble with the law, etc. In Texas, the testimony of these students reading such things as solid D grades into the court record painted a picture that these students did not deserve to pass regardless of their test scores" (quoted in Graham 2001). While Phillips's strategy was "not taken seriously at NCS," according to a spokesperson for NCS Pearson (quoted in Graham 2001), it nevertheless unveils a strategy to deflect responsibility for actions that harm students onto the students themselves. This constitutes a form of thinking comparable to "double-think" that Sandoval (2000) called the "late-capitalist retranslation of difference [, which] allows hierarchical and material differences in power between people to be erased from consciousness, even while these same economic and social privileges are bolstered" (73).

## A Word on Correlation, Cause, and Dependence

The theme often promoted by the TEA and its business partners is the formulation that as accountability measures and standards become more stringent over time, achievement increases, dropout rates decrease, and the "gap" closes. The inference of such a statement is that accountability causes gains in achievement. The TEA made the same argument in the *GI Forum* case: improved National Assessment of Education Progress scores and increased participation by students of color in AP courses and on the SAT occur as accountability measures are implemented and made more stringent over time—thus establishing a causal relationship. Present in the implied correlation between achievement levels and the implementation of accountability measures is the assumption of *cause*, an assumption made often in the statistical correlation in social sciences, policy making, and commonsense uses of correlation. Indeed, Huff (1993 [1954]) called the conflation of correlation with causality a "post hoc fallacy" (93). Interestingly enough, the scholar credited for constructing the concept of correlation—after whom the correlation coefficient is named—Karl Pearson, believed correlation to be a replacement of causality. Philosophically influenced by Austrian physicist Ernst Mach and German socialism, Pearson critiqued "the old idea of causality" as too subjective and in need of replacement by contingency and correlation. For Pearson, causalities were no more than concepts "converted into a dominant reality" (Desrosières 1998: 111).

It is possible to argue that the conflation of causality and correlation, despite Pearson's conceptualization of correlation as contingency, derives from the emergence of correlation as a way of theorizing racial dependence. According to statistical historians, the statistical concept of *correlation* was Karl Pearson's mathematical formalization of Sir Francis Galton's concept of regression (MacKenzie 1981; Desrosières 1998). MacKenzie (1981) contended that Galton's preoccupation with eugenics "led him to develop radically new concepts," and that "eugenics made the understanding and measurement of statistical dependence *as a phenomenon in its own right* a central goal of statistical theory" (71).[10] The appeal of Galton's theory of regression, besides its racial overtones and articulation of "Edwardian" social efficiency (Porter 2002), was that it "opened up areas of common measurement" and provided an "instrument of proof" (Desrosières 1998: 124, 125). Yet, these very tools of constructing common measurement and documentation of proof were rearticulated in the 1950s within a "sociology of inequality" (146). Using correlation within such a sociology of inequality has been a central strategy in combating racism and contesting the production of truth about the (commonsensical) correlation between accountability measures and improved achievement across racial and economic groups. In a forum, which I attended, on the testing system in Texas organized by Drs. Valenzuela and Marshall during the 78th legislative session, one of the most compelling uses of statistical data was that by Dr. Richard Valencia, an educational psychologist at the University of Texas. When newspapers headlined the success of third graders on the new TAKS, he suggested that this heralding of success "led to a false sense of security," constituting "a blatant case of misleading journalism."[11] His evidence consisted of disaggregated data on the "failure" of the third-grade TAKS in Austin schools, showing that while Whites in Austin failed at a 4 percent rate, Hispanics failed at a 15 percent rate, Blacks at an 18 percent rate, and Hispanics taking the Spanish TAAS at a 25 percent rate. He then took the failure rates of the top 10 percent and the bottom 10 percent of schools, finding that the schools at the top (0 percent failure rate) had a population that was 8 to 27 percent Hispanic and African American and that the schools at the bottom (25 to 45 percent failure rate) had a population that was 98.5 to 99 percent Hispanic and African

American. The crescendo of his testimony was the statistical fact that the correlation of percentage of students failing and the percentage of Hispanic and Black students in the school population was $y = .70$, a "very high correlation."

## Conclusion

In this chapter, I examined the formation of statistical truth as a hegemonic process of "making hold," what Desrosières defined as *objectification*. Statistical tools or techniques such as progress, sampling, standard error of measurement, and correlation provide means for negotiating and solidifying truth. The statistical notion of progress underlined the formation of truth about testing, particularly in proving the effectiveness of the testing system and the overall educational system. Underlying the common sense of the statistical notion of progress in educational reform is minority failure, as the performance of students of color is often marked as a mode of comparison. In terms of the statistical tool of sampling, polls provide a means for representing a collective will, as well as for interpellating or persuading subjects. The poll by TPERF that concluded, "Texans are saying, 'Don't mess with testing,'" was a means not only for representing or projecting a collective Texas habitus, but also for shaping a particular structure of feeling. Knowing the persuasive capacity of polls, I collected alternative poll data as a statistical counterdiscourse. In addition to the tool of polls that represent a collective will, the statistical tool of standard error of measurement allows for the solidifying of objects, which in testing systems are particular test scores. As a technique of mediating the contradiction between what is measurable and what is immeasurable, standard error of measurement served as a way for the Texas Education Agency and the State Board of Education to negotiate the new, more difficult standards of the TAKS, tempering possible objections to the testing system in the context of widespread panic over potential massive failures. Providing a means for defining validity and causal relationships, statistical correlation served as a mode for MALDEF to challenge the validity of testing in Texas, using correlation to show that the high school exit-level tests were neither valid nor psychometrically sound. The commonsensical conception of correlation as cause has provided a way for supporters of testing to argue that the accountability system itself has caused improvements in the educational system. At the same time, Valencia used correlation as a statistical counterdiscourse, representing the presence of structural racism (as an underlying causal agent). The ruling of the *GI Forum* case in favor of the TEA, despite the abundance of statistical evidence provided by MALDEF, demonstrated the need for a strategy beyond the formation of a statistical counterdiscourse. In the next chapter, I discuss the formation of another strategy used by Representative Olivo to counter both the harmful effects of high-stakes testing and the hegemonic statistical discourses of the state: *narrative*.

# 6 / Between Women and
## the State of Texas

*Representation and the*
*Politics of Experience*

America's measurement of me has lain like a barrier across
the realization of my own powers.

—Audre Lorde (1984: 147)

I'll end with a story for the record. Teachers are being
instructed to have their bags ready, in case kids vomit. If
kids vomit, they are told to put the test inside that bag.

—Representative Dora Olivo, April 30 testimony[1]

Collecting narratives of students' experiences with testing lay at
the heart of Representative Dora Olivo's political strategy to gar-
ner support for the multiple-criteria bills. The "children's stories"
aimed not only to deconstruct statistical testing discourses, but also to
document the extent to which continual testing and fetishization of the
resulting statistics objectifies and dehumanizes students, as well as
alienates teachers and school administrators. This focus on countering
statistical discourse with narratives of experience signaled a shift from
the method of countering the hegemonic statistical discourses of testing with statistical subjectivity or statistical counterdiscourse that had
been so central in the *GI Forum* case. According to Peters (1997), the
polar opposite of statistics is narrative (78), and I would politicize this
polarity, suggesting that testimonials often become the counterdiscourse or the *contre-histoire* of statistics, a way of asserting or reinserting
agency.[2] Even the common U.S. colloquialism of "becoming a statistic"

signifies a loss of agency, a slippage into determinism and anonymity, and a subject position to be avoided (Woodward 1999). This tension between determinism and free will has laced the history of statistics as an administrative science (Desrosières 1998; Hacking 1991). According to Desrosières (1998), "[I]n 1753, a plan to take a census of the population was violently denounced by the Whig party as 'utterly ruining the last freedoms of the English people'" (24).[3] By positioning stories as political testimonies, the strategy of collecting stories not only brought visibility to the implications of knowledge production, but also gave me the impression that this strategy emerged from a "womanist" (Walker 1983: xi) politics, a politics of *transfrontera* (Saldívar-Hull 1999).

## Imagining Feminism, Imagining Transfrontera

The full-time staffers for Representative Olivo were women, and midway through the session, only women of color. While there were several men deeply embedded in the Representative's political network, especially from MALDEF, it was the presence of women that made the deepest impression on me. The team that the Representative built was made up of Latina, Black, and White women, some representing the major civil rights organizations, some teachers or administrators from the public schools, and others university professors. The lobbyists visiting the office that seemed to give the most support to the multiple-criteria bills were women, from organizations made up of, for example, midwives, retired teachers, and interior decorators. I believe that the bill brought together these women because of Representative Olivo's racial and gendered identity, since the bill was written in the context of Prado's ruling on the *GI Forum* case on racial discrimination. All of the women remarked, "We love your sign," which read, "Let teachers make the final decisions, NOT corporate test makers." A common sentiment spoken in the office was that women do all the work—taking care of children, educating them, and working, which reminds me of these lines from Anzaldúa's "To Live in the Borderlands Means You": "*Cuando vives en la frontera* / People walk through you, the wind steals your voice / You're a *burra, buey*, scapegoat" (1999: 216). For me, these women, particularly in the office, lived on the *frontera*, a space that made me interrogate the line between state and civil society. Because of the breakdown of border-making processes of nation-states with globalization, Trouillot (2001: 133) has suggested that anthropologists need to "look for state processes and effects in sites less obvious than those of institutionalized politics and established bureaucracies." While I agree with Trouillot, I found that government sites, such as Representative Olivo's office, because of the "trajectory" (Omi and Winant 1994)[4] of racial politics in which people of color are literally incorporated by the U.S racial state, can be viewed themselves as a type of border site, in the Anzaldúan sense. Kaplan, Alarcon, and Moallem (1999) conceptualized this border site as a place "between woman and nation" that "refers to a particular space of the performative and performativity where woman and nation intersect in specific ways" (6). In this space, the Latina Representative is both of the state, yet not of the state, both "disordering" the "'pedagogy' of the nation-state" (7) and revealing the ability to "maneuver creatively to cross boundaries and position [herself] . . . as [a member] . . . of diverse rather than singular communities" (12). For me, the office represented a disordering in which "unofficial" people could use computers and be welcomed in what I experienced as an atmosphere of family, yet it was also a site of political business and very difficult work,[5] where I was educated by the staff about the workings of Texas government.

Perhaps "imagining" (Kaplan, Alarcon, and Moallem 1999) the office as *transfrontera*, engaged in the feminist politics of opposing statistical objectification through narrative, falls into the trap of "romanticizing resistance" and calling movements by women *feminist*, which according to Abu-Lughod (1990) attributes to the women "forms of consciousness or politics that are not part of their experience" (47). At the same time, Behar (1993) has proposed interrogating those instances of "no name feminism" (276). While we never spoke of feminism,[6] I felt that the movement's politicization of experience as a way of challenging the depersonalizing system of high-stakes testing mirrored feminist politics and theorizing. The child-centered focus of the particular educational politics supported by the movement echoes that of women's political organizing around education in Texas historically, in particular the women's club movement of the Progressive Era, the epistemological basis for which McArthur (1998: 65) attributed to "long involvement in the child study movement and direct observation through school mother's clubs." Additionally, the strategy of collecting children's stories echoes feminist use of experience as a way of breaking the silence imposed by intersecting patriarchal, imperialist/capitalist, and racial systems of oppression. As MacKinnon (1995 [1982]) wrote, "Women's experience of politics, of life as sex object, gives rise to its own method of appropriating that reality: the feminist method" (535). For Anzaldúa

(1983), "The danger in writing is not fusing our personal experience and world view with the social reality we live in, with our inner life, our history, our economics, and our vision" (172). Not only did the movement center narrative to challenge official knowledge, but testimonies and political statements, such as the sign that read "Let teachers make the final decisions, NOT corporate test makers," critiqued official knowledge with an attention to "perspectivist" and "situated" knowledge, a position articulated by feminists to critique and deconstruct scientific objectivism (and objectification), positivism, and universalism (Collins 1998; Haraway 1988; Harding 1991; Lewis 1973; Sudbury 1998).

## Measuring Silences

> **Amarillo Principal:** Don't lose sight of the kid. We can talk statistic here, statistic there . . .
> **Representative Harold Dutton:** Thank you for putting a face on this.[7]

According to Spivak (1988), the "task of measuring silences" pays attention to both "what refuses to be said," in terms of "collective ideological refusal," and "what cannot be said," in terms of "subaltern consciousness" (286, 287). This task of measuring silences interrogates the ways in which silence and secrecy embedded in the production of discourses both secure the hegemony of a particular discourse and contain possibilities for the disruption of those very discourses (Foucault 1978).[8] These stories simultaneously experientially deconstructed (Cook 1995) the statistical "pedagogy of the nation-state" (Kaplan, Alarcon, and Moallem 1999: 7) and revealed the ways in which statistical discourses on testing silenced (the effects on) children's embodied subjectivities. Consider, for example, one of the stories collected by Representative Olivo for a Web site: "One fourth grader was sick with the flu and throwing up. He missed school on test day. He is a very good Math student. The teacher called and insisted that his mother bring him to school to take the test because they need his high score to help the school's rating. He did go to school and threw up three times while he was taking the test" (quoted in Olivo 2003).

When the Texas Education Agency released the results that 89 percent of the third graders passed the first administration of the reading TAKS test, an *Austin American-Statesman* article ran with the headline "Students Rise to the Challenge of Tougher Test in Reading: Third

Graders Breeze through State's New Assessment Tests" (Blackwell 2003). The story above about the fourth grader challenges the claim that a statistical product such as 89 percent automatically signifies that students "breeze through" high-stakes tests. In fact, situations of children's sickness, such as those the stories reveal, become erased in the race to produce statistics. Despite the statistical discourse of progress and projections of "data-driven public school improvement," despite the TPERF survey meant to confirm the consensus (53 percent) of Texans that "[s]tandardized testing helps schools improve" and "Texans are saying, 'Don't mess with testing'" (TPERF 2002b), parents are leaving the public school system because the price of this "improvement" or the "collateral damage" (see McNeil 2000a: 189, 281n1; Saltman 2000) is their children's health and well-being: "I'm a parent who is—as I like to say—a refugee from the public school system. . . . [L]ast year was a living hell. By the end of the year we were so close to putting our fourth-grade son on anti-depressants. Instead we switched him to a Montessori school, and he's flourishing. We moved our second-grade daughter to the Montessori in October, and she is equally happy to be free from the constant pressure of perfectionism." Yet another parent was a "refugee":

> My daughter has just withdrawn her girls from public school and moved to a small private school. The oldest is a third-grader who has been having difficulties in completing assignments within the appropriate time. Her teacher advised her parents that she would not pass the TAKS test and recommended they seek medical intervention in the form of psychiatric drugs. Concurrently, she began suffering from chest pains that led to a complete evaluation by a pediatric cardiologist. However, once she was removed from the stressful situation she was experiencing in the public school, the pain went away![9]

Is it simply irony that the very political proponents of increased testing in the legislative session were also proponents of vouchers, given that the very mechanism of testing in this case becomes a force for driving parents and teachers away from public schools?

The narratives of children's painful experiences[10] as agentic (Asad 2000) reinsert subjectivity into a political terrain occupied with statistical objectification, whereby the action to "put a face on" testing is not simply aesthetic, but political (Lowe 1996: 156, 157). According to

Croissant (1998), "Children are growing up cyborg between the extremes of disembodiment presented by the possibilities of life in cyberspace and the complete reduction to embodiment posited for production workers subject to the machinations of hypermobile global capital in export zones" (285).[11] The stories reveal the extent to which statistical fetishism or statistical panic has generated the disembodiment of children from their scores to the point that test administration not only operates through a sort of objectifying violence (see Anzaldúa 1999: 59) that harms children but also normalizes the desensitization of that pain. For example, the Texas Education Agency's rationale for offering the TAAS eight times is that the probability that a student "on the bubble" would pass the test increases to 99.6 percent after eight attempts at taking the test (TEA, Student Assessment Division 2000: 37). However, one of the stories told to Representative Olivo deconstructed such a theory:

> About ten years ago I worked with a principal who adopted one of our school's students. This student came from a very poor and abusive home. When she was taken in by this principal and his family she became a happier person, however was still behind academically. She had started school late (at the age of ten), her grandmother had never seen the need to send her to school or to allow her anytime to study at home (I had this child in 5th grade). By the time this child was a senior she had to pass the TAAS exit. Well, she didn't pass. She retook the test and retook the test. . . . After her third failure notice she tried to commit suicide. She wanted so badly to pass the test and keep on learning. She however was never given that little bit of hope she needed so badly.[12]

In Lipman's (2004) ethnography of schooling in Chicago, a fifth-grade teacher tearfully recounted a story of a student who had committed suicide because of failure on a test (102). Simultaneously, the desensitized and computer-generated discourse of statistics, the governance by the removed "expert," and the construction of students as each an assemblage of statistical factors (Castel 1991) enables the enactment of violent disembodiment *because* pain is silenced. By speaking from that silenced space, the children's stories enact an objection, an opposition to this violence and an experiential deconstruction of the statistical discourse of testing.

## Positioning (in) Alienation

> The possessing class and the proletarian class represent one and the
> same human self-alienation. But the former feels satisfied and self-
> affirmed in this self-alienation, experiences the alienation as a sign of
> *its own power*, and possesses in it the *appearance* of a human
> existence. The latter, however, feels destroyed in this alienation,
> seeing in it its own impotence and the reality of an inhuman
> existence.
>
> — Karl Marx, "Alienation and Social Classes" (1978 [1844]: 133)

Marx's characterization suggests that an examination of children's experiences of objectification, dehumanization, or disembodiment (alienation) is only partial. Objectification is not simply an effect, but a practice, an enactment of desire, by which, ironically, the depersonalization
(of students) within a singular numerical outcome becomes the route
for creating a particular individuality as hero.[13] Underlying the decades-
long accountability movement for increased standardized testing is a
desire or fantasy that top-down, data-driven, and emotionally detached
reform can produce miracles and heroic myths. One example is the
figure of Joe Clark hailed in the film *Lean on Me*, as the story centers
on the success of his military-style discipline in raising students' test
scores. While Clark's expulsion of three hundred students brought praise
from Reagan's then education secretary Bill Bennett, one school official
remarked that the mass expulsion was "an easy way to raise average
scores" (Kozol 1991: 163). Similarly, in the 2000 presidential election,
George W. Bush proudly assumed credit for raising test scores in Texas,
what would be called the "Texas Miracle" (see Haney 2000 for a critique), and, once elected, he was deemed the "Education President."
These "miracles" are symptomatic of the elements of what Helmreich
(1998) suggested constitutes Western (imperialist) self-alienation and
Euro-American masculinity: "emotional detachment, escape and autonomy, . . . calculative rationality, . . . objectifying, instrumentalizing,
and dominating the world" (70).

The alienation produced in the desire for miracles facilitates the production of a black box (Latour 1987)[14] around testing, hiding the complex process by which scores are formed and obtained. At a House Public Education Committee hearing on accountability, a representative of
the Texas Business and Education Council cited transparency as the
key to the success of the test-based accountability system, since results

were "clear and understandable," presented in such a way that was "not so complex" and characterized by "openness." However, as Butler (1993) asked, "[W]hat *has to be excluded* for those economies [of discursive intelligibility] to function as self-sustaining systems?" (35). The stories disrupted the hegemonic notion that test-based statistics were simply the manifestation of objective progress, as had been the dominant discourse behind the "Texas Miracle." The stories suggested that not only was the discourse of accountability both the simulation of (Baudrillard 1983) and self-alienation from accountability, but also that subjects/students were being positioned by teachers and administrators for (or in order to produce) a particular discourse:

> I . . . had a principal inform me my son does not perform well on standard[ized] tests, but he's an A-B student, an A-B honor student. And he said it's a good thing that my son is in fourth grade and not in the third grade [where he would not be promoted without passing the test]. Not only do the kids have the negative effect, I mean, also the administrators are indicating the negative effects that this test has because it's a good thing that my son is in fourth grade and not in third grade. (Tressy Murray, April 30 testimony)

> I have a third grader this year that informed me that if he did not do well on the TAKS that I was not to argue with the school. Instead, we are to move to another school if he and others do not perform well . . . , per an announcement by a classroom teacher. This would also increase the institutional score (if he were to perform less well than anticipated or fail). In fact, you could have a quite homogeneous little group of students who perform well on standardized exams in a particular school, and perhaps those that do not, will attend private schools. (RLH, quoted in Olivo 2003)

> In October, the principal of a school in El Paso placed four third graders back in second grade. She was convinced that they would not be able to pass the test.[15]

As Booher-Jennings (2005) remarked in her ethnography of an urban elementary school in Texas, such practices of manipulating student bodies have "at the core . . . a deference to data—which are understood solely as quantitative outcomes on multiple-choice, or 'TAKS-formatted,' tests—and their neutrality and objectivity" (261). The desires for statistical miracles then structure the way that school officials approach their jobs, rendering work in school alienating (Lipman 2004; Booher-Jennings 2005), as seen in the case of Rod Paige, who, as superintendent of the Houston Independent School District, pressured school administrators and teachers to raise scores and lower dropout rates at any cost (see Chapters 3 and 4). The contradiction of objectification is evident in teachers' own accounts of the experience of testing. A Texas professor sent to Representative Olivo some of the following stories:[16]

> A teacher told me that she feels so ashamed of herself because as the children enter her classroom each morning, she mentally sorts them, saying "I need to work with that one today to prepare for the test" or "This one already knows the information, I don't need to work with him" or "This one probably won't pass anyway, so I won't work with him." She blames the testing system for making her stoop so low.

> One very good teacher who usually works with student teachers from the university told me, "Don't give me a student teacher in the spring. I am ashamed for them to see what I have to do to drill the children for this test."

The teachers were fully aware of and bothered by their acts of positioning and objectifying their students in order to produce institutional scores, yet teachers' own "authorship" of institutional scores disappeared in the statistical aggregates and reports.

In opposing Representative Olivo's multiple-criteria bills, a *Houston Chronicle* editorial (2003b) claimed that "injecting a subjective measure into the equation—along with all the politics and bias that would entail—lamentably would gut the accountability system crucial to improving the quality of education all children receive." Constructing a binary between accountability and subjective measures, and, also important, between quality and the subjective, the editorial assumed that the process of test-score production is itself absent of politics and bias. The deployment of the objectivity of testing and relevant data as the only true sources of accountability supports the erasure of authorship, context, and social relations of power (Hubbard 1990). As Haraway (1988) argued, the "god-trick" of objectivity that "promises transcendence" functions as "a story that loses track of its mediations just where someone might be held responsible for something" (579).

Additionally, such appeals to objectivity and the loathing of subjectivity trivialize teachers' work and professional judgments, and one common discourse produced by accountability proponents is the rhetoric of "teacher-proofing" curricula (McNeil 2000a). In the proceedings of SCOPE, which enacted sweeping reforms that set the foundation for the test-based accountability system, claims of objectivity justified the exclusion of teachers and school administrators from the process (Newman 1987: 93). Such a sentiment echoed in the ruling of Judge Prado in the *GI Forum* case: "[T]he State need not equate its test on the basis of *standards it rejects*, such as subjective teacher evaluations" (*GI Forum et al. v. Texas Education Agency et al.* 87 F. Supp. 2d 667, 683 [2000]; my italics). Additionally, some proponents of accountability construct subjectivity in teaching as frivolity. For example, Brad Duggan of the organization Just for the Kids told the *Texas Observer* about testing, "You do lose some of the spontaneity and fun, . . . [but] the trade off is worth it" (Bernstein 2002). Assistant Secretary of Education Susan Neuman, in a 2002 speech before the University of the Pacific in California, suggested that the accountability measures in the No Child Left Behind Act, "if implemented the right way, will put an end to creative and experimental teaching methods in the nation's schools," according to Balta (2002). Apparently, the assistant secretary remarked, "It [the No Child Left Behind Act] will stifle and hopefully it will kill (them)" (quoted in Balta 2002).

## Essentialism, Standpoints, and the Politics of Representation

In the face of objectification, the activism of the women organized by Representative Olivo articulated the necessity of experience as the basis for claiming the authority from which to speak about students' learning in two ways. First, the activists argued that teachers' and parents' knowledge of students constituted better and more authentic knowledge of student educational progress than that produced by distant, removed testing corporations. Second, in their testimonials, the women activists established their positionalities as mothers and teachers as the basis for their authority to both speak about the impact of testing on students and serve as students' advocates in the legislative arena.

Just as Haraway (1988) suggested that situated knowledge yields better knowledge, the movement for Representative Olivo's bills on multiple criteria proclaimed that teachers' and parents' situated knowledge of student progress constituted better knowledge. In a "Sample Resolution" handed out to supporters, part of a document entitled "Organizer's Tool Kit," the privileging of situated knowledge as better knowledge is present:

> Whereas, a student's overall academic record yields comprehensive and complete data about academic performance—reflecting evaluations based on multiple criteria, professional judgments, and observations by parents/caregivers;

> > We should trust our professionals to judge student learning. Teachers are trained to use multiple criteria to assess students. They recognize that students have different learning styles, and they know how to modify assessments accordingly. They conduct ongoing, timely evaluations as they grade student work; judge portfolios, projects, and presentations; administer teacher-made and local assessments, diagnostics, and inventories; and interact with their students on a daily basis—all examples of existing multiple criteria. We should trust the judgment of our parents/caregivers, too. They are their children's first teachers, and know their strength and weaknesses better than anyone else.

One of the main discursive constructions by the movement for multiple criteria was in fact the opposition between a situated teacher and a distant, removed corporation. The position stated in a memorandum to "Friends of Multiple Criteria" was that "[t]his would return true decision-making authority to the real professionals—our teachers, not corporate test-makers."

In testimony before the Texas House Public Education Committee in favor of Representative Olivo's bill, all of the witnesses were women, four of whom spoke from the standpoint of mothers. The testimonials, as experiential narratives, grounded testing within a sense of the "embodied subjectivities" (Gilroy 1993: 76; Lowe 1996: 156), or the corporeality of students. One especially moving testimony came from a former superintendent of Laredo, Sylvia Bruni, who delivered her case late into the night, after hours of waiting to testify. Despite testifying before what appeared to be only half of the Public Education Committee, she intimated her story for the record:

> This is a more, personal . . . issue. It impacts me as a grandmother, mother, and as a teacher, because I still consider myself an educator. I'm raising a granddaughter, who is now eight years old, very bright, very clever, easily, easily eligible for the gifted and talented program in her school. About two weeks before the test . . . we began to hear the anxiety, that was developing in this child, and here is a little girl, who is clever, who was reading, whose Christmas gift to me when she was in Kindergarten, a Kindergartner, was that she read her first book. She's able to read and she reads fluently, but she was so obsessed over the possibility of failure, and you ask, "Why obsessed?" We think it was because the sense of anxiety basically pervades the entire system. When I wrote the letter that is on the back page of the testimony, I wrote it after an evening that had her crying literally for two hours straight. And as I told [the] Representative . . . , that evening, I said all of the sudden the Mother took over. I've understood the reasoning behind the legislation logically and intellectually. That night, I understood it emotionally. She [the granddaughter] just went through the TAKS math test today. Last night, she prayed for over ten minutes. That's a long time for a nine year old to pray. My point here is very simply this: that when you're dealing with an eight-year-old mind, who still believes in Santa, and the Tooth Fairy, and the Easter Bunny, who has that level of maturity, it is impossible, literally impossible, they are not developmentally ready to be able to reason their way through the fear of failure. It's simply not possible. (Sylvia Bruni, April 30 testimony)

Clearly, she spoke from her position as a grandmother, mother, and teacher, imparting knowledge available from only her standpoint. As she stated, once "all of the sudden the Mother took over," she understood the rationale for supporting the multiple-criteria legislation emotionally. Her self-positioning and self-identification (Rouse 1995) were in fact staking a claim of epistemic privilege from her experience, an experience that she uses here to deconstruct, both discursively and materially, the statistical objectification of children, as well as to make a truth

claim. Contextualizing children's experiences in terms of their development, she reminded the committee that "an eight year-old mind . . .
still believes in Santa, and the Tooth Fairy, and the Easter Bunny." The
cadence with which she said "Santa" echoed the loving communication between a grandmother and her grandchild, but also invoked
memories of childhood, humanizing the experience of facing failure
based on a single test. The story also indicated that the weight of testing
manifests itself in the very bodies of children and adolescents, as her
granddaughter was "crying literally for two hours straight" and "prayed
for over ten minutes" before taking the test.

At the committee hearing of the multiple-criteria bills on April 30,
2003, alongside Sylvia Bruni, three other witnesses spoke from the standpoint of mothers. One began her testimony, "I'm here tonight just because I was a parent of a child that turned eighteen and had a difficult
time taking that TAAS test." After stating her positions as a faculty
member and researcher on issues of testing, Dr. Valenzuela concluded
her testimony as a representative of her child:

> I am also a mother. I have a daughter [ten years old] in the dis-
> trict here and her teacher, my daughter's teacher, . . . says that
> just two days ago that she dedicated 90 hours, 90 hours to test
> preparation, and then to testing, and then to giving back the
> students the results of the test. And in her mind this involves
> disciplining the minds and the fingers, the habits of small chil-
> dren, [and it is] an injustice not to teach a test. And this is at one
> of the best schools, elementary schools in Austin Independent
> School District and I just want to quote my daughter who's in
> that class, by just concluding with these personal statements
> that she herself wrote and would have testified on had it not
> been so late. But, I'll end with this personal account. She wrote,
>
> > A couple of weeks ago, while my class was taking a prac-
> > tice TAKS test, my friend started crying in front of the
> > class because she missed all the questions on the test.
> > She kept on repeating that she just couldn't think. When
> > I take the TAKS test, I usually get headaches from stress.
> > Though some questions are easy, some are really hard
> > and some just don't make any sense. My teacher spent
> > about 90 hours preparing us for the test, in fact today

and tomorrow we've been taking the test, which means
we lose close to 100 hours. While we're taking the test
and while we're preparing, we could be learning more
for the next grade. A test can only show us if our answers
are right or wrong. It doesn't teach us anything. (April
30 testimony)

For Spivak (1988), "radical practice should attend to [the] . . . double
session of representations" (279), given two distinct senses of representation: political representation as proxy, and philosophical and artistic
re-presenting (275). In the case of testimony for the multiple-criteria
bills, parents stood as political representatives of their children by representing their stories. At a meeting on Black education in the Austin
Independent School District, a Black female middle school principal
admonished the crowd, "We are what's wrong with the children. We've
sold them out. . . . Kids look to us to speak up [in their behalf]." This
taking on the role of political representatives may in fact be part of the
tradition of vindicationist politics and that experiential deconstruction
within this vindicationist politics calls for all to be representatives and
critically (counter-hegemonically or oppositionally) re-present the world
in ways that "disorder" hegemonic re-presentations.[17] According to Asad
(2000), "An agent suffers from the pain of someone she loves—a mother,
say, confronted by her wounded child. That suffering is a condition of
her relationship. . . . She lives a relationship. . . . The other's hurt . . . is
a practical condition of who she and her suffering child are" (42).[18] It is
this condition to which parents appealed when re-presenting and representing their children, such as the following introduction to one of the
children's stories: "As the mother of a third-grader, I have experienced
first hand the negative impact that the stress this new mandatory testing
program places upon students" (Olivo 2003).

One rhetorical device used for dismissing narratives such as these is
the differentiation between the "anecdotal" and "hard data," in which
hard data is often equated with quantification. Mulvenon, Stegman, and
Ritter (2005) challenged the veracity of reports of experiences of test-
based anxiety: "A commonly held belief, and oft-reported element, is
that standardized testing is creating an increased level of anxiety within
the educational community and having a detrimental impact on student achievement. For students, most of these reports are anecdotal with
a story of a child who has experienced a restless evening, vomiting, or

other physical maladies associated with a stressful event." The authors concluded that their survey results revealed that "the oft-cited increased anxiety levels among students were nonexistent. Isolated cases of trauma associated with testing probably exist, but overwhelmingly most students reported no additional anxiety due to standardized testing" (58). In many ways, the authors limited hard data about student anxiety to that which is quantifiable and produced in survey data, not only obscuring the narrative or literary quality inherent in interpreting data (whereby the authors construct a narrative about anxiety from the results of their survey), but also subordinating contextualized, experiential narratives to the authors' narrative constructed through their interpretation. For Lowe (1996), testimonies and testimonials, as political acts emerging from complex embodied, material, and social conditions, challenge the limits placed on what counts as "legitimate knowledge" (157). Interestingly enough, it is exactly the delimiting of knowledge about education to the easily quantifiable that both shapes the conditions from which the testing stories emerge (e.g., dehumanization of students) and comes under direct challenge by the stories. At a televised book signing on March 12, 2007, David Berliner, coauthor of *Collateral Damage: How High-Stakes Testing Corrupts America's Schools*, remarked:

> I want to say something about the stories and newspaper articles we used in this book. Some could easily criticize this, and some-one has, that it's merely stories. When you have a thousand or two thousand or three thousand stories all on the same phe-nomena, all going the same way, when does it become hard data? I think it's a very important question because this not about quantifiable effects, it's about the stories people are tell-ing about what's happening in their schools. And one such story can be ignored, and ten can be ignored, but literally hundreds should not be ignored.[19]

Narratives, testimonies, and the parents' stories in and of themselves are not "innocent"; rather, they are caught up in a politics of representa-tion or a "politics of location" (Mohanty 1992; Sudbury 1998). Accord-ing to Spivak (1988), in accounting for the two senses (and the poli-tics) of representation, theories "must note how the staging of the world in representation—its scene of writing, its *Darstellung*—dissimulates the choice of and need for 'heroes,' paternal proxies, agents of power—

*Vertretung*" (279). One question that emerges, then, is to what extent do the need for heroes and the choice of representatives silence the subaltern more? At the voucher hearing, for example, most of the parents supporting vouchers were Latino and Black, and the sponsor of the bill, who in a sense represented their cause, was the chair of the Public Education Committee. Many of the parents spoke about the public schools not meeting the needs of their children, particularly those with learning and physical disabilities. One mother, a divorcée, raising a child with a disability, said, "My daughter is falling behind. She had problems following directions. The teachers didn't have time for her. She fell through the cracks." Why was the meeting on vouchers a space for so many parents to voice their concerns about the troubles their students encountered in public schools, and why were only invited experts allowed to testify at the meetings on finance and accountability? When witnesses were called to the lectern to testify, their names were frequently mispronounced, an act that, while on the surface appeared innocent, to me felt dismissive, a feeling paralleled by the lack of attentiveness given to one of the voucher supporters who testified completely in Spanish. At one of the meetings on school finance, committee member Hochberg asked Carolyn Hoxby, a presenter from Harvard, "Who do you represent? . . . I just wanted the father of the plan to be recognized." At once this question revealed to me the immediate (sexist) assumption that plans are only "fathered" and that perhaps we must indeed question ourselves about the ways in which our re-presentations conceal these "fathers" and "the choice of and need for 'heroes,' paternal proxies," as Spivak called them. One of the many groups of parents and students at the voucher hearings sporting T-shirts in support of vouchers was Black Alliance for Educational Options, which the online newspaper the *Black Commentator* (2002) called a "Trojan Horse" due to its being funded by famed economist Milton Friedman (see Chapter 4) and also financially supported by President Bush.

Admittedly, the witnesses for Representative Olivo were themselves organized through networks, and politically, we needed the stories to appear to be representative of a collective and widespread set of experiences for students. In political arenas, where establishing a "collective will" (Mouffe 1979) is critical to passing a law, the projection of an essential experience posed in a causal relationship with a particular law may perhaps be necessary. Yes, we were involved in a counter-hegemonic process, necessitating negotiation. In the Capitol, political networks and the structure of the legislative process, which I found favored a mobile, middle-class lobbyist, produced which experiences would be heard and which testimony would go into the public record. I found that, in the Capitol, the subaltern cannot speak, and ironically, I found myself in that very place.

## The Subaltern Cannot Speak

On the day that the multiple-criteria bills were scheduled to be heard (April 29), Representative Olivo asked me to testify, given that I was researching high-stakes testing and its effects on students of color. As I had gotten used to my role as an intern, simply filing documents and taking my place behind the scenes, down in the office without windows to the outside world, only televisions and live digital playing on the Internet, this role frightened me. Me, testify? Despite my intent to take a stand, I was terrified at the prospect of speaking. I had seen how the Public Education Committee treated women witnesses; the only time I recall a committee member raising his voice was at a Latina witness. Further, subjective testimony often brought dismissive reactions or intimidating deconstructing questions that seemed prosecutorial in tone, resembling a cross-examination. After all, I was simply a fly-on-the-wall anthropologist, right? Nevertheless, I began writing my testimony, linking what I thought were research findings with a personal experience as a tutor seeing a Latina student experience not passing the TAAS and having the threat of not graduating. I convinced myself that I could still "go on the record" by giving written testimony without speaking if I became too nervous. I even filled out a witness form and ran off copies of my testimony. The presence of so many others, particularly women, started to embolden me to testify—how could I let the Representative down? Likewise, the young White student from San Antonio who had become famous for not taking the TAKS field test was there. Many people—mostly women—had come in from out of town to testify. I came from San Antonio. However, the night drew longer and longer, and each hour we heard that the floor activity would cease and allow committee hearings.[20] It was a struggle for the bills to even be heard. It was rumored in the office that the committee chairman said, "Sure, she'll get her hearing," on the last day of the session, which would guarantee not having a hearing at all. It seemed that night that the bills were destined not to be heard as the hours passed. At 9 P.M. the young San

Antonio student and her father began to leave—she needed to go to school in the morning. After an hour or so, she came back and we all clapped. Other witnesses started going home, too, especially mothers, and finally the student and her father really did have to leave and drive back to San Antonio. It was approximately 1 A.M. when the floor activity stopped and Representative Olivo came to the office to give us word of whether or not there would be a committee hearing that night. Some of the women from the NAACP and the office found out that I (a young woman) was driving back to San Antonio that night alone and insisted that I follow another group heading back to San Antonio. The last I heard, as I loaded up my things, was that there would not be a committee hearing that night. I could still testify. However, I learned the following morning that Representative Olivo kept fighting to have a hearing because key witnesses had *flown* in from different parts of Texas and needed to speak that night. I missed my chance! I felt not only that I let the Representative down, but, for my ethnography, I missed a key event—despite the fact that it was taped, and I could gain access to it. While I thought that going home that night was a detriment to my study, I realized that I experienced what it felt like *not* to be able to speak: like those parents who worked full-time and could not wait all day to testify at a hearing; those who lived away from Austin and could not make the trip in order to testify or perhaps whose disabilities prevented them from testifying; those children, like the student from San Antonio, who could not stay up until 1 A.M. to testify. It made me reflect on the broader structure of the meetings, and the claims of openness and transparency that masked the more obscure structure of meetings, when, for instance, a witness from the Eagle Forum insisted that the public had no access to the committee substitutes being heard.

Not only did my experience shed light on the ways in which the subaltern cannot speak, but the committee substitute for one of the multiple-criteria bills also shed light on this. One of the Black mothers testifying for the multiple-criteria bills was going over the bills and noticed something. One of the intents was to give parents more say in the decision of promoting their child. As the law stands, if a child fails the test three times, he or she can be promoted only if a committee made up of the student's teacher, principal, and parent decides *unanimously* to *promote*. The second substitute for the promotion multiple-criteria bill replaced *promotion* with *retention*, in other words, changing the law to state that the committee must unanimously vote to retain a student.

Thus, a parent's decision cannot be outweighed by the teacher and principal. In the final substitute, the language read that the committee must decide *by majority* to retain. When the mother saw this, she said that such language would not change the current law—a principal could lean on the teacher to support retaining a student despite the opposition of the parent (see Fine 1991),[21] in which case the parent could still not speak. She even hesitated at supporting the bills but decided to proceed in testifying for the bills. The nature of substitutes is that they are compromises, negotiations that in the political process can lose some of their more radical edges. In Representative Olivo's case, the opposition to *any* change in the law regarding promotion of third, fifth, and eighth graders—due in part to the weight of Washington—ruled out even these compromises. The bills, though they became attachments, were tabled ultimately by the Public Education Committee chairman himself, a way of silencing both the critique of high-stakes testing and also a possible reform measure that could prevent teachers and children from feeling alienated and objectified.

## Conclusion

I argue that the strategy for gaining support for the multiple criteria paralleled feminist politics of *transfrontera*, as a coalition composed mostly of women, as well as feminist critiques of objectivism. At the forefront of the movement for multiple criteria were children's stories and the politicization of experience as a way of opposing the governmental objectification, commodification and exploitation, and objectivist production of truth characteristic of testing and its statistical discourse. The stories functioned as experiential deconstruction, mirroring the feminist use of experience as a source of politics and knowledge formation. By measuring silence, accounting for authorship, and using a particular standpoint from which to act politically, the narratives also echoed feminist theories on silence, critiques of scientific discourse, and conceptions of situated knowledge. However, the use of stories in support of vouchers necessitates a critical view of issues of representation, in the two senses of re-presenting experience and becoming a political representative of that experience. In critically viewing uses of experience, we have to account for the "staging" of those stories, who makes that staging possible, and who stands to benefit (and at whose expense). In many cases, due to the structure of the committee meetings, many parents and students cannot speak. While acknowledging these issues of representation, it was ultimately the acts of retelling experience, of *contre-histoire*, that were called upon to disrupt the hegemony of high-stakes testing. Though the bills were not successful, the politicization of experience, as a measuring of silences, still has the potential to loosen the holds of statistical discourse and its objectification.

# 7 / Conclusion

## Summary

In this book, I have argued that statistical objectification works to maintain the hegemony of the high-stakes testing system in Texas. In one sense, statistics objectify Texas students, teachers, and the public, inscribing them as objects of governance. I came to this conclusion by using Abu-Lughod's (1990) suggestion of viewing resistance as diagnostic of power, seeing the forms of resistance against testing as resistance against being transformed into a statistic, as one student put it, as "a name and a score." I found that Texas students, their parents, their teachers, and others were engaging in resistance against what Foucault (1983) called the "submission of subjectivity." Statistics on testing also generate what Woodward (1999) called "statistical panic." This structure of feeling constructed by the Texas Education Agency and the media enforced widespread test anxiety across Texas, which both imparted fear on children and their parents, teachers, and administrators and served as a political rallying point for the movement for multiple criteria. I argue that the panic generated from statistics on testing allowed for teachers and administrators to target students of color as at risk of failure and render them invisible through the policy of pushing out.

Statistical discourse on testing not only objectifies students as things, but provides the conditions for the commodification of knowledge, as testing corporations, such as NCS Pearson, profit in the millions from testing. By incorporating students, teachers, administrators, state agency workers, and even school communities within a system of competition, the state of Texas has not only shielded the testing system from criticism, but also created a rewards-sanctions system that only supports the profitability of testing. I claim that statistics are key to the profitability of testing because within the postmodern informational economy, statistics provide a means for commodifying (objectifying, in a Marxist sense) social facts. The profitability of testing and data-processing companies is accompanied by the neoliberal imperative to privatize public functions, that is, redistributing funds directed toward public services to private companies. While statistics historically became integral to the government with the development of the welfare state, neoliberals have recuperated statistical discourses that oppose social welfare, specifically Malthusianism and eugenic meritocracy, while emphasizing the need for economic efficiency through the statistical discourse of quality control. As Castel (1991) suggested, preventive policies tend to dissolve subjectivity by reducing individuals to statistical factors and transforming intervening specialists, such as teachers, to mere executants, while overemphasizing the role of administrator and creating opportunities, as Apple suggested, for the managerial middle class. Through this recuperation, neoliberal discourses delegitimize public schools as social welfare by reducing education to statistical factors, claiming to prove both the inefficiency of equitable district funding and the inevitability of "minority failure" (see McDermott 1997). An additional component to the delegitimizing of public education is the gendered devaluing of teaching, an occupation of predominantly women, as too subjective.

Along with objectifying subjectivities and labor, statistical discourses objectify truth through a hegemonic struggle (over the production of truth). Statistical materialism has historically been a key tool in establishing hegemony, by representing the collective, or "national-popular," will and functioning as a popular religion or way of viewing the world. Statistical discourses have also been central in educating consent, or, as Woolf (1989) suggested, "affirming consensus" and in constituting a tool of moral self-government and self-identification. In terms of testing, statistics, which Asad (1994) suggested is the modern language and politics of progress, are central to the construction of the concept of minority failure. The statistical tools of representativeness via polls and sampling were central in constructing the idea of a collective will that the TPERF claimed could be summarized as "Texans are saying, 'Don't mess with testing.'" For the TEA, the statistical tool of standard error of measurement was central in stabilizing the testing system in

Texas, particularly guarding against challenges to the legitimacy and validity of both the new TAKS test and the accountability system empowered the same year the TAKS was introduced to keep third graders from being promoted to the next grade. The validity of the testing system also depended on the statistical tool of correlation, which functions as ideological glue in that it constructs relationships between quantifiable entities, as well as commonsensically suggests a relationship of cause. The hegemony of statistical materialism can also be attributed to statistical subjectivity, or the use of statistics as a mode of resistance, such as that by MALDEF, teachers, and even myself. However, I question the extent to which the practice of statistical subjectivity supports a form of self-government that functions like symbolic violence.

In Chapter 6, I describe the goal of the movement toward passing the multiple-criteria bills: to oppose objectification through the collection of children's stories. This use of experience embodied a feminist politics, serving as a tool of experientially deconstructing the statistical objectification of students. The children's stories reveal the ways in which the silence of being "outside measure" serves as its own technique of power. The stories also reveal the ways in which statistical discourse aids in the denial of authorship and responsibility, particularly in the positioning of students by teachers and administrators in order to obtain a particular statistical output or discourse. Third, the stories reveal the political necessity of arguing from a position of epistemic privilege, in terms of establishing the (largely parental) authority to both represent children in political arenas and re-present children's experiences in the context of the testing regimes (in which the hegemonic statistical "truth" varies from the children's experiential "truth"). This politics is not without contradictions, and to a certain degree in the Texas Legislature the subaltern cannot speak.

At the conclusion of this project, I pose the very question to myself that I posed of other texts: What are the political implications of my project? This question can be interpreted in a variety of ways, and in this chapter, I address four different interpretations of what is meant by *political implications*. In one sense, the question asks what my project and theorization about statistics implies about the state of educational reform. Second, it asks what I am suggesting about the use of statistics in political and educational arenas. Third, what do I envision as the political effect or consequences of this project? Finally, what does my project imply about practicing anthropology as cultural critique and as activism and what are the kinds of effects on anthropology that I envision my work producing?

## "What Are You Afraid Of?": Statistical Objectification and the Progress of Education

> House Public Education Committee Chairman: Isn't it fair to
> state that your position [is basically] the fear of the unknown?
> Wayne Pierce of the Equity Center: No, it's the fear of past
> experience. [Laughter][1]

According to Foucault (1988b), one of the traps into which intellectuals are summoned or interpellated by those who govern is to assume a position of prophesying, of providing visions of the future upon being asked, "'Put yourselves in our place and tell us what you would do'" (52). This position is a trap because as governed, intellectuals have limited (or are refused) access to knowledge. For Popkewitz (1999), intellectuals envisioning social change often reinforce the conception of individuals as governable objects amenable to (and malleable in terms of) social administration, which itself is viewed as a form of salvation, of producing individual freedom: "When we hear the rhetorical claims that research needs to be practical to help identify successful teaching, or, in a related variant, the writing of the last chapter of a book that outlines what needs to be done to bring the prophesies in existence, we need to recognize that acting as oracles and the prophesies are effects of power constructed by the joining of the twin registers of administration and freedom that we associate with . . . modernity" (27). As both subject to governance and complicit in governing, intellectuals outlining proposals for social change often leave unchallenged the ways in which notions of empowerment and giving voice can reinforce systems of power (Spivak 1988). In considering the political implications of my work, I position myself not as an oracle, elaborating the unknown, but rather as an interpreter of the history of the present, afraid, like Wayne Pierce, of past experiences. What I am afraid of[2] is that the testing regimes' method of statistical objectification—as a form of governance, commodification, and the hegemonic formation of truth—is, in the name of "progress," hardening or further sedimenting educational segregation.[3] This fear comes not from a dystopic prediction of the future or the unknown, but rather from past experiences and contradictions involved in methods of social reform. As Orfield (1996) warned of the resurgence of the *Plessy v. Ferguson* doctrine in present educational policy, the surge of the racially realigned Republican Party in the second post-Reconstruction era (Marable 1991) echoes the period of post-Reconstruction that witnessed state retrenchment of civil rights gains (DuBois 1962 [1935]). While the ubiquity of statistical knowledge is made possible by post–world war advances in probability calculus and the late-capitalist informational economy, Dickens's (1996 [1907]) critique of statistics in *Hard Times* is nevertheless applicable today, at the same time as Malthusian and eugenic-meritocratic statistical discourses have resurfaced. The efforts after the *Brown* decision to evade desegregation also serve as cautionary tales, with the construction and subsequent deconstruction of the statistical concept of racial discrimination.

As I conjecture in Chapter 2, testing may very well be part of that process of evading desegregation. Further, the statistical objectification of failures and successes, particularly within evaluative accountability systems, has serious implications for segregation. In promotion of his school accountability act before the National Governor's Meeting, President Clinton (1999) described the content of his plan: "It says that school districts accepting federal money must end social promotion, turn around or shut down failing schools, ensure teachers know the subjects they're teaching, have and enforce reasonable discipline codes, and empower parents with report cards on their schools." While the proposals may sound appealing, closing down failing schools only masks the conditions that create that failure. Threats of school closure in the name of efficiency mask and depersonalize the racial, political, and material context in which those schools exist—as well as the ways in which private corporations benefit from this (production of) failure. School closures, like the pushing out of students of color, which I discuss in Chapters 3 and 4, reproduce the forms of marginalization, displacement, and erasure characteristic of U.S. racialization. This could be no clearer than for the residents of East Austin. In the 1970s as part of the desegregation court negotiations between the school board of the Austin Independent School District and the Department of Health, Education, and Welfare, St. John's Elementary, Kealing Middle School, and Anderson High School, the segregated Black schools, were all closed in the name of achieving racial balance. However, as Wilson and Segall (2001) documented, the loss of these schools, particularly Anderson High School, signaled the loss of a community center and a site of cultural history. As Jackson (1979) wrote, the fact that there would be "no secondary school with a Black heritage" meant that the "cost of desegregation [was] too high in the Black community" (94, 97). School closure continues to haunt the East side. Since the 1990s, one of the high schools with the highest percentage of Black students in the district has been under the threat of closure due to its poor statistical output, its low-performing status—its high dropout rate and low enrollment. After a low-performing rating, another east-side high school with a large Black population lost its Liberal Arts Academy, a magnet established to redress segregation. The achievement gap on the east side prompted a group of Black community leaders to call for privatization and even secession of the east side from the Austin Independent School District. Some even viewed the rejection of these proposals by the superintendent and school board as refusing to address the concerns of the east side. With the continued pressure from the No Child Left Behind Act for statistical production, in the form of "adequate yearly progress" reports, the threat of school closures may reproduce the type of devastation experienced in East Austin and similar communities, for whom school closure means the loss of culturally historic community centers—particularly when we historicize the movement for public education by ex-slaves in the pre- and post-Reconstruction era (DuBois 1962 [1935]; Anderson 1988) and by internally colonized U.S. Mexicans since the Treaty of Guadalupe Hidalgo (San Miguel and Valencia 1998). At the same time that failing schools are under the threat of closure, in the past regular session, House representatives sponsored bills, such as HB 973, to exempt schools achieving exemplary status from civil rights obligations.

My argument is that the statistical objectification of progress, whether it be racial balance, closing the achievement gap, accountability ratings (and their sanctions-rewards system), or adequate yearly progress measures, is a constituent part of the process by which minority failure becomes "institutionally overdetermined" (McDermott 1997). As Desrosières (1998) argued, statistical objectification is a process of "making *things that hold*," based on their predictability or probability, that renders manageable the social realm in which the "solidity, durability, and space of validity" of objectified things that hold depends on the strength and "breadth of investment (in a general sense) that produced them" (9–11). We should read accountability regimes in terms of the statistical objectification, or making hold, of failure, based, first, on the predictability and probability that standardized testing reflects (or is highly correlated with) (parental) socioeconomic status (MacKenzie 1981: 43). Second, objectification is based on the differential objectification of students and alienation of teachers in order to manage them.[4] Third, objectification is based on the "possessive investment" (Lipsitz 1998) by the neoliberal and neoconservative historic bloc not only in segregation (as an expression of racial capitalism) but also in exploiting the educational realm within the late-capitalist informational economy. Finally, the objectification operates to make hegemonic, that is, to solidify, validate, and make durable, the truth of failure—particularly the inevitable failure of liberal reforms within the public school to correct racial inequality—and the progress instituted by the establishment of accountability systems. The statistical objectification, or making hold, of minority failure perpetuates the individualization of failure and success via a "deficit-thinking" model (Valencia 1997) of approaching educational reform that prevents critical analysis of the ways in which closure and privatization of public schools harden segregation and devastate our communities.[5]

## Measuring Political Implications: Navigating the Spaces Beyond Measure and of Multiple Measures

In his discussion of the "political implications of knowledge," Kelley (2002) wrote that he "worries" that young intellectuals tend to believe that their production of knowledge constitutes "'droppin' science' on the people [that] will generate new liberatory, social movements," when really it is the "social movements that generate new knowledge, new theories, new questions" (9). While Denzin (1997) argued that anthropologists as cultural critics have an "obligation to create a body of work that embodies a particular ontological, epistemological, and political vision of how things can be made better" (226), I agree with Kelley. It has really been the movement against the racial discrimination caused by the testing system in Texas and for multiple measures or multiple criteria, rather than my work, that has provided (and will continue to provide) both a vision and a method for opposing the statistical objectification caused by high-stakes testing.

Perhaps, by envisioning the opposition to testing as an opposition to statistical objectification (as the suppression of subjectivity, as the commodification of children's knowledge, and as the production of truths that secure the hegemony of the testing regime), I am suggesting a vision similar to that of Hardt and Negri (2000) of "beyond measure" (356–359). For Hardt and Negri, "beyond measure" represents a "new place in the non-place," a construction of the value of labor in terms of virtuality and possibility, emerging from the "vitality of the productive context, the expression of labor as desire, and its capacities to constitute the biopolitical fabric of Empire from below" (357). "Beyond measure" represents a politics that neither accepts the West's "abhor[ration of] the immeasurable" (355) nor rests purely on the deconstruction of measure by privileging that which is "outside measure" ("the impossibility of power's calculating and ordering production at a global level") (357). Does not this "beyond measure" sound something like Gilroy's (2000) political call for a beyond-race or antirace politics, opposing race essentialism due to its inevitable fascistic potentialities, and supporting, rather, the construction of a diasporic, deterritorialized consciousness? Should I title this work *Against Statistical Discourse* in rearticulation of Gilroy's *Against Race?* The answer is no. It is my conclusion that neither position (against race or against statistics) recognizes the historic struggle for hegemony and the processes of rearticulation that preclude erasure of these discourses.

Gilroy's *Against Race* does not examine statistics as one of the primary tools for essentializing race, not only in terms of essentializing racial inferiority (see Gould 1996), but also in terms of providing a basis for truth claims in antiracist politics, for example, in the tradition of Ida B. Wells-Barnett. While many regard Wells-Barnett's *Red Record* (1991 [1895]) as a politics of naming the injustice of lynching and the invisibility of racist violence through reporting the statistics on lynching, I see it as also calling into question the reality or truthfulness—as she says in her autobiography, "to tell the truth freely" (Wells-Barnett 1970: 69–75)— of a statistical discourse that justified lynching as a protective force against the "dangerous" and "brutish" Black man, whose life could justifiably be taken due to his "nature" as a rapist. First, she recognizes that objectivity itself is denied to her and uses the statistics on lynching compiled by the *Chicago Tribune* "in order to be safe from the charge of exaggeration" (1991 [1895]: 148). In her autobiography, Wells-Barnett (1970) remarked on the way that statistical reporting on lynching formed a type of symbolic violence, "Like many another person who read of lynching in the South, I had accepted the idea that meant to be conveyed that though lynching was irregular and contrary to law and order, unreasoning anger over the terrible crime of rape led to the lynching; that perhaps the brute deserved death anyhow and the mob was justified in taking his life" (64).

Wells-Barnett documented the cases of lynching to reveal not only the cases of wrongful accusations of rape, but also the nature of lynching as a tool of a broader racial violence used against both men *and* women. I see Wells-Barnett as using *statistical subjectivity*, at the same time critiquing both the politics of *measure*, which not only racializes Black men as rapists, but also serves as a form of self-government in which Black people accept this racialization; and also the politics of *outside measure*, which both inscribes invisibility onto the racial body and silences the centrality of violence to U.S. racism. As Urla (1993) suggested, "In asking how quantifying techniques and discourses operate as technologies of power, we cannot assume that quantification is always a form of domination imposed upon an unwilling and silent populace. There is no doubt that statistical surveys have most often served various state interests. However . . . minorities may also turn to statistics as a means of *contesting* state power and hegemonic constructions of social reality" (837). This contradiction and the problematic stance of "against" statistics (and race for that matter) were made clear to me by the politics of Ward Connerly, who recently argued that statistics on race inhibit a truly colorblind society (Murphy 2003). Connerly actually obtained 980,000 signatures to place a referendum on the California ballot prohibiting the collection of racially based statistical data, coincidentally, at the same time of the vote to recall then governor Gray Davis. While the referendum failed,[6] it points out a contradiction: On the one hand, statistics are involved in a "politics of containment" (Collins 1998: 35), such as that used to objectify children in testing regimes; on the other hand, there is an *alternative* politics of containment of which Ida B. Wells-Barnett was a part (or pioneer). That alternative politics uses the statistical objectification of racism, that is, (strategic) race essentialism—to *name* violence or discrimination—as an alternative form of surveillance, as a form of containing or governing those committing racist acts. It is the same alternative politics of containment that has produced this very study and other projects of "studying up." It is also the politics of using the state as a site of resistance, particularly when appealing to maintaining social welfare policies.[7] I consider the politics of constructing an alternative politics of containment as a reappropriation of statistical objectification. Hardt and Negri (2000) conceptualize reappropriation as "free access and control over knowledge, information, communication, and affects" and the "right to reappropriation is really the multitude's right to self-control and autonomous self-production" (407). Thus, unlike "beyond measure," which is a site "autonomous from any external regime of measure," the alternative politics of containment through statistical objectification—a politics that politicizes *measure* and *outside measure*—constitutes rather a reappropriation of the regime of measure. In *Mathematics and the Struggle for Black Liberation*, Anderson (1970) argued that math is essential to understanding the technological advances and politics of the twentieth and twenty-first centuries. Math education, for Anderson, should be a broad community project, beginning with the demystification of math and a radical historiography of the origins of mathematical concepts in precolonial African, Arab, Indian, and Chinese civilizations (22). For Anderson, "Understanding statistics is also vital because much of the current statistical analysis is interpreted by whites to further justify our 'need' for a colonial, oppressed existence" (26). For civil rights activist Bob Moses, math education through (Ella Baker's model of) community organizing, which he has done in the Algebra Project, is a central project for countering economic disenfranchisement (Moses and Cobb 2001).[8] In *How to Lie with Statistics*, Huff (1993 [1954]) argued that "arbitrarily rejecting statistical methods makes no sense. . . . That is like refusing to read because writers sometimes use words to hide facts and relationships rather than to reveal them" (121). Instead, he provided questions for interrogating the truth of particular statistical fact productions. I view the critique of statistical objectification and the outlining of the ways in which statistics are reappropriated as attempting to engage in work that King et al. (2002) call the third shift, which, like the graveyard shift, "pulls together the work done by the earlier shifts throughout the day, and also prepares operations for the next day. Hence this shift often carries the responsibility for both 'breaking down' prior activities and production modes and 'setting up' the subsequent work activities for the day shift" (404). In the move against high-stakes testing, this reappropriation is encapsulated in the movement for multiple measures, or multiple criteria.

Like Hardt and Negri's concept of *beyond measure*, the movement for multiple measures seeks the radical and plural democratization of regimes of knowledge.[9] For LaClau and Mouffe (1985), radical and plural democracy is based on "the strategy of construction of a new order" that starts from the negativity of deconstruction (189), a strategy that articulates King et al.'s (2002) conception of the third-shift.[10] While leaving open a critique of utopia, radical and plural democracy nevertheless must be constituted by a utopian, "radical imaginary" (LaClau and Mouffe 1985: 190). It also rejects the idea that there is "*one* politics of the Left" (179), and articulates its political struggle through a "polyphony of voices" (191). As I discuss in Chapters 3 and 6, the multiple-measures, or multiple-criteria, movement began with the experiential deconstruction and refusals of objectification caused by the testing system. The politics of deconstruction, as I discuss in Chapter 2, served as a basis for constructing a new formation within the system, a reappropriation of the regime of measure articulated through utopian visions of love and passion. The late U.S. senator Paul Wellstone (D-MN), sponsoring a bill for multiple measures, proclaimed that he was motivated by the fact that "education is my passion," and he thanked his audience for their "love of children and . . . passion to do what is right" (Wellstone 2000). In Texas, a witness for multiple criteria ended her speech by thanking the committee for "letting me spew my passion." Positions of support for multiple measures have emphasized the productive capability of the multitude of students, (re)defined education as desire and development of creativity and talent, and stressed the importance of school communities in structuring educational goals. Wellstone (2000) described education as "a process of shaping the moral imagination, character, skills, and intellect of our children." Multiple measures could counter the construction of children in terms of "deficits" and "limited promise," in which "Children are measured by their score, not their potential, not their diverse talents, not the depth of their knowledge and not their character." In support of the bill, the National Council of Teachers of Mathematics (2000) admonished high-stakes tests for "not [being] aligned with school and community goals," while Kelly Burk (2000), speaking on behalf of the National Education Association, opposed the manner in which high-stakes testing "stifles creativity, impacts the ability of teachers to meet the unique needs of individual students, and provides an incomplete—and perhaps inaccurate—picture of students' knowledge and skills." As Valenzuela (2002) argued, instituting a policy of multiple measures is ethical, democratizes decision-making authority, expands the methods by which students can express their performance levels, and increases the validity and reliability of educational decisions (107–108).

Given this take on multiple measures, I see the expression of statistical subjectivity through statistical counterdiscourse as a form of what Sandoval (2000) called "meta-ideologization," a "political activity that builds on old categories of meaning in order to transform them into . . . something else" (85). Statistical discourse as a "visualization technology" (Helmreich 1998: 101) is a way of factually objectifying, in the sense of Desrosières, certain forms of objectification that are silenced and individualized and that, when meta-ideologized, can turn the gaze toward objectifying processes, such as racism. However, statistical counterdiscourses as discourses also carry with them silences that can "loosen . . . [their] holds" (Foucault 1978: 101). One of those silences is the historical formation of statistics as a tool of governmentality. Wishing that large numbers of students would fail the TAKS in order to maintain statistical panic, as did one supporter of the multiple criteria bills, is one of the ways in which even an oppositional politics does not attend to this silence. In using statistics, we often operate within hegemonic modes of knowledge production, producing statistical discourses from sites of power. This is part of the contradictory position of being incorporated within the state, in which we simultaneously not only reform the state, but also govern those acts that are racist, discriminatory, and unjust. However, using the science of the state (as well as reforms of the welfare state) does not automatically solve differentials in power created and maintained by the state (and I say this while writing from a state university). Second, the pedagogical functioning of statistical discourse, as a scientific discourse, silences and requires the invisibility of revolutions, disjunctions, and contradictions (see Kuhn 1996 [1962]). Statistics are often *decontextualized*, and users can report the best data in order to conjure a particular image, in order to perform statistical magic. Third, statistical counterdiscourse often leaves unchallenged the "*socio-logos*" of race (Silva 2001) and the politics of progress embedded in statistics. We are then left reproducing the reduction of racism and realities of race and segregation to statistically objectifiable *difference* that ultimately produces a White "norm" as the universal signifier.

Thus, meta-ideologization through statistics must be accompanied by an explicit critique of statistics, the same type of practice as autoethnography (McClaurin 2001). The use of ethnography as cultural critique *is* a meta-ideologization of anthropology as an inherently colonizing and assimilating force, which in order to be a form of cultural critique now requires a reflexivity and explicit critique of its historical formation. Through the productive power of double consciousness, it is possible, then, for the ethnographic (re)production (or representation) of experience to be a powerful political tool against statistical objectification, a tool of experiential deconstruction—as was shown by Representative Olivo's strategy. By recognizing the politics of experience, we engage in what Sandoval (2000: 83) has called "democratics," or the appeal to and "centering of identity in the interest of egalitarian justice." It is this appeal to a radical democratic vision of education that the movement for multiple criteria embodies.

However, experiential deconstruction must also attend to the politics of representation (Spivak 1988), through not only the deconstruction of re-presentations, but also the material analysis of hegemony and (the formation of) the historic bloc that simulates and projects a collective will, which supposedly represents Black and Latino collectivities, while reinforcing the production of male (administrative) heroes, such as presidents, governors, superintendents, and legislators. There must also be analysis of the reification of the politics of progress, a politics that not only allows for the use of testing statistics and dropout rates to operate as a discourse network, but also allows for students of color to become targets for state intervention, to become *desaparecidos* and *olvidados*.

These techniques (meta-ideologization, experiential deconstruction, democratics, and semiology, or a sign reading of representation) are exactly the four techniques of Sandoval's (2000) "methodology of the oppressed." Refusing to dismiss the use of statistics as *essentially* bad or narratives as *essentialist* is possible through *differential movement*, a form of "tactical subjectivity" (59) centering on a "both, and" epistemology, characteristic of U.S. Third World feminists politics. This is what Ida B Wells-Barnett practiced in the *Red Record*, in which she not only collected statistics on lynchings, but also re-presented the stories of those lynchings to experientially deconstruct a particular (statistical) discourse of the justifiably lynchable Black male rapist. Her project was an inherently political and very personal one, connected to a democratic ethos. Like DuBois, Wells-Barnett challenged the construction of a particular truth, by politically producing truth, exactly what Foucault (1984a)—nearly fifty years later—called the "constitut[ion] of a new politics of truth" (74). As Sandoval (2000) wrote, "The 'truth' of differential social movement is composed of manifold positions for truth: these positions are ideological stands that are viewed as potential tactics drawn from a never-ending interventionary fund, the contents of which remobilizes power. . . . The differential mode of social movement and consciousness depends on the practitioner's ability to read the current situation of power and self-consciously choosing and adopting the ideological stand best suited to push against its configurations, a survival skill well known to oppressed peoples" (60).

Thus, I do not support an antistatistics stance that would only support Ward Connerly's vision for a world blind to racism. Instead, I envision a politics that would re-articulate or meta-ideologize statistical discourse within a reflexive statistical counterdiscourse, necessarily accompanied by a recognition of the politics of experience. This first includes an ethnographic re-presentation of experiential narratives and accounts of experiential deconstruction (of statistical objectification). Second, it refuses (a desire for) alienation by reinserting authorship and attention to the issues of power inherent in being a re-presenter of social experience and reality, but also in assuming the political role as representative. By reappropriating the regime of measure and by de-mystifying and politicizing the formation of statistical knowledge, perhaps we can also reappropriate a sense of accountability that demands not only statistical reflexivity (a political recount), but also a narrative or ethnographic/qualitative index of public school reform, whereby democratic schooling on the one hand and the "democratization of oppression" (see Sandoval 2000: 73–74) and privatization on the other are disarticulated or disassociated. The very formation of the coalition in support of multiple criteria (and in opposition to the objectifying measures of high-stakes testing) suggests that all students are being objectified, and that the politics of experience, as a measuring of silence, may be the downfall of high-stakes testing.

## Sister Inside/Outside of the Confessional: Reflections on "Ethical Ambitions"

> Our vision was to penetrate the power structure. The situation of la raza has always been one of exclusion from government, not lack of willingness to participate. But participation only serves to legitimize the current public policy of that institution. One changes nothing fundamentally—one only makes minor reforms.
>
> —José Angel Gutiérrez (1998: 180)

Just as Gutiérrez struggled with the extent to which reforming the state would constitute revolutionary change, so I struggle with the question of the extent to which reforming anthropology by participating in efforts to reform the state can be revolutionary.[11] I began with what Bell (2002) called "ethical ambitions," envisioning my project as part of the Gramscian or Freirian project of producing knowledge for the sake of consciousness-raising, *conscientização* (Foley 2002: 471), believing that charting statistical objectification as one method by which the Right is maintaining the hegemony of the testing regime can challenge the common sense of that regime. Ultimately, I see my project as concurrent with that outlined for *Critical Race Theory* by Crenshaw et al. (1995):

"to use the critical historical method to show that the contemporary structure of civil rights rhetoric . . . [is] a collection of strategies and discourses born out of and deployed in particular conflicts and negotiations"; and by doing so to take part in the process of creating a critical vocabulary with which to oppose racism (xvi, xxi, xxvii). For me, naming statistics as discourses embedded in cultural processes of negotiation and hegemony provides a vocabulary with which to critique neo-hereditarian (Herrnstein and Murray 1994; see also Valencia and Solórzano 1997) and cultural-determinist (D'Souza 1995) statistical arguments claiming to prove the existence of racial supremacy and inferiority. However, watching the proceedings, I recognized that this project may not be politically tenable, for instance, as a standpoint for testifying at a Public Education Committee hearing or in court because my valorization of the experiential deconstruction of testing statistical discourse could be rearticulated in such a way as to support the deconstruction of statistical proofs of racial discrimination. More important, my vocabulary may be untenable in political arenas such as public hearings because it targets an audience of scholars who already distinguish the Foucauldian notion of discourse from the use of discourse in the broader sense as public discussion or debate, and who are well versed in Gramscian theories of hegemony. One of the questions to be answered in future research projects is mapping out the ways in which these theories are already integrated and could be integrated into a vocabulary useful in those political arenas.

I chose anthropology as "home-work" (Viswewaran 1994) and "studying up" (Nader 1972; Helmreich 1998) as a way of countering colonial relationships and the problematic of possessing more privilege than subjects, inherent in the ethnographic process. In terms of "de-colonizing anthropology," I could neither avoid the problematic of entering different cultures nor escape those relationships of power that Behar (1993) called the "webs of betrayal" constructed by ethnographers "seeking out intimacy and friendship with subjects on whose backs, ultimately, the books will be written [and] upon which their productivity as scholars in the academic marketplace will be assessed" (297). First, observing committee meetings, I instantly became aware that the legislature, with its rules, language, and culture, in many ways did not constitute a "home," and I felt that I had not attained what Briggs (1986) called "metacommunicative competence" (61–92). Not only did I not always speak and understand the culture of the Capitol, but my inability to speak or understand Spanish also attributed to a failure to attain metacommunicative competence within the meetings and the multiple-criteria movement, for which I *was* called out. At many times I felt like *la vendida*[12]—a word I did know—hiding my true interest in studying statistics by suggesting that I was studying power relationships in the educational system, in large part because I felt that my questioning of statistics could be considered detrimental to the tradition of people of color of using statistics in antiracist politics.[13] Conducting ethnography did at many times feel to me as Trinh (1989) described it, as spying, or "legal voyeurism" (68, 69), and I asked myself whether or not I would want someone watching me work, enabled to engage in "academic colonialism" (Marcus 1998 [1994]: 188), assimilating and rearticulating my words into their theoretical formations. I felt that "studying up" does *not* resolve the problem of writing on the backs of those with whom ethnographers establish close relationships, an issue with which Gusterson (1996: 151, 167) also dealt in his ethnography of a weapons lab, as he was caught in between the intimate relationships established with lab employees and his engagements with anti–nuclear weapons activism. My notebooks often felt as the dividing line between insider and outsider, as one person at the rally thought I was a news reporter although I wore the Texans for Quality Assessment T-shirt. I feel as did Behar (1993: 302): that in me there is no heroine. I questioned my own position in and impact on the movement, particularly since I hesitated to speak formally and did not do all that I could to testify at the committee hearing on the multiple-criteria bills. Unlike ideal activist anthropology, I chose this topic without consulting activists or organizations, without obtaining their stamp of validity, and without even discussing my interpretations with them. Instead I searched for an "open problem"[14] and assimilated my politics and the movement of others into that problem. As I come to the conclusion, I must be accountable to community politics, but also produce academically rigorous and valid work—at the same time that communities are *imagined*, and *rigor* and *validity* are positivist social constructions. Some questions for further research that I might investigate are the following: How does the community with which I worked on this project view my conclusions about testing and multiple criteria? What is their critique of my work? And what projects do they view as necessary research in the movement against the harmful effects of testing?

In some sense this project could be viewed as failure (Visweswaran 1994) in terms of its limited utility in political arenas such as public hearings and because of its inability to decolonize anthropology or achieve truly dialogical activist anthropological research. At the same time, the movement for multiple criteria also failed to transform the testing regime through the legislative process in the 77th and 78th regular legislative sessions. However, as Bell (2002) wrote, "I do not believe that earlier attempts to combat social injustices were failures, even if they did not realize their goals, or once achieved, proved of only temporary value. I say so harking back to our discussion of faith and remembering this: If our goal is greater than ourselves, our own comfort or gain, and we continue to strive for it, then as feminist leaders proclaimed, failure becomes impossible" (164).

For Bell, "failure" not only teaches activists lessons on the necessity of humility and self-critique, but also leads to the realization that activism is a continuing process, not simply a question of winning and losing. In a symposium I attended, Latinos and Educational Equity, held by the Center for Mexican American Studies on January 26, 2001, a heated debate on the Texas testing system and the *GI Forum* case ensued between the leading MALDEF attorney and a key expert for the Texas Education Agency, who had worked with MALDEF before and had been honored by the *Journal of Black Issues in Higher Education*. To my recollection, the debate began with the question on why the TEA should not place a moratorium on the testing system until the problems of racial and economic inequality could be resolved. Suddenly, "Who won?!" exploded into the air out of the mouth of the TEA expert, intended to imply that justice determined the right(eous) ness of the testing system. However, its deployment on the mostly Mexican American audience for me seemed ironic and (unintentionally) insensitive, symptomatic of racialization and the forms of erasure on which tales of American victory and justice are written (see Montejano 1986; San Miguel and Valencia 1998). Speaking to women of color, Míranda (2002) told us, "[T]he *erasure* of aboriginal literature defines *you*. You are constituted by erasure; you negotiate not just your own histories and oppression, but a huge national fantasy on which those histories and oppressions rest, a fantasy that surrounds you in every detail of your daily life" (200–201).

In a quintessential United States fashion, the question of who won belies the presence of an "oppositional culture" within institutions (Willis 1981 [1977]) and the functioning of state processes such as litigation and the bill processes as "cooling-out" (Clark 1961), needed to resolve contradictions within the state.[15] It was the movement that taught me the meaning of the ethics of "evolving faith" (Bell 2002: 75–93), "middle voice" (Sandoval 2000: 154–157), the "sojourner" (Collins 1998:

231), and the "subject-in-process" (Visweswaran 1994: 62). At a conference sponsored by Dr. Valenzuela, held during the 78th regular session, a representative of the Texas Parent-Teacher Association who worked closely with Representative Olivo on her bill said to the audience, "Don't tell the Representative I said this, but these bills won't pass." However, fully aware of the potential that the bills would not pass, Representative Olivo never stopped fighting for the bills. In fact, at the prospect of the bills not passing, one of the women in the Representative's office suggested that if the bills were not passed, maybe it was time for a boycott. I learned from this experience that my project is not simply a work in progress,[16] but a *work in process*, a process of *disordering*,[17] engaging in what Maya Angelou called "deep talk," which King et al. (2002) define as follows: "the ever-deepening spiral of revelation, truth telling, truth seeking, meaning making, and planning. There may never be an answer, at least no one answer. But the process itself is generative and leads to the discovery of new possibilities, of identity, voice, community, and action" (404).

## Situating the Non-Place

> Struggle is par for the course when our dreams go into action. But unless we have the space to imagine and a vision of what it means fully to realize our humanity, all the protests and demonstrations in the world won't bring about our liberation.
>
> —Robin D. G. Kelley (2002: 198)

Writing this book is as much about self-transformation (Foucault 1988a: 14; Anzaldúa 1983: 169) as it is about the ethical transformation of anthropology (Trinh 1989: 71)[18] or the transformation of our educational system. Before I began working at the Capitol, discussions of love in theory and activism, such as that by Sandoval (2000), did not appeal to me, as a woman feeling that love can hide abusive relationships. I tend to see utopia as a dangerous reflection of Western escapism that has supported the "spatial confinement of the native" (Mohanram 1999: 184), from the frontier dreams (Garza-Falcon 1998: 122) to the spatialization of race and class in segregation (Sugrue 1996) to the "colorblind bind" occurring in the rearticulation of the racial equality arguments of Thurgood Marshall and the NAACP (Baker 1998: 208–228). However, the experience of working in the Capitol disrupted the postmodern pessimism, or dystopia, into which I descended, not only by working with

Representative Olivo, but also by working with the men and particularly the women of the movement. I cannot truly conclude this study without the following story about the ethic of love (Collins 1998: 200). I had begun falling into a slight depression in the Capitol, developing chest pains not only from the stress that looms in the Capitol air and in the division of labor, but also from watching the process and the bills being passed—in the broader context of the war on Iraq, which I believed a travesty of justice. On an early April afternoon, we were on an errand to find the "women with the pink crosses," in support of legislation to help the women of Juárez. We found the two women, one of whom was a Latina legislative aide, who talked to me at length about education, expressing her support for the multiple-criteria bills because her daughter was a teacher on the south side of San Antonio. She spoke of her daughter calling her in tears because of the limited resources of the school and her inability due to testing to use innovative methods of teaching, "you know, like Jaime Escalante," the math teacher in the film *Stand and Deliver*. At the end of our conversation, she hesitated and said, "Let me give you a heart." Pulling out a small red heart, whose glassy contours resembled candy, she said to me, "Here is my heart because I love you. God bless you." For nearly an hour, I clenched the heart in my fist, feeling as if she had read through my smiling face and found that my heart was breaking there in the Capitol,[19] but also feeling as if she had restored hope in the emptiness I felt surrounded me in the office without windows. For me, the gift supplied me with what Bell (2002) termed the nourishing "energy of passion" (22–24, 32). At that moment, I understood Sandoval's (2000) emphasis on love, desire-in-resistance, and her definition of love as revolutionary hope and faith (140). As Cherríe Moraga (1983) wrote, "But what I really want to write about is faith. . . . I am not talking here about some lazy faith, where we resign ourselves to the tragic splittings in our lives with an upward turn of the hands or a vicious beating of our breasts. I am talking about believing that we have the power to actually transform our experience, change our lives, save our lives. Otherwise, why write this book? It is the faith of activists I am talking about" (xviii).

# Chronology

## Timeline of Testing in Texas
## 1970–2003

1970      U.S. District Court rules in *United States v. Texas* that the Texas Education Agency must desegregate schools in Texas.

1979      District court orders Austin Independent School District to desegregate through busing.

1979      William Clements is the first Republican governor since Reconstruction. He runs on an antibusing platform.

1980      Texas Legislature passes the Equal Educational Opportunity Act, which establishes the first state-mandated testing system, the Texas Assessment of Basic Skills.

1982      Mark White is elected governor of Texas. Teacher-led organizations were crucial in mobilizing votes for White, as he ran on a platform that promised to raise teachers' salaries.

1983      Governor Mark White creates the Select Committee on Public Education to reform the educational system and appoints billionaire Ross Perot to lead the committee. Texas Legislature passes House Bill 72, which includes teacher certification exams, a no-pass, no-play rule, and new state-mandated exams (Texas Educational Assessment of Minimum Skills, or TEAMS) that at the high school level require passage for a diploma.

1984      The Mexican American Legal Defense and Education Fund (MALDEF) along with the Equity Center file suit against the state of

Texas in order to equalize funding between poor and rich Texas districts in *Edgewood v. Kirby*.

1990    In *Edgewood v. Kirby*, the Texas Supreme Court deems the Texas school finance system unconstitutional. The court orders the legislature to devise a finance bill that would successfully equalize "adequate" and "efficient" funding.

1990    The State Board of Education approves a more difficult statewide testing system, the Texas Assessment of Academic Skills (TAAS). The approval comes despite statewide poor performance on the 1989 TEAMS and projections that on the new high school exit exams at least 73 percent of African Americans and 67 percent of Hispanics (versus 50 percent of Whites) would fail the math portion of the test; at least 53 percent of African Americans and 54 percent of Hispanics (versus 29 percent of Whites) would fail the reading section; and at least 62 percent of African Americans and 45 percent of Hispanics (versus 36 percent of Whites) would fail the writing section (*GI Forum et al. v. Texas Education Agency et al.* 87 F. Supp. 2d 667 [2000]).

1995    The Supreme Court finally approves legislation to equalize funding according to *Edgewood v. Kirby*. The bill, dubbed "Robin Hood," contains the provision of an accountability system in which schools and districts are given ratings based on the state-mandated test, the TAAS, dropout statistics, and school attendance rates.

1995    The NAACP files a complaint with the Office of Civil Rights concerning the disproportionate racial impact of the TAAS test and reaches a settlement with the Texas Education Agency on the agreement that the agency would provide proper remediation for students who failed the TAAS.

1997    MALDEF files suit against the Texas Education Agency in *GI Forum et al. v. Texas Education Agency et al.*, claiming that the TAAS exit exam (which high school students were required to pass in order to graduate) disproportionately impacted African American and Mexican American students.

1999    Under the leadership of Governor George W. Bush, the Texas Legislature passes the "no social promotion bill," requiring third-, fifth-, and eighth-grade students to pass the state-mandated exam in order to be promoted to the following grade. The high school exit exam was to be taken in the eleventh grade, and the Texas Education Agency was to develop a more rigorous standardized test, which would become the Texas Assessment of Knowledge and Skills (TAKS).

2000      Judge Edward Prado dismisses the plaintiffs' case in *GI Forum et al.
          v. Texas Education Agency et al.*, ruling that:

> In short, the Court finds, on the basis of the evidence pre-
> sented at trial, that the disparities in test scores do not result
> from flaws in the test or in the way it is administered. In-
> stead, as the Plaintiffs themselves have argued, some minor-
> ity students have, for a myriad of reasons, failed to keep up
> (or catch up) with their majority counterparts. It may be, as
> the TEA argues, that the TAAS test is one weapon in the
> fight to remedy this problem. (*GI Forum et al. v. Texas Edu-
> cation Agency et al.* 87 F. Supp. 2d 667 [2000])

2003      The TAKS is first administered. For the first time, third-grade stu-
          dents are required to pass the TAKS in order to move to the fourth
          grade.

2003      MALDEF and a state representative try to pass a multiple-criteria bill
          that would allow a committee of a student's teacher, parents, and
          principal to decide whether or not a child should be promoted after
          the first failure on the TAKS versus the third failure on the TAKS.
          The bill would empower parents by requiring a unanimous decision
          to *fail* versus a unanimous decision to *promote*. The bill is not passed
          by the House Public Education Committee, and attempts to pass the
          provisions as an attachment to another bill are thwarted by the House
          Public Education Committee chair.

Sources: Davidson 1990; *Handbook of Texas Online*, http://www.tsha.utexas.edu/
handbook/online/ (accessed February 20, 2006); McNeil 2000a; Texas Education
Agency, "Timeline of Testing in Texas," www.tea.state.tx.us/student.assessment/resources/
studies/testingtimeline.pdf (accessed February 20, 2006).

# Notes

## Chapter 1

1. This is a pseudonym.
2. On October 25, 2002, Senator Wellstone died tragically in a plane crash in Minnesota.
3. In 1997, Congress commissioned the report in light of proposals for national tests. According to the mandate, the National Academy of Sciences was "to conduct a study and make written recommendations on appropriate methods, practices, and safeguards to ensure that . . . existing and new tests that are used to assess student performance are not used in a discriminatory manner or inappropriately for student promotion, tracking, or graduation" (Public Law 105-78, 105th Cong., 1st sess. (November 13, 1997), 111 Stat 1506).
4. In Texas, testing data are disaggregated by race, socioeconomic status, gender, language proficiency, special education status, and at-risk status.
5. My location within this intellectual genealogy comes from the fact that I was a student of both Drs. Valencia and Valenzuela. Their classes, testimony, and research inspired my own choice to study testing in Texas as a problem of racial inequality.
6. By 1810, probability calculus synthesized the earlier studies of the "degree of certainty" by judges and philosophers and that of "empirical combinations of imperfect observations" intended to determine accuracy by astronomers and physicists—a synthesis referred to as the Gauss-LaPlace synthesis (Desrosières 1998: 62).
7. Foucault (1991) referred to Le Vayer's conception of "three fundamental types of government: . . . the art of self-government, connected with morality; the art of properly governing a family, which belongs to economy; and finally, the science of ruling the state, which concerns politics" (91).

8. Apple's (2001) work on the formation of the Right's historic bloc in gaining hegemony in educational reform is precisely such a Gramscian approach, which I consider indispensable in understanding the hegemony of the marketization of education and its materialization in the reproduction of inequities in education.

9. Arguably, this project gave birth to social sciences in terms of underlying the notion of society (Desrosières 1998: 77–79; Porter 1995: 37).

10. This genealogy traces the following schools of educational theory: Parsonian structure-functionalism; structuralist Marxism and correspondence / social reproduction theory; structuralist conflict theories / cultural capital; Frankfurt School critical theory / poststructuralism; Gramscian British cultural studies; (postmodernist) critical pedagogy; and race, gender, and class analysis.

11. According to Johnston (2002), the method of discourse analysis emerged in linguistics during the 1960s, emphasizing the need to contextualize sentences by examining the broader text (68). With the "narrative turn," the concept of "culture as text" spread to literary, historic, and social scientific disciplines, resulting in the development of qualitative "'macro' discourse analysis" of social movements that "intensely analyzes textual materials with the goal of laying bare the relationships between movement discourse and the discursive field of the broader culture" (68, 69). Blommaert et al. (2001) differentiated between two forms of discourse analysis: "critical discourse analysis" (CDA) in Europe, which focuses on textual analyses, interpreting "ideology-as-mystification" and promoting a political strategy of "deconstruct[ing] . . . the discourse of oppressive commercial and state institutions"; and "linguistic anthropology" (LA) in the United States, which focuses on ethnographic analyses of meaning, interpreting "culture-as-ideology" and promoting a political strategy of advocating against the oppression of linguistic minorities (5, 6).

12. In *Archaeology of Knowledge* (1972), Foucault uses the metaphor of archaeology to describe a method for analyzing particular discursive practices. The method he calls archaeology "uncovers" the "regularity" of discourses (144); locates and describes the "contradictions," "dissensions," and "oppositions" inherent in discourse (149–154); describes the local "play of analogies and differences" ("isomorphisms," "models," "isotopia," "shifts," and "correlations") (160–161); establishes the limitations of and changes to discursive practices ("emergences," "derivations," "transformations," and "ruptures") (168–176); and analyzes how discursive practices appropriate the "ideological functioning of science" (183–186).

13. Foucault (1984b) defined genealogy in "Nietzsche, Genealogy, History" as an "analysis of descent" that is "situated within the articulation of body and history," in which "*emergence* designates a place of confrontation"; that records the history of violent relations of force in which rules of, directions of, and participation in discourses are imposed and changed; that forces proximity of the historian to history; and that becomes "parody," dissociates continuities, and "sacrifice[s] . . . the subject of knowledge" by attending to the dynamics of power and injustice by which producers of knowledge become producers of

knowledge (76–97). According to Stoler (1995), in his lectures on race, Foucault clarified the difference between the complementary strategies of archaeological and genealogical analysis: whereas archaeology involves the "analysis of local discursivities," genealogy involves analysis of "tactics whereby, on the basis of these discursivities, the subjugated knowledge would come into play" (60).

14. It may be argued that the upheaval in the sciences and anthropology was in fact this vindicationist literature finally breaking through disciplinary barriers, no less part of a broader struggle against colonization in Africa and Asia.

15. Robinson wrote, "The development, organization, and expansion of capitalist society pursued essentially racial directions, so too did social ideology. As a material force, then, it could be expected that racialism would inevitably permeate the social structures emergent from capitalism. I have used the term 'racial capitalism' to refer to this development and to the subsequent structure as a historical agency" (2000: 2).

16. See Foucault's (1978: 16–17) critique of the "repressive hypothesis," in which he showed that talking about sex was not censored in the Victorian Era, but, in fact, discourses of sexuality were everywhere.

17. See also the appendix of the second edition of Jay MacLeod's (1995) *Ain't No Making It*, in which he describes his dilemma of profiting from the stories of students he studied while the students had encountered serious financial hardship since the first publication of his book.

18. See Jones (1993) and Fry (2001 [1975]) for the example of the Tuskegee Experiment, in which Black men exposed to syphilis were denied treatment in order for researchers to study the progression of the disease.

19. This term is used by Kritzman (1988) in his introduction to Foucault, describing Foucault's work as analyzing the "politics of experience." I did not use quotation marks in the text itself because my theorization and knowledge of the politics of experience originates not from Foucault, but from feminists, and particularly feminists of color (e.g., see Collins 1990; Mohanty 1992; Sudbury 1998).

20. I kept myself from recording my observations of the workplace, feeling that to do so would violate my commitment to Freire's vision of not making the people with whom you are working objects of study. I also viewed my positioning in terms of a "drawbridge" (Sudbury 1998: 181–182). Speaking of coalitional politics, Anzaldúa contended, "Many of us choose to 'draw up our own bridges' for short periods of time in order to regroup, recharge our energies, and nourish ourselves before wading back into the frontlines. . . . The other option is being 'down'. . . . [which] may mean a partial loss of self. Being 'there' for people *all the time, mediating all the time* means risking being 'walked on,' being 'used'" (Anzaldúa 1990: 223). I knew that as a volunteer I could be exploited as a free laborer, yet at the same time, as a writer-ethnographer, I had the potential to exploit those with whom I worked.

21. Denzin (1997) did recognize this crisis in his reprinting of a poem by Floyd Red Crow Westerman of the Dakota Nation called "Here Come the Anthros" (214–215).

22. This term goes unquestioned by McClaurin but is interrogated in *Between Woman and Nation* (Kaplan, Alarcón, and Moallem 1999), following Partha Chaterjee's notion of "imagined community." I put it in quotation marks here because I became involved in a political movement in Texas formed by a multiracial coalition, made mostly of women, who came together after a charge that testing in Texas constituted racial discrimination. My birthplace and place where I grew up is not Texas, but Columbus, Ohio; thus, I cannot authentically assert that Texas, where I have lived for six years, is my "home." I also felt that if perhaps I was a teacher or a mother of a child in public school, I would have more at stake in the testing system and thus a deeper understanding of the processes of objectification occurring due to the testing system. In Chapter 6, I explore the idea of "imagined community" in the context of the multiple-criteria movement.

23. Charles Lam Markmann, in translating Frantz Fanon's *Peau Noire, Masques Blancs* into English (as *Black Skin, White Masks*), translated Fanon's chapter title "L'experience vecue du noir," in which "l'experience vecue" is literally "the lived experience," as "The Fact of Blackness."

24. Hardt and Negri (2000) used the term "from below" to refer to the "multitude," masses, or oppressed (357). Sandoval (2000: 74) suggested that the vertical metaphors of *up* and *below* have been replaced with horizontal metaphors of *margin* and *center*. The critique by Kaplan, Alarcón, and Maollem (1999: 8) of the metaphor of *marginality* as "complicit with the discourse of the nation-state" may also apply to the vertical metaphors of *up* and *below*. I use them to suggest not only my differential movement between science and activist anthropologies, but also my positionality as both of the state (as intern and university student) and not of the state (as Black woman of the petit bourgeoisie). This conceptualization is in concert with the "in-betweenness" or "double concept of borders" (9) that Kaplan, Alarcón, and Maollem argued should replace *marginality*.

## Chapter 2

1. Attached to the promise of funding were the skepticism and fears of corruption, which for politicians necessitated evaluation through an outcomes model or evidenced by standardized tests (Sacks 1999, Wong and Nicotera 2004, Lemann 1999). Sacks (1999: 75) suggests that in that sense, "[t]he Elementary and Secondary Education Act, then, had perhaps an unquantifiable impact on the expansion of standardized testing in schools."

2. Menchaca argued that under the Spanish in Mexico, slaves were granted some legal rights and that "people who were one-sixteenth Black were legally classified as Spaniards" (2001: 61). Also, the church prevented slave owners from revoking these rights, such as the granting of freedom to the offspring of a Black male slave and a Mexican Indian woman—no such provision existed for Black women (62). By the time of Mexican independence, slavery was re-

formed to such an extent that the government emancipated any slave entering Mexico, Mexican-born children of slaves at the age of fourteen, and even adult slaves "after serving ten additional years . . . in bondage" (163).

3. While lynching is often thought to have been used against men only, Ida B. Wells-Barnett (1991 [1895]) provided several examples of women being lynched.

4. For DuBois, this alliance undermined a "general strike" against the southern plutocracy.

5. Garza-Falcon (1998) noted that the practice of passing property rights through women in Mexican society led many Anglo men to marry Mexican women and thus obtain their land.

6. According to Kluger (1975), while the district court in *Mendez* ruled that the "separate but equal" doctrine was unconstitutional, the court of appeals ruled that segregation of Mexicans in California was illegal, not because "separate but equal" was unconstitutional, but because there was no provision in California law allowing for racial segregation (399).

7. Crenshaw uses this term to designate the intersection of race and gender, particularly the refusal of the court to allow for that intersection to be recognized. The dichotomization of race and gender to me parallels the dichotomization of race and class that prevented the legitimation of a concept of segregation as possessing racial and class dimensions.

8. A case in point is West Lake in Austin, which refused to desegregate in the 1970s and broke away from the Austin Independent School District, forming its own district in the west center of the city.

9. Greenberger (1993: 264–265) provided the text of the amendment as follows:

> Notwithstanding any other provision of this title, it shall not be an unlawful employment practice for an employer to give any professionally developed ability test to any individual seeking employment or being considered for promotion or transfer, or to act in reliance upon the results of any such test given to such individual, if—
> (1) in the case of any individual who is seeking employment with such employer, such test is designed to determine or predict whether such individual is suitable or trainable with respect to his employment in the particular business or enterprise involved, and such test is given to all individuals seeking similar employment with such employer without regard to the individual's race, color, religion, sex, or national origin, or
> (2) in the case of any individual who is an employee of such employer, such test is designed to determine or predict whether such individual is suitable or trainable with respect to his promotion or transfer within such business or enterprise, and such test is given to all such employees being considered for similar promotion or transfer by such employer without regard to the employee's race, color, religion, sex, or national origin.

10. See Ken Biggs, Lonestar Internet, Inc, "H Ross Perot," http://www
.famoustexans.com/rossperot.htm (accessed January 14, 2008) and David T
Likken, "A Professional Autobiography: Do the Mistakes of Youth Become the
Wisdom of Old Age?" http://home.fnal.gov/~lykken/Autobiography.pdf (accessed January 14, 2008). I find this interesting given the comment in Richards,
Shore, and Sawicky (1996) that the roots of performance contracting (the basis
of privatizing public schools) originated in the Pentagon with former members
of the Department of Defense.

11. This was mentioned to me in an interview with MALDEF attorney
Leticia Saucedo. The same strategy was tried in GI Forum but denied by Judge
Prado.

12. This was also written in an Achieve, Inc. (2002) document and in an
article by Braceras (2002) in which she said, "The Texas accountability system
was enacted in response to a series of court challenges to the constitutionality
of the financing of the Texas educational system" (1130). Additionally, Braceras
wrote, "As in the case of Texas, the Massachusetts testing regime was adopted
as part of an overall reform package and in response to litigation challenging
the constitutionality under the state law of the state's public financing system"
(1136).

13. In Esdall and Faler 2002.

14. He wrote, "As their numbers dwindle in the Legislature, so does the
Capitol clout wielded by white Democrats."

15. One person informed me that Republicans supported this bill so heavily not only because of the funding of their campaigns by insurance companies, but also because Democrats both received significant contributions from
trial attorneys and may in fact have occupations as trial attorneys. The limit on
malpractice suits, which was part of the national Republican agenda as well,
could then translate into the limiting of Democratic legislators. Supporting
this theory, Elliot and Ratcliffe (2003) wrote, "The debate was highly personal
for many of the lawyers who serve in the Legislature. Some of the HB 4 supporters make their livings defending corporations, while some of those most
strongly fighting the bill work at law firms that represent injured persons."

16. The makers of the cards smartly refrained from designating any of the
Black Democrats as spades.

17. I read the redistricting bill in the context of voter intimidation tactics
employed by Republicans in the 1980s (see Davidson 1990: 235, 236).

18. The home-rule school district was, according to A. Phillips Brooks
(1995b), the cornerstone of George W. Bush's campaign for Texas governor in
1995. The home-rule district was part of SB 1, a law with sweeping educational
reforms, led by Republican senator Bill Ratliff and Democratic representative
Paul Sadler. An amendment by Black Democratic representative Sylvester
Turner to remove the home-rule district from the education reform bill was
defeated. Representative Turner remarked, "Don't throw me back to the 1950s"
(quoted in A. Phillips Brooks 1995b).

19. I expand on this bill Chapter 4.

## Chapter 3

1. This rally countered the suggestion by Wat (2003) that the antitesting movement was mostly White, with the exception being California.

2. Peter is a pseudonym. The sign bore the actual name of the student.

3. Ironically, by the end of the 2003 Texas legislative session, I felt that the movement embodied the feminist *critique* of Foucault's own submission of subjectivity in his work, particularly his writings on "docile bodies" (see Deveaux 1994).

4. Curtis (2002) critiqued Foucault's notion of "population" as ahistoric, a problem stemming from Foucault's conflation of populousness (in mercantilism, in which populousness signals wealth), the social body, and population. For Curtis, population is only made possible by (1) the construction of equivalences within a nation or the creation of "a common abstract essence" and (2) the merging of administrative statistics with the calculus of probabilities; thus, the emergence of *population* is historically located in the twentieth century. Stoler (1995: 39) also critiqued Foucault's notion of the emergence of population as ahistorical, but she critiqued Foucault's distinction between the social body and population. In Desrosières (1998), the adunation of France signaled the transformation of administrative statistics from the "mirror of the prince" to the "mirror of the nation," which I believe is the distinction that Foucault is making between statistics within sovereignty and those within government (or the "governmentalization of the state"). Also, Cohen (1982) provided evidence that in the late eighteenth century, statistics in the United States were used to create a homogenous national essence. Thus, here I connect Foucault's notion of governmentality (specifically, the relation of population to government) to the concept of *nation*. This is also a synthesis of Gramsci's (1971: 123–206) analysis of Machiavelli and the "modern prince" and Foucault's (1991) analysis of Machiavelli and the sovereignty-government distinction. The problem of locating statistics historically is rooted in the very emergence of statistics, which Woolf (1989) described as "provid[ing] a classic example of the nonlinearity of scientific evolution" (592).

5. Foucault (1991) referred to Le Vayer's conception of "three fundamental types of government: . . . the art of self-government, connected with morality; the art of properly governing a family, which belongs to economy; and finally, the science of ruling the state, which concerns politics" (91).

6. The 1983 report by the National Commission on Education, *A Nation at Risk*, argued that the achievement levels of U.S. students lagged behind those of students across the world, and consequently provided the impetus for and "instigated more than 300 state and national business reports and commissions assessing public schools" (Bartlett et al. 2002: 11).

7. The field test is a process of testing the test "in the field," or testing the questions with students in real testing situations.

8. Blalock and Haswell number the student response according to page from 1 to 20, and student number from 1 to 402 or as (page-student number).

Interestingly, the enumeration provides student anonymity as a form of protection of privacy, in contrast to the kind of student anonymity critiqued by Dickens through his character of Gradgrind.

9. This is a play on words, since statistical significance is a formal concept within mathematical statistics. I am referring not to this formal concept, but to a commonsensical notion of significance.

10. This quote is taken from Confrey 2001.

11. In light of this evidence, Judge Prado wrote in his summary opinion:

> Plaintiffs have failed to make a causal connection between the implementation of the TAAS test and these phenomena, beyond mere conjecture. In other words, Plaintiffs were only able to point to the problem and ask the Court to draw an inference that the problem exists because of the implementation of the TAAS test. That inference is not, in light of their evidence, inevitable. The Defendants hypothesize . . . just as plausibly, for example, that the ninth grade increase in drop outs is due to the cessation of automatic grade promotion at the beginning of high school in Texas (*GI Forum, et al v. Texas Education Agency, et al.* 87 F. Supp. 2d 667, 676 [2000]).

12. See Saldívar-Hull's (2000) use of the definition of *desaparecidos* (183n22). Also, according to Adorno and Horkheimer (1979 [1944]), "All objectification is a forgetting" (230).

13. As Robinson (2000 [1983]) suggested, "From the twelfth century forward, it was the bourgeoisie and the administrators of state power who initiated and nurtured myths of egalitarianism while seizing every occasion to divide peoples for the purpose of their domination. The carnage of wars and revolutions precipitated by the bourgeoisies of Europe to sanctify their masques was enormous" (26).

14. I experienced this firsthand when, in one of my undergraduate biology classes, the professor posed the following question: "What is the most common disease among humans? [pause] Did I say humans? I meant Caucasians." The answer was cystic fibrosis.

15. I video recorded and transcribed this segment, which appeared on January 7.

16. See reports by Intercultural Development Research Association (Johnson 2003).

## Chapter 4

1. This is also Davidson's (1990) argument about the realignment of the Republican Party in Texas.

2. An example is given by Morantz (1996), where in Charlotte, North Carolina, the "business elite urged the Chamber [of Commerce] to help dismantle the race- and class-desegregated educational system, which they believed to be impeding educational success by lowering educational standards" (185).

3. See McDermott 1997.

4. As mentioned in Chapter 1, Foucault 1984a describes the "political economy of truth," as defined by the preeminent role of scientific discourse, the production of truth by dominant political and economic institutions (such as the university, military, and media), as well as its "immense diffusion and consumption" through educational and informational systems that in turn make it an "issue of a whole political debate and social confrontation" (73).

5. This comment was made during the committee hearing on vouchers (see Chapter 2).

6. I use "administrative science" to reinforce Desrosières's distinction between the developments of two forms of statistics: the *administrative science* used by states and the *probability calculus* developed by mathematicians, as well as astronomers, physicists, and social scientists.

7. See Curtis (2002), who argued against Foucault's historicization of "population," which Curtis describes as a phenomenon of the nineteenth century. Curtis argued that Foucault conflates population with "populousness."

8. In "Race, 'Culture,' and Mestizaje: The Statistical Construction of the Ecuadorian Nation, 1930–1950" Clark (1998) wrote that in 1950, "[t]he census thus became part of Ecuador's long-standing effort to join the community of nations" (194).

9. Foucault's concepts of "rupture and recuperation," according to Stoler (1995), exemplify a "key insight" in understanding how "racism appears *renewed* and *new* at the same time," accommodating the "fundamental paradox" whereby racism "effectively incorporates emancipatory claims" (89).

10. Metcalf (2002) said of the use of the term *sanctions* in accountability rhetoric, "Predictably, CEO's bring to education reform CEO rhetoric: stringent, intolerant of failure, even punitive—hence the word 'sanction' as if some schools had been turning away weapons inspectors" (18). Metcalf pointed to the merging of corporate and market metaphors with those of war, as did McNeil (2000a) and Saltman (2000) in their use of the war terminology "collateral damage."

11. Blalock and Haswell number the student response according to page from 1 to 20, and student number from 1 to 402 or as (page-student number).

12. Hardt and Negri (2000) argued that FDR's welfare state "invested social relations in their entirety, imposing a regime of discipline accompanied by greater participation in the process of accumulation," and that it was one of the first expressions of "Empire" (242).

13. As I mention earlier, this is one of the conditions to which Hardt and Negri (2000) point in their discussion of the transformation into an informational economy.

14. In Texas, the Ten Percent Plan was designed after *Hopwood v. Texas*, 78 F. 3d. 932 (5th Cir. 1996) eliminated affirmative action in admissions to still provide a way for disadvantaged students (of color) to attend college. According to the plan, students graduating in the top 10 percent of their class earned automatic entry into the University of Texas system. However, Republicans in the

Texas Legislature introduced legislation in the 78th legislative session that would restrict those included in the top ten to only those high school students who complete a college-preparatory curriculum (the recommended curriculum for graduation versus the required curriculum). However, given that many predominantly impoverished and minority schools do not offer the recommended curriculum, passage of the law would then oppose the intent of the plan.

15. For Hardt and Negri (2000), "Fear of violence, poverty, and unemployment is in the end the primary and immediate force that creates and maintains these new segmentations. . . . As we argued earlier, the fundamental content of the information that the enormous communication corporations present is fear. The constant fear of poverty and anxiety over the future are the keys to creating a struggle among the poor for work and maintaining conflict among the imperial proletariat. Fear is the ultimate guarantee of the new segmentations" (339).

16. Woodward (1999) argued that in the postmodern economy, health industries project endless statistics in order to commodify fear, in what she calls "the pricing of panic," or the production of risk as commodity. However, this commodification of risk is part and parcel of insurance technologies developed in the nineteenth century (see Ewald 1991). Daston (1988) historicized insurance even further back to the "sale of maritime insurance and annuities . . . known since ancient times and revived in the fourteenth century by Italian entrepreneurs" (9).

17. For instance, Gould (1996) and Roberts (1997) discussed the case of Carrie Buck, whose right to reproduce was taken away due to her low IQ. While eugenics evokes these policies of sterilization, MacKenzie's point is that eugenics was much broader than sterilization, akin to DuBow's (1995) contention that racial science was not simply inconsequential pseudo-science, but gave birth to disciplines, particularly physical anthropology.

18. Russett (1989) attributed the pessimism of nineteenth-century social sciences to the application of the Second Law of Thermodynamics, which contained a principle that "when all mechanical energy had been transformed into heat at a uniformly low temperature life on earth would cease" (128). For Russett, the restrictive model of physics dominated social scientific ideology, versus the expansive view of biology (126). Additionally, as Protestantism infected capitalism, Calvinist determinism invaded social science despite the attempts of scientists to eschew religion as irrational (203).

19. See also Achieve, Inc. (2002) and Braceras (2002: 1130, 1136).

20. Shewart's observations echo Hacking's (1991) description of the "taming of chance" and the "erosion of determinism."

21. This is unlike Marshall, who sees an absence of physical constraints. Physical repression and discipline in education continually occur, particularly in schools with majority Black and Latino populations, spaces into which police and metal detectors have entered. See Devine 1996.

22. As Robinson (2000 [1983]) wrote, "From the twelfth century forward, it was the bourgeoisie and the administrators of state power who initiated and nurtured myths of egalitarianism while seizing every occasion to divide peoples for the purpose of their domination" (26).

23. One notable aspect of the politics of education in the 78th legislative session was the presence of only one woman on the Public Education Committee, Representative Glenda Dawson. At the first committee meeting, I noted that she had not spoken throughout the entire meeting, and even qualified it at the end by saying that she did have a voice.

24. According to Russett (1989), it was G. Stanley Hall's conception that "women were designed to be racial conduits rather than racial catalysts" (61).

## Chapter 5

1. At the meeting, the testimony of Dr. Angela Valenzuela exposed this contradiction, in which she historicized vouchers and Milton Friedman's proposals as a tool of evading desegregation orders, while acknowledging parents' disappointment with the current system. For Valenzuela, the accountability system allowed discrimination inherent in the current system to be "mask[ed] . . . through fuzzy math," but vouchers, which themselves were tools of evading the achievement of racial equality, were neither the answer to alleviating discrimination, nor the answer to providing more resources for students with disabilities (which was the argument of many of the Latino parents testifying for vouchers). (Her testimony, which, by the way, opened the door for the use of Spanish in following testimonies, seemed to be rushed.)

2. Cohen (1982) suggested that "in the 1790's, statistical thought offered a way to mediate between political ideas based on a homogeneous social order and economic realities that were fast undermining hegemony" (173).

3. The authors cited the National Research Council's *High Stakes: Testing for Tracking, Promotion, and Graduation*.

4. In the areas of employment and education, the cases that set this notion were *Griggs v. Duke Power Co.* (401 U.S. 424, 91 [S. Ct. 849] 1971), *Swann v. Charlotte-Mecklenburg Board of Education* (402 U.S. 1, 91 [S. Ct. 1267] 1971), *Wright v. Council of Emporia* (407 U.S. 451, 92 [S. Ct. 2196] 1972), and *Keyes v. Denver School District I* (413 U.S. 189, 93 [S. Ct. 2686] 1973) (see Freeman 1995).

5. D'Souza, in *The End of Racism* (1995), argued that proportionality or statistical representation should *not* qualify as proof of discrimination, yet he uses exactly statistical proportions and representation to prove the inferiority and pathology of Black culture.

6. Although Hardt and Negri (2000) proposed that postmodern racism is (Balibar's (1991) theory of) "differentialist racism" based on a "theory of segregation, [but] not on hierarchy" (193), I think that rather than "racism without the races," postmodern racism is more race without the racisms. Thus, I think

of the "new" racism as not simply "differentialist racism," but a *deferentialist* racism, a racism that moves at a differential to racism, denies that it exists, but retains the old forms of racial discourse.

7. Elul cited the following cases: *Quarles v. Oxford Mun. Separate School District* (1989); *Montgomery v. Starkville Mun. Separate School District* (1987).

8. In the decision, Prado cited the Report of Dr. Uri Treisman, testifying for the TEA, as acknowledgment of testing as past discrimination. In his testimony, cited in Gomez, Kastely, and Holleman (2000), Treisman argued, "The use of standardized tests in American education has a complex history. On the one hand, it is a well documented fact that they have served as principal instruments of discrimination and disenfranchisement. However, it is equally true and well-documented that such tests have been used to create more equitable access to higher education and career opportunities for immigrant and minority populations" (212).

9. See the discussion of "individualization [that] is 'descending'" versus "ascending" in Foucault 1995 (1978), 192–194.

10. Galton developed the concept of statistical dependence in his formulation of the concept of a statistical tendency or "regression" toward a mean or average, characterized by French engineer Emile Cheysson as "a kind of fatal, irresistible regression, of the individual type toward the average type of his race" (Desrosières 1998: 122). According to Desrosières, "The aim of statistical tools was to measure and undo the effects of heredity. If men could be classified in order, from the very best to the very worst, the technique of regression showed the proportion of specific qualities and defects in both good and bad that was preserved by heredity. . . . This led eugenicists to prophesy, using science to support their remarks, a bleak long-term future: if nothing was done, the quality of the English nation would inexorably decline" (128).

11. Quotes from Dr. Valencia are those I recorded in my notes while attending the forum entitled, "Forum on High-Stakes Testing, Accountability, and Minority Youth: A Forum for Discussion of the Issues" on March 25, 2003 at the University of Texas at Austin.

## Chapter 6

1. From this point forward, "April 30 testimony" designates witnesses testifying for the multiple criteria bills before the House Public Education Committee in a hearing on April 30, 2003. I transcribed the testimonies from a video-tape, and the testimonies are also available on the Texas House Web site: www.house.state.tx.us/committees/audio78/broadcasts.php?session=78& committeeCode=400.

2. Asad (2000: 29) suggested that social scientists appeal to narrative when statistics appear to rob subjects of agency.

3. Ironically, with the rise of Quetelet, it is the British sense of statistics as political arithmetic, mainly quantitative, and not the German sense of statistics as description that becomes the hegemonic sense of statistics.

4. According to Omi and Winant, "By 'trajectory,' we mean the pattern of conflict and accommodation which takes shape over time between racially based social movements and the policies and programs of the state" (1994: 78).

5. Representative Olivo even said to one male visitor who came, then quickly left in the midst of us scrambling to put together packets, "If you can't stand the heat . . ."

6. Because feminism is often associated with abortion rights, for example, the Christian, particularly Catholic, positionality of women in the office who opposed abortion might prevent them from identifying as feminist.

7. This exchange occurred at the Public Education Committee meeting on March 4, 2003, during testimony regarding Dutton's bill (HB 381) on counting dropouts.

8. For Foucault (1978), "[S]ilence and secrecy are a shelter for power, anchoring its prohibitions, but they also loosen its holds and provide for relatively obscure areas of tolerance" (101).

9. These stories came from an untitled document that I was given in addition to the "Organizer's Toolkit."

10. It may be, following Scott's (1991) conception of experience as discursively constructed, that the conflicts between the discourse of child abuse (a historical construction perhaps tied to the struggles against child labor) and the statistical discourse of testing "produce" the experiences. However, as Stone-Mediatore (1998) argued in critique of Joan Scott, "Equating experience with representations of experience . . . obscures the role of subjective experience in motivating and informing intervention in representational practices" (120). It is the experience of students that facilitates the conflict of the statistical discourse of testing and the discourse of child abuse.

11. For Davis-Floyd and Dumit (1998), "cyborgification" is a product of the technocratic model of envisioning human biology, stemming from both the Cartesian mind-body split and the gendered conception of women's bodies as "defective machine(s)" (4). In the early twentieth century, educational reformers used standardized testing as a method of extending that technocratic model to school systems, thereby constructing children as machines. Foucault (1995 [1978]) talked about the way in which discipline (of the examination) assigns an "aptitude" and thus "dissociates power from the body" (138). With the rise of the computer, the disembodiment of children accompanying technocratic disciplining in schools has reached new levels.

12. See note 9.

13. Foucault (1995 [1978]) talked about different types of individualization: the heroic autobiography and the numbered case handed out by the examination.

14. According to Latour, "The word **black box** is used by cyberneticians whenever a piece of machinery or a set of commands is too complex. In its place, they draw a little box about which they need to know nothing but its input and output" (1987: 2–3). Latour also used the term *black box* to refer to moments in which "many elements are made to act as one" (131).

15. These stories are from a handout that I was given while observing a staff member compose Representative Olivo's Web site.

16. Ibid.

17. See Collins's (1990) discussion of the conception of "lift as we climb" within Black women's organizational style. The origins of this conception lie within the vindicationist politics of the early twentieth century.

18. It must be noted that parent-child relationships do *not* absolve the problem of representation, given that mother-child and father-child relationships can be abusive and exploitative.

19. I video-taped and transcribed this segment of C-SPAN2, *Booknotes*, March 12, 2007.

20. Committee meetings are open for public debate. Floor activity refers to the meeting of the full House, and while the public can observe the proceedings, only the representatives take part in debate.

21. Fine (1991) found that in many cases, Black and Latino parents suspected that their children's teachers held racist views of them, preventing parents from establishing automatic (and uncritical) alliances with teachers.

## Chapter 7

1. This exchange occurred at the first meeting, on February 4, 2003, on HB 604, the sunset of the Robin Hood bill. Wayne Pierce as representative of the Equity Center had teamed with MALDEF in the *Edgewood* case that spawned the establishment of the finance equity law.

2. It is interesting that the committee continued to pose the question of "fear of the unknown" and "What are you afraid of?" in later meetings, particularly on the reincarnation of HB 604 in HB 5 and the voucher, or "freedom scholarship," bill, HB 2465.

3. Here, as in Chapter 2, I see segregation as an intersection of race and class—not in terms of *either* racial segregation *or* class segregation, but in terms of *both/and*.

4. Here, I use *differential* in reference to the conception by Hardt and Negri (2000) of racism as a "strategy of differential inclusion" (194). As I suggest in Chapters 3 and 4, while all students are objectified by the testing process, some students, particularly students of color, are objectified as invisible, as outside measure.

5. As Bourdieu and Passeron (1977) argued, technocratic, statistical conceptions of failure and educational output fail to provide a full understanding of failure and further preclude an "analysis of the educational system's system of functions" (154, 184).

6. See the exit poll conducted by the *Los Angeles Times* (2003) showing the racial, geographic, gender, and party breakdown for the support of Connerly's Proposition 54 (along with the recall vote).

7. This is particularly true given Desrosières's (2000) suggestion that the statistical concepts of unemployment and inequality were developed largely in

the context of Roosevelt's New Deal, becoming "commonplace in all Western countries after 1945" (199).

8. I refer here to DuBois's (1962 [1935]) term *economic enfranchisement* because I think it expresses the sense in which Moses uses it. For DuBois, while freed Blacks were politically enfranchised, they never achieved economic enfranchisement or economic emancipation that would guarantee the "real end to slavery" (351). Moses and Cobb (2001) wrote, "What is central now is the need for economic access; the political process has been opened—there are no formal barriers to voting, for example—but economic access, taking advantage of new technologies and economic opportunity, demands as much effort as the political struggle required in the 1960's" (6). In this sense, "math literacy . . . is the key to the future of disenfranchised communities" (5).

9. LaClau and Mouffe defined radical and plural democracy as a "strategy of the construction of a new order" (1985: 189) that depends on the "multiplication of political spaces and the preventing of the concentration of power in one point" (178); "the autonomization of the spheres of struggle"; the "social appropriation of production" (178); and the "construction of a new common sense" (183). I see these elements corresponding to Hardt and Negri's (2000) notion of *beyond measure* as a constituent-versus-deconstructive power formed from the multitude within Empire (59) and from below (357); as possessing collectivity (405), community, cooperation, and "expansive commonality" (358), and political autonomy (407). There are differences between *beyond measure* and *radical and plural democracy*, such as Hardt and Negri's focus on a "new city" and "global citizenship," whereas LaClau and Mouffe problematized the notion of citizenship and unitary subject (185), "society in general" (180), and "the totalitarian myth of the Ideal city" (190). LaClau and Mouffe differentiated radical and plural democracy from liberal democracy, and I stress this distinction given Frederic Jameson's conception of postmodern capitalism as the "democratization of oppression that none can escape" (Sandoval 2000: 36). While both concepts are characterized as "non-place," neither concept—radical and plural democracy or beyond measure—projects an uncritical utopian project. Where for LaClau and Mouffe utopianism fails to acknowledge diverse and various spaces (1985: 190), for Hardt and Negri, utopianism seeks an "outside," which is an impossibility in Empire, and instead beyond measure comes from within and is material (2000: 46, 58, 65).

10. Perhaps part of the third shift required in critiquing and producing statistics is to engage in mathematical education and literacy, instead of going beyond mathematics. In fact, mathematics can be seen as both an expression of the virtual (Hardt and Negri's "beyond measure") and a practice of the third space, or third shift, which King et al. (2002) likened to "deep talk," which emphasizes the "generative" process in which "there may never be an answer, at least not one answer" (404). I spent the last year of my training as a mathematics major envisioning spaces representable only as amoebas, conjecturing about the contents and dimensions of those spaces, where numbers were themselves assumptions in need of definition. In my topology class, my professor told

us that he could not imagine why physicists tried to take these abstract mathe-matical spaces and apply them to real life. Perhaps this study could be critiqued as a "pure" mathematician's objection to "applied" mathematics, since I once intended to obtain a doctoral degree in pure mathematics.

11. Perhaps my self-reflectivity, both in this section and throughout the text, can be subjected to the critique of reflexivity in ethnographic accounts: that it engages in "ethnographic self-indulgence" (Bruner in Denzin 1997: 218) and simply constitutes a "confessional text" (see Denzin 1997: 221). Visweswaran (1994) as well as Caplan (1988–1989) and Wolfe (1992) (see Denzin 1997: 221) argued that these critiques tend to be deployed against feminist writings, while reflexive ethnographies by men tend to be characterized as "experimental," cre-ating paradigms, genres, and "vital technique(s)" (Marcus and Cushman 1982 in Visweswaran 1994). The use or deployment of the term *confession* to de-scribe feminist reflexivity is interesting given Foucault's (1978) conception of the confession as "the standard governing the production of the true discourse on sex" (63). For Foucault, psychological and psychiatric sciences absorbed the confession into their discourse, through the institutionalization of the clinical oral examination; the interpretation of the telling of personal histories that could reveal hidden causes, which were largely sex related; and the "medical-ization of the effects of the confession," wherein confessions produced thera-peutic and healing effects (65–67). Interestingly, the practices of orally examin-ing and interpreting personal histories to reveal hidden truths are constitutive of the ethnographic project. Rosaldo (1976) suggested, "[T]he prevailing an-thropological view is as follows: place a tape-recorder in front of Mr. Non-literate Everyman and he will tell the 'real truth' about his life," and through ethnography we can elicit "a revelation of the dark and hidden depths of . . . intimate and private being[s]" (quoted in Behar 1993: 272). I consider feminist reflexivity to be a search or a call for ethical practices within ethnography/an-thropology that is both confessional and not confessional. The confession, as a form of "asceticism" within Christian ethics, is a means for self-purification, a liberatory revealing of the hidden of the self, a means to an end (Foucault 1984: 354, 355). In one sense, so-called confessional texts do have a therapeutic and cleansing value for the ethnographer. However, according to Visweswaran (1994), the discomfort caused by feminist "confessional" texts within anthro-pology rests in their critique of the ethnographer-as-self because "calling them-selves into question" (31) simultaneously questioned the limitations of ethno-graphic understanding itself, thus precluding any confessional purification of anthropology (see also Enslin 1994; Gordon 1993). As Sister Insider/Outsider (see Lorde 1984), I am both inside and outside the confessional, inside and outside anthropology. Being raised as a Black Catholic, I have a sense of ethics unquestionably shaped by (Western) Christian ethics, at the same time that I consider myself coming from a Black radical tradition deeply inspired by lib-eration theology (see Cook 1995) that focuses not only on self-critique, but also a critique of the power of the Church (Bell 2002: 80, 81). These confessions of my failures to decolonize anthropology are admittedly a form of Christian as-

ceticism, a therapeutic telling of the truth of my experience, yet also an admission of the painful experience of double consciousness, of the inability of my Black skin to shed the White mask (Fanon 1967; Sandoval 2000) or to escape the oppressor within (Lorde 1984; Smith 1998).

12. According to Anzaldúa (1983), "I can write this and yet realize that many of us women of color who have strung degrees, credentials and published books around our necks like pearls that we hang onto for dear life are in danger of contributing to the invisibility of our sister-writers. 'La Vendida,' the sell-out" (167).

13. For this political reason, I expanded my vision to include Urla's (1993) concept of "statistical subjectivity," but also to suggest that the challenge of statistics was neither new nor originated in my research. However, if DuBois found himself rearticulated by Southern lawyers fighting desegregation (Kluger 1975: 546), then I must accept that by the very act of writing, our work—particularly the work of people of color, who are at once hypervisible and invisible (Lorde 1984: 42)—enters into a charged political field and is always susceptible to critique and rearticulation.

14. In mathematics, research depends on finding an "open problem," one that no one else has solved. I found that by going to social science, I could not avoid the pressure to find an "open problem" or "nuance" in the field.

15. As I learned for the first time over the session, the committee chair makes the decision as to which bills come before the committee. While the notion of a public committee hearing makes the process appear democratic, the selection of bills seemed totalitarian in my view. Not only were Representative Olivo's bills not heard until late into the session, but the hearings were scheduled on a day in which House proceedings extended beyond midnight. Further, committee deliberations and voting could take place on the House floor, where the public was not permitted, and often at times when not all committee members, particularly dissenting members, were present—as was the case with the passing of Representative Grusendorf's HB 2465, the "freedom scholarship," or voucher, bill.

16. See Chapter 5 for a critique of the notion of progress.

17. As Pérez (1999) wrote, "Our social psychological, and spiritual well-being continues to depend upon the discursive disordering of 'power's' collectively imposed imaginings" (39).

18. For Scheper-Hughes (1995), "the ethical" is "precultural to the extent that our human existence as social beings presupposes the presence of the other" (419). However, responding to Scheper-Hughes, Ong questioned this conception of "precultural," being "uncomfortable with her sense of political righteousness," asking "What are the political implications of an anthropologist's firm moral position in the face of the actual play of negotiation, contradiction, and interchange with other moralities?" (in Scheper-Hughes 1995: 429). By this critique Ong does not imply abandoning ethics; rather, she calls into question a type of moralizing that reproduces the ideology of Third World "development" in need of salvation by the West, which is present in

Scheper-Hughes's article. For Ong, "an ethical anthropology must be more aware of the local effects of geopolitics, transnational capitalism, and rescue anthropology" (in Scheper-Hughes 1995: 430). Ong's concept of ethics is similar to Foucault's concept of ethical self-criticism that abandons the search for universality and authenticity in favor of historically investigating the constitution of (our)selves as subjects (McNay 1992: 98).

19. On the hearing for the Head Start bill, 2210 in the U.S. House, Representative Maxine Waters descended to the podium after other Black and Latino representatives presented the case opposing the privatization of funds for Head Start, and said, "This is breaking my heart." I recorded these comments while viewing House proceedings on C-SPAN, July 24, 2003.

# Bibliography

Abu-Lughod, Lila. 1990. The Romance of Resistance: Tracing Transformations of Power through Bedouin Women. American Ethnologist 17(1):41–55.

Achieve, Inc. 2002. Aiming Higher: Meeting the Challenges of Educational Reform in Texas. http://www.tea.state.tx.us/curriculum/aimhitexas.pdf. Accessed December 4, 2002.

Adorno, Theodor, and Max Horkheimer. 1979 [1944]. Dialectic of Enlightenment. John Cumming, trans. London: Verso.

Alonso, William, and Paul Starr, eds. 1987. The Politics of Numbers. New York: Russell Sage Foundation.

Althusser, Louis. 1971. Lenin and Philosophy and Other Essays. New York: Monthly Review Press.

Anderson, James D. 1988. The Education of Blacks in the South, 1860–1935. Chapel Hill: University of North Carolina Press.

Anderson, S. E. 1970. Mathematics and the Struggle for Liberation. The Black Scholar. 2:20–27.

Anzaldúa, Gloria. 1983. Speaking in Tongues: A Letter to Third World Women Writers. In This Bridge Called My Back: Writings by Radical Women of Color. 2nd Edition. Cherríe Moraga and Gloria Anzaldúa, eds., pp. 165–176. New York: Kitchen Table, Women of Color Press.

———.1990. Bridge, Drawbridge, Sandbar or Island: Lesbians of Color Hacienda Alianzas. In Bridges of Power: Women's Multicultural Alliances. Lisa Albrecht and Rose Brewer, eds., pp. 216–231. Philadelphia: New Society Publishers.

———. 1999. Borderlands/La Frontera: The New Mestiza. 2nd Edition. San Francisco: Aunt Lute.

Appadurai, Arjun. 1993. Number in the Colonial Imagination. *In* Orientalism and the Post-Colonial Predicament. Carol A. Breckenridge and Peter van der Veer, eds., pp. 314–339. Philadelphia: University of Philadelphia Press.

Apple, Michael W. 2001. Educating the Right Way: Markets, Standards, God, and Inequality. New York: RoutledgeFalmer.

Apple, Michael W., and Lois Weis. 1983. Ideology and Practice in Schooling. Philadelphia: Temple University Press.

Archibald, George. 2004. School Reform Breaks "Segregation": Paige Likens Opposition to Era of Racism. Washington Times. January 8: A3. http://www.lexisnexis.com/universe. Accessed January 9, 2004.

Aronowitz, Stanley, and Henry Giroux. 1991. Postmodern Education: Politics, Culture, and Social Criticism. Minneapolis: University of Minnesota Press.

Asad, Talal. 1994. Ethnographic Representation, Statistics, and Modern Power. Social Research 61(1):55–88.

2000 Agency and Pain: An Exploration. Culture and Religion 1(1):29–60.

Asad, Talal, ed. 1973. Anthropology and the Colonial Encounter. London: Ithaca Press.

Asbury, Charles A. 1978. An Essay on the Proper Relation between Testing and School Desegregation: A Non-Technical Opinion. Journal of Negro Education 47(1):69–71.

Ascher, Carol. 1990. Can Performance-Based Assessments Improve Urban Schooling? ERIC Digest 56.

Austin Chronicle. 2002. AISD's Haves and Have Nots. Austin Chronicle. March 22. http://www.austinchronicle.com/issues/dispatch/2002-03-22/pols_feature4.html. Accessed April 21, 2002.

Bacon, David. 2001. The Trouble with Testing. La Prensa San Diego. November 21. http://www.laprensa-sandiego.org/archieve/november21/TESTING.HTM. Accessed November 17, 2004.

Baker, Lee. 1998. From Savage to Negro. Berkeley: University of California Press.

Baker, R. Scott. 2001. The Paradoxes of Desegregation: Race, Class, and Education, 1935–1975. American Journal of Education 109(3):320–343.

Balandier, George. 1966 [1951]. The Colonial Situation: A Theoretical Approach. *In* Social Change: The Colonial Situation. Immanuel Wallerstein, ed., pp. 34–61. New York: Wiley.

Balibar, Etienne. 1991. Is There a "Neo-Racism"? *In* Race, Nation, Class: Ambiguous Identities. E. Balibar and E. Wallerstein, eds., pp. 17–28. London: Verso.

Balta, Victor. 2002. End Creative Teaching, Official Says. The Record. (Stockton, CA) October 25: B1, B4.

Bartlett, Lesley, Marla Frederick, Thaddeus Gulbrandsen, and Enrique Murillo. 2002. The Marketization of Education: Public Schools for Private Ends. Anthropology and Education Quarterly 33(1):5–29.

Baudrillard, Jean. 1983. Simulations. Paul Foss, Paul Patton, and Philip Beitchman, trans. New York: Semiotext(e).

Beaumont Enterprise. 2003. Test Misleads about Extent of Learning. Beaumont Enterprise. (Beaumont, TX) April 4.

Behar, Ruth. 1993. Translated Woman: Crossing the Border with Esperanza's Story. Boston: Beacon Press.

Bell, Derrick. 1995. Serving Two Masters: Integration Ideals and Client Interests in School Desegregation Litigation. In Critical Race Theory: The Key Writings That Informed the Movement. Kimberlé Crenshaw et al., eds., pp. 5–19. New York: The New Press.

———. 2002. Ethical Ambition: Living a Life of Meaning and Worth. New York: Bloomsbury.

Bernal, Ernesto. 1999. Item-Factor Analysis of the 1977 Exit-Level Tests. Plaintiff's Expert Witness Testimony (Exhibit P1). In GI Forum et al. v. Texas Education Agency et al., No. Civ A, SA-97-CA1278-EP, 2000 WL 222268 (W.D. Tex. January 7, 2000).

Bernstein, Jake. 2002. Test Case: Hard Lessons from the TAAS. Texas Observer. August 30, 94(16):4.

Black Commentator. 2002. Trojan Horse Watch: Bush Funds Black Voucher Front Group, Your Tax Dollars Pay for Propaganda Blitz. November 14. http://www.blackcommentator.com/16_thw.html. Accessed November 19, 2002.

Blackwell, Kathy. 2003. Students Rise to Challenge of Tougher Test in Reading: Third Graders Breeze through State's New Assessment Tests. Austin American-Statesman. March 19: B1.

Blalock, Glenn, and Rich Haswell. 2002. Student Views of TAAS. http://comppile.tamucc.edu/TAAS/index.html. Accessed October 23, 2002.

Blanton, Kevin Carlos. 2000. "They Cannot Master Abstractions, but They Can Often Be Made Efficient Workers": Race and Class in the Intelligence Testing of Mexican Americans and African Americans in Texas during the 1920s. Social Science Quarterly 81(4):1014–1026.

———. 2003. From Intellectual Deficiency to Cultural Deficiency: Mexican Americans, Testing, and Public School Policy in the American Southwest, 1920–1940. Pacific Historical Review 72(1):39–62.

Blauner, Robert. 1987. Colonized and Immigrant Minorities. In From Different Shores: Perspectives on Race and Ethnicity in America. Ronald Takaki, ed. pp. 149–160. New York: Oxford University Press.

Blommaert, Jan, James Collins, Monica Heller, Ben Rampton, Stef Slembrouck, and Jef Verschueren. 2001. Discourse and Critique: Part I. Critique of Anthropology 21(1):5–12.

Booher-Jennings, Jennifer. 2005. Below the Bubble: "Educational Triage" and the Texas Accountability System. American Educational Research Journal 42(2):231–268.

Bourdieu, Pierre. 1977. Outline of a Theory of Practice. Richard Nice, trans. Cambridge: Cambridge University Press.

Bourdieu, Pierre, and Jean-Claude Passeron. 1977. Reproduction in Education, Society, and Culture. Richard Nice, trans. London: Sage.

Bowles, Samuel, and Herbert Gintis. 1976. Schooling in Capitalist America: Educational Reform and the Contradictions of Economic Life. New York: Basic Books/Harper.

Braceras, Jennifer. 2002. Killing the Messenger: The Misuse of Disparate Impact Theory to Challenge High-Stakes Educational Tests. Vanderbilt Law Review 55(4):1111–1203. http://www.lexisnexis.com/universe. Accessed October 23, 2002.

Bracey, Gerald W. 2002. The 12th Bracey Report on the Condition of Public Education. Phi Delta Kappan 84(2):135–150.

Briggs, Charles. 1986. Learning How to Ask: A Sociolinguistic Appraisal of the Role of the Interview in Social Science Research. Cambridge: Cambridge University Press.

Brooks, A. Phillip. 1995a. Senate Approves Education Overhaul: Sweeping Measures Eases No-Pass, No-Play and Loosens State Control of the Schools. Austin American-Statesman. March 28: A1. http://www.lexisnexis.com/universe. Accessed June 4, 2004.

——. 1995b. Black, Hispanic Lawmakers Fail to Kill Home Rule. Austin American-Statesman. May 5: B3. http://www.lexisnexis.com/universe. Accessed June 4, 2004.

Browne, Kingsley R. 1993. Statistical Proof of Discrimination: Beyond "Damned Lies." Washington Law Review 68(3):477–558. http://www.lexisnexis.com/universe. Accessed April 7, 2004.

Burchell, Graham, Colin Gordon, and Peter Miller, eds. 1991. The Foucault Effect: Studies in Governmentality. Chicago: University of Chicago Press.

Burk, Kelly. 2000. In Support of the Fairness and Accuracy in Testing Act. Testimony on Behalf of the National Education Association. http://www.nea.org/lac/testimon/fairness.html. Accessed April 9, 2003.

Butler, Judith. 1993. Bodies That Matter: On the Discursive Limits of "Sex." New York: Routledge.

Caplan, Patricia. 1988–1989. Engendering Knowledge: The Politics of Ethnography. Anthropology Today 4(5):8–12; 4(6):14–17.

Castel, Robert. 1991. From Dangerousness to Risk. In The Foucault Effect: Studies in Governmentality. Graham Burchell, Colin Gordon, and Peter Miller, eds., pp. 281–298. Chicago: University of Chicago Press.

Cherry, Robert. 1997. Myrdal's Cumulative Hypothesis: Its Antecedents and Its Contemporary Applications. In A Different Vision: Race and Public Policy. Vol. 2. Thomas D. Boston, ed., pp. 17–37. London: Routledge.

Cicotti, Giovanni, Marcello Cini, and Michelangelo de Maria. 1976. The Production of Science in an Advanced Capitalist Society. In The Political Economy of Science: Ideology of/in the Natural Sciences. Hilary Rose and Steven Rose, eds., pp. 32–58. London: Macmillan.

Clack, Cary. 2003. Parents Supportive of Daughter's Plan to Boycott TAKS. San Antonio Express News. February 1: B1.

Clark, A. Kim. 1998. Race, "Culture," and Mestizaje: The Statistical Construction of the Ecuadorian Nation, 1930–1950. Journal of Historical Sociology 11(2):185–211.

Clark, Burton R. 1961. The "Cooling-Out" Process in Higher Education. In Education, Economy, and Society. A. H. Halsey, Jean Floud, and C. Arnold Andersen, eds., pp. 513–523. New York: Free Press.

Clifford, James. 1988. The Predicament of Culture: Twentieth Century Ethnography, Literature, and Art. Cambridge, MA: Harvard University Press.

Clinton, William. 1999. Remarks at the National Governors' Association Meeting. Weekly Compilation of Presidential Documents. March 1. 35(8):275(4).

Cockerill, Bill. 1977. Segregation in Austin Hits All-Time High: History Student's Study Blames Administrative Practices. Daily Texan. June 6.

Cohen, Patricia Cline. 1982. A Calculating People: The Spread of Numeracy in Early America. Chicago: University of Chicago Press.

Collins, James. 2001. Selling the Market: Educational Standards, Discourse, and Social Inequality. Critique of Anthropology 21(2):143–163.

Collins, Patricia Hill. 1990. Black Feminist Thought: Knowledge, Consciousness, and the Politics of Empowerment. New York: Routledge.

———. 1998. Fighting Words: Black Women and the Search for Justice. Minneapolis: University of Minnesota Press.

Confrey, Jere, dir. 2001. Systemic Crossfire: Students Speak Out on TAAS. SYRCE, Department of Curriculum and Instruction, University of Texas at Austin.

Confrey, Jere, Angela Valenzuela, and Alba Ortiz. 2002. Recommendations to the Texas State Board of Education on the Setting of the TAKS Standards: A Call to Responsible Action. November 12. Paper presented at the State Board of Education meeting (Austin, Texas), November 14.

Cook, Anthony E. 1995. Beyond Critical Legal Studies: The Reconstructive Theology of Dr. Martin Luther King, Jr. In Critical Race Theory: The Key Writings That Informed the Movement. Kimberlé Crenshaw et al., eds., pp. 85–102. New York: The New Press.

Cook, Glenn. 2005. Title I at 40. American School Board Journal. 192(4):24–26.

Copelin, Laylan. 2003. Lawmakers Will Jump into TAKS Debate: Rally against Such "High Stakes Testing" Is Planned for Saturday. Austin American-Statesman. January 22: B1.

Cox, Oliver. 1948. Caste, Class, and Race: A Study in Social Dynamics. New York: Monthly Review Press.

Crenshaw, Kimberlé. 1995. Mapping the Margins: Intersectionality, Identity Politics, and Violence Against Women of Color. In Critical Race Theory: Key Writings That Formed the Movement. Crenshaw, Kimberlé, Neil

Gotanda, Gary Peller, and Kendall Thomas, eds., pp. 357–383. New York: The New Press.

Crenshaw, Kimberlé, Neil Gotanda, Gary Peller, and Kendall Thomas, eds. 1995. Critical Race Theory: Key Writings That Formed the Movement. New York: The New Press.

Croissant, Jennifer L. 1998. Growing Up Cyborg: Developmental Stories for Postmodern Children. In Cyborg Babies: From Techno-Sex to Techno-Tots. Robbie Davis-Floyd and Joseph Dumit, eds., pp. 285–300. New York: Routledge.

Curtis, Bruce. 2002. Foucault on Governmentality and Population: The Impossible Discovery. Canadian Journal of Sociology 27(4):505(30).

Danziger Kurt. 1997. Naming the Mind: How Psychology Found Its Language. London: Sage.

Daston, Lorraine. 1988. Classical Probability in the Enlightenment. Princeton, NJ: Princeton University Press.

Davidson, Chandler. 1990. Race and Class in Texas Politics. Princeton, NJ: Princeton University Press.

Davis, Angela. 1983 [1981]. Women, Race, and Class. New York: Vintage Books.

Davis, Charles Edwin. 1975. United States v. Texas Education Agency et al.: The Politics of Busing. PhD Dissertation, University of Texas, Austin.

Davis-Floyd, Robbie, and Joseph Dumit. 1998. Cyborg Babies: From Techno-Sex to Techno-Tots. New York: Routledge.

Denzin, Norman K. 1997. Interpretive Ethnography: Ethnographic Practices for the 21ˢᵗ Century. Thousand Oaks, CA: Sage Publications.

Desrosières, Alain. 1998. The Politics of Large Numbers: A History of Statistical Reasoning. Camille Naish, trans. Cambridge, MA: Harvard University Press.

Deveaux, Monique. 1994. Feminism and Empowerment: A Critical Reading of Foucault. Feminist Studies 20(2):223–247.

Devine, John. 1996. Maximum Security: The Culture of Violence in Inner City Schools. Chicago: University of Chicago Press.

Dickens, Charles. 1996 [1907]. Hard Times. London: Everyman.

Donato, Ruben. 1997. The Other Struggle for Equal Schools: Mexican Americans during the Civil Rights Era. Albany: State University of New York Press.

Donzelot, Jacques. 1991a. The Mobilization of Society. In The Foucault Effect: Studies in Governmentality. Graham Burchell, Colin Gordon, and Peter Miller, eds., pp. 169–179. Chicago: University of Chicago Press.

———. 1991b. Pleasure in Work. In The Foucault Effect: Studies in Governmentality. Graham Burchell, Colin Gordon, and Peter Miller, eds., pp. 251–280. Chicago: University of Chicago Press.

Dowdell, Erika, Albert Cortez, Lenina Nadal, and Penda Hair. 2001. Symposium Proceedings: Building a Multiracial Social Justice Movement Session One: Accessing Higher Education as a Multiracial Movement: The

Importance of Student Movements. NYU Review of Law and Social Change 27: 5–30. http://www.lexisnexis.com/universe. Accessed June 22, 2003.

Downing, Margaret. 2002. Wake-Up Call: The TAKS Field Test Results Were So Gawd-Awful They May Become a Catalyst for Good. Houston Press. November 28. http://www.lexisnexis.com/universe. Accessed November 17, 2004.

Drake, St. Clair. 1980. Anthropology and the Black Experience. The Black Scholar 11(7): 2–31.

D'Souza, Dinesh. 1995. The End of Racism: Principles for a Multiracial Society. New York: Free Press.

DuBois, W.E.B. 1962 [1935]. Black Reconstruction in America, 1860–1880. New York: Russell and Russell.

DuBow, Saul. 1995. Scientific Racism in Modern South Africa. Cambridge: Cambridge University Press.

Dumit, Joseph, and Robbie Davis-Floyd. 1998. Introduction. Cyborg Babies: Children of the Third Millenium. In Cyborg Babies: From Techno-Sex to Techno-Tots. Robbie Davis-Floyd and Joseph Dumit, eds., pp. 1–18. New York: Routledge.

Dumit, Joseph, with Sylvia Sensiper. 1998. Living with the "Truths" of DES: Toward and Anthropology of Facts. In Cyborg Babies: From Techno-Sex to Techno-Tots. Robbie Davis-Floyd and Joseph Dumit, eds., pp. 1–18. New York: Routledge.

Easlea, Brian. 1990. Patriarchy, Scientists, and Nuclear Warriors. In Issues in Feminism: An Introduction to Women's Studies. S. Ruth, ed., pp. 70–82. Mountain View, CA: Mayfield Publishing.

Eaton, Tim. 2003. Study: Risks Exist if Kids Repeat Grade: Third Graders Must Pass TAKS Test for Promotion. Corpus Christi Caller-Times. March 23. http://c4.zedo.com//ads2/f/20832/3853/172/0/1620000215/0/162/185/zz-V1-pop1048595224956.html. Accessed March 25, 2003.

Edelman, Marian Wright. 2002. Mr. President, We Want Our Slogan Back. National Catholic Reporter. August 2: 25.

Elliot, Jane, and R. G. Ratcliffe. 2003. House Approves Cap on Malpractice Awards. Houston Chronicle. March 29:A1. http://www.lexisnexis.com/universe. Accessed June 2, 2004.

Elul, Hagit. 1999. Making the Grade, Public Education Reform: The Use of Standardized Testing to Retain Students and Deny Diplomas. Columbia Human Rights Law Review 30: 495–536. http://www.lexisnexis.com/universe. Accessed November 8, 2001.

Enslin, Elizabeth. 1994. Beyond Writing: Feminist Practice and the Limitations of Ethnography. Cultural Anthropology 9(4):537–568.

Epstein, Barbara. 1995. Why Post-Structuralism Is a Dead End for Progressive Thought. Socialist Review 25(2):83–119.

Esdall, Thomas B., and Brian Faler. 2002. Lott Remarks on Thurmond Echoed 1980 Words: Criticism Unabated Despite Apology for Comment on Former Dixiecrat's Presidential Bid. Washington Post. December 11: A6. http://www.lexisnexis.com/universe. Accessed September 6, 2004.

Ewald, François. 1991. Insurance and Risk. In The Foucault Effect: Studies in Governmentality. Graham Burchell, Colin Gordon, and Peter Miller, eds., pp. 197–210. Chicago: University of Chicago Press.

Fabian, Johannes. 1983. Time and the Other: How Anthropology Makes Its Object. New York: Columbia University Press.

Fanon, Frantz. 1967. Black Skin, White Masks. Charles Lam Markmann, trans. New York: Grove Press.

Farr, J. Steven, and Mark Trachtenberg. 1999. The Edgewood Drama: An Epic Quest for Education Equity. Yale Law and Policy Review 17(2):607–727.

Feinburg, Stephen E. 1992. A Brief History of Statistics in Three and One-Half Chapters: A Review Essay. Statistical Science 7(2):208–225.

Feldstein, Ruth. 2000. Motherhood in Black and White: Race and Sex in American Liberalism, 1930–1965. Ithaca, NY: Cornell University Press.

Fine, Michelle. 1991. Framing Dropouts: Notes on the Politics of an Urban Public High School. Albany: State University of New York Press.

Fischer, Frank. 1990. Technocracy and the Politics of Expertise. Newbury Park, CA: Sage.

Fischer, Michael M. J. 1991. Anthropology as Cultural Critique: Inserts of Science, Visual-Virtual Realities, and Post-Trauma Polities. Cultural Anthropology 6:525–537.

Foley, Douglas E. 2002. Critical Ethnography: The Reflexive Turn. Qualitative Studies in Education 15(5):469–490.

Fordham, Signithia, and John Ogbu. 1986. Black Students' School Success: Coping with the "Burden of 'Acting White.'" Urban Review 18(3):176–206.

Foucault, Michel. 1972. The Archaeology of Knowledge and the Discourse on Language. A. M. Sheridan Smith, trans. New York: Pantheon Books.

———. 1978. The History of Sexuality. Vol. 1. Robert Hurley, trans. New York: Vintage Books.

———. 1983. The Subject and Power. In Michel Foucault: Beyond Structuralism and Hermeneutics. 2nd Edition. H. Dreyfus and P. Rabinow, eds., pp. 208–226. Chicago: University of Chicago Press.

———. 1984a. Truth and Power. In The Foucault Reader. Paul Rabinow, ed., pp. 51–75. New York: Pantheon.

———. 1984b. Nietzsche, Genealogy, History. In The Foucault Reader. Paul Rabinow, ed., pp. 76–100. New York: Pantheon.

———. 1984c. On the Genealogy of Ethics: An Overview of Work in Progress. In The Foucault Reader. Paul Rabinow, ed., pp. 340–372. New York: Pantheon.

———. 1988a. The Minimalist Self. In Michel Foucault: Politics Philosophy Culture: Interviews and Other Writings. Lawrence Kritzman, ed., Alan Sheridan and others, trans., pp. 3–16. New York: Routledge.

———. 1988b. An Aesthetics of Existence. *In* Michel Foucault: Politics Philosophy Culture: Interviews and Other Writings. Lawrence Kritzman, ed., Alan Sheridan and others, trans., pp. 47–53. New York: Routledge

———. 1988c. Politics and Reason. *In* Michel Foucault: Politics Philosophy Culture: Interviews and Other Writings. Lawrence Kritzman, ed., Alan Sheridan and others, trans., pp. 57–85. New York: Routledge.

———. 1988d. On Power. *In* Michel Foucault: Politics Philosophy Culture: Interviews and Other Writings. Lawrence Kritzman, ed., Alan Sheridan and others, trans., pp. 96–109. New York: Routledge.

———. 1991. Governmentality. *In* The Foucault Effect: Studies in Governmentality. Graham Burchell, Colin Gordon, and Peter Miller, eds., pp. 87–104. Chicago: University of Chicago Press.

———. 1994 [1971]. The Order of Things: An Archaeology of the Human Sciences. New York: Vintage Books.

———. 1994 [1973]. The Birth of the Clinic: An Archaeology of Medical Perception. A. M. Sheridan Smith, trans. New York: Vintage Books.

———. 1995 [1978]. Discipline and Punish: The Birth of the Prison. 2nd Edition. Alan Sheridan, trans. New York: Vintage.

Fraser, Steven, ed. 1994. The Bell Curve Wars: Race, Intelligence, and the Future of America. New York: Basic Books.

Frasier, Mary M. 1997. Multiple Criteria: The Mandate and the Challenge. Roeper Review. 20(2):A-4(3).

Freeman, Allan D. 1995. Legitimizing Racial Discrimination through Anti-Discrimination Law: A Critical Review of Supreme Court Doctrine. *In* Critical Race Theory: The Key Writings That Informed the Movement. Kimberlé Crenshaw et al., eds., pp. 29–45. New York: The New Press.

Freire, Paulo. 1993 [1970]. Pedagogy of the Oppressed. New York: Continuum.

Fry, Gladys-Marie. 2001 [1975]. Night Riders in Black Folk History. Chapel Hill: University of North Carolina Press.

Gardner, H. 1983. Frames of Mind: The Theory of Multiple Intelligences. New York: Basic Books.

Garza-Falcon, Leticia. 1998. Gente Decente: A Borderlands Response to the Rhetoric of Dominance. Austin: University of Texas Press.

Gilroy, Paul. 1993. The Black Atlantic: Modernity and Double Consciousness. Cambridge, MA: Harvard University Press.

———. 2000. Against Race: Imagining Political Culture beyond the Color Line. Cambridge, MA: Belknap Press.

Gluckman, Amy. 2002. Testing . . . Testing . . . One, Two, Three. Dollars and Sense: The Magazine of Economic Justice 239 (January–February). http://www.dollarsandsense.org/archives/2002/0102gluckman.html. Accessed July 13, 2002.

Gomez, Placido, Amy Kastely, and Michelle Holeman, eds. 2000. The Texas Assessment of Academic Skills Exit Test—"Driver of Equity" or "Ticket to

Nowhere"? Scholar: St. Mary's Law Review on Minority Issues 2: 187–247. http://www.lexisnexis.com/universe. Accessed February 7, 2002.

Gordon, Colin. 1991. Governmental Rationality: An Introduction. *In* The Foucault Effect: Studies in Governmentality. Graham Burchell, Colin Gordon, and Peter Miller, eds., pp. 1–51. Chicago: University of Chicago Press.

Gordon, Deborah A. 1993. Worlds of Consequences: Feminist Ethnography as Social Action. Critique of Anthropology 13(4):429–443.

Gough, Kathleen. 1968. Anthropology and Imperialism. Monthly Review 19(11):12–27.

Gould, Stephen Jay. 1996. The Mismeasure of Man. New York: W. W. Norton.

Graham, Chad. 2001. Testing Service Not Revamping Practices in Iowa City. Associated Press State and Local Wire. April 12. http://www.lexisnexis.com/universe. Accessed February 18, 2008.

Gramsci, Antonio. 1971. Selections from the Prison Notebooks of Antonio Gramsci. Quintin Hoare and Geoffrey N. Smith, eds. and trans. New York: International Publishers.

——. 1988. An Antonio Gramsci Reader: Selected Writings, 1916–1935. David Forgacs, ed. New York: Schocken Books.

Greenberger, Steven R. 1993. A Productivity Approach to Disparate Impact and the Civil Rights Act of 1991. Oregon Law Review 72:253–322.

Greene, Linda. 1995. Race in the Twenty-First Century: Equality through Law? *In* Critical Race Theory: The Key Writings That Informed the Movement. Kimberlé Crenshaw et al., eds., pp. 292–301. New York: The New Press.

Gusterson, Hugh. 1996. Nuclear Rites: A Weapons Laboratory at the End of the Cold War. Berkeley: University of California Press.

Guthrie, James W. 1994. Do America's Schools Need a "Dow Jones Index"? Clearing House 68(2):98–103.

Gutierrez, Bridget. 2002. Staggering Failure Rate Feared on TAKS Test. San Antonio Express-News. December 18: 1A.

——. 2003a. Updated: TAKS Proves Tough for Many High School Students. San Antonio Express-News. May 30. http://news.mysanantonio.com/story.cfm?xla=saen&xlb=320&xlc=1004533. Accessed June 2, 2003.

——. 2003b. TAKS Produces Massive Failures. San Antonio Express-News. May 31. http://news.mysanantonio.com/story.cfm?xla=saen&xlb=320&xlc=1004781. Accessed June 2, 2003.

——. 2003c. 11,000 Fail Final TAKS Try: These Third-Graders Will Be Retained Unless Parents Appeal and Win. (Correction appended.) San Antonio Express-News. July 24: 1B.

——. 2003d. 537 Failed TAKS for 3rd-Graders in County; but Official Says Passing Rate of 97% Exceeded Expectations. San Antonio Express-News. July 25: 1B.

Gutiérrez, José Angel. 1998. The Making of a Chicano Miltant: Lessons from Cristal. Madison: University of Wisconsin Press.

Gwaltney, John Langston. 1980. Drylongso: A Self-Portrait of Black America. New York: Vintage Books.

Habermas, Jurgen. 1989. The Public Sphere. In Jurgen Habermas on Society and Politics: A Reader. S. Seidman, ed., pp. 231–236. Boston: Beacon Press.

Hacking, Ian. 1991. How Should We Do the History of Statistics? In The Foucault Effect: Studies in Governmentality. G. Burchell, C. Gordon, and P. Miller, eds., pp. 181–195. Chicago: University of Chicago Press.

Haggerty, Kevin D. 2002. The Politics of Statistics: Variations on a Theme. Book Reviews. Canadian Journal of Sociology 27(1):89–105.

Hale, Charles R. 2001. What Is Activist Research? Items and Issues 2(1–2):13–15.

Haney, Walter. 1999. Supplementary Report on Texas Assessment of Academic Skills Exit Test (TAAS-X). Plaintiff's Expert Witness Testimony (Exhibit P52) in GI Forum et al. v. Texas Education Agency et al., No. Civ A, SA-97-CA1278-EP, 2000 WL 222268 (W.D. Tex. January 7, 2000).

———. 2000. The Myth of the Texas Miracle in Education. Education Policy Analysis Archives 8(41). http://epaa.asu.edu/v8n41/. Accessed August 24, 2000.

Haraway, Donna. 1988. Situated Knowledges: The Science Question in Feminism and the Privilege of Partial Perspective. Feminist Studies 14(3):575–599.

Harding, Sandra. 1991. Whose Science? Whose Knowledge? Thinking from Women's Lives. Ithaca, NY: Cornell University Press.

Harding, Sandra, ed. 1993. Racial Economy of Science: Toward a Democratic Future. Bloomington: Indiana University Press.

Hardt, Michael, and Antonio Negri. 2000. Empire. Cambridge, MA: Harvard University Press.

Hardy, Lawrence. 2003. Helping Students Destress. Education Digest 68(9):10–17.

Harris, Ernest. 1992. The One City Plan That Has Worked: Segregation in Austin. Austin Chronicle. February 28: 7–9.

Heise, Michael. 2002. Educational Jujitsu: How School Finance Lawyers Learn to Turn Standards and Accountability into Dollars. Education Next 2(3):30–35.

Helmreich, Stefan. 1998. Silicon Second Nature: Culturing Artificial Life in a Digital World. Berkeley: University of California Press.

Herman, Ken. 2003. Vanishing at Capitol: The White Democrats: As GOP Burgeons, Opposition Members Tend to Be Minorities. Austin American-Statesman. March 1. http://www.lexisnexis.com/universe. Accessed June 2, 2004.

Herrnstein, Richard J., and Charles Murray. 1994. The Bell Curve: Intelligence and Class Structure in American Life. New York: Free Press.

Higham, Scott, and Robert O'Harrow Jr. 2005. Contracting Rush for Security Led to Waste, Abuse. Washington Post. May 22: A01.

Hinds, Michael deCourcy. 2002. 2002 Carnegie Challenge: Teaching as a Clinical Profession: A New Challenge for Education. New York: Carnegie Corporation of New York. http://www.carnegie.org/pdf/teachered.pdf. Accessed November 21, 2004.

Houston Chronicle. 1999. Austin ISD Indicted in TAAS Probe: Official, System Accused of Manipulating Test Data. Houston Chronicle. April 7. http://www.lexisnexis.com/universe. Accessed May 5, 2002.

———. 2003a. State Budget Process: Wake Us from the Nightmare. Houston Chronicle. March 3. http://www.lexisnexis.com/universe. Accessed March 9, 2004.

———. 2003b. Rating TAKS: State Mustn't Waver in Reaching Accountability Goals. Houston Chronicle. April 18: A36.

Hubbard, Ruth. 1990. The Politics of Women's Biology. New Brunswick, NJ: Rutgers University Press.

Huff, Darrell. 1993 [1954]. How to Lie with Statistics. Irving Geis, illus. New York: W. W. Norton.

Hughes, Shannon, and Jason Bailey. 2002. What Students Think about High-Stakes Testing. Educational Leadership 59(4):74–76.

Jackson, Robena Estelle. 1979. East Austin: A Socio-Historical View of a Segregated Community. Thesis, University of Texas, Austin.

Johnson, Charles S., and Horace Mann Bond. 1934. The Investigation of Racial Differences Prior to 1910. Journal of Negro Education 3(3):328–339.

Johnson, Roy. 2003. Schools Continue to Lose Students: Texas Public School Attrition Study, 2002-2003. IDRA Newsletter. October 2003. San Antonio: Intercultural Development Research Association. http://www.idra.org/IDRA_Newsletter/October_2003_Self_Renewing_Schools_Holding_Power/Schools_Continue_to_Lose_Students/. Accessed November 28, 2008.

Johnston, Hank. 2002. Verification and Proof in Frame and Discourse Analysis. In Methods of Social Movement Research. Bert Klandermans and Suzanne Staggenborg, eds., pp. 62–91. Minneapolis: University of Minnesota Press.

Jones, James. 1993. The Tuskegee Syphilis Experiment: "A Moral Astigmaticsm." In The Racial Economy of Science: Toward a Democratic Future. S. Harding, ed., pp. 275–286. Bloomington: Indiana University Press.

Joyce, Matt. 2003. Opponents of New Statewide Testing Rally at Capitol. Associated Press. http://www.substancenews.com/Feb03/testrally.htm. Accessed November 17, 2004.

Kamin, Leon J. 1974. The Science and Politics of I.Q. Potomac, MD: L. Erlbaum Associates.

Kaplan, Caren, Norma Alarcón, and Minoo Moallem. 1999. Introduction: Between Woman and Nation. In Between Woman and Nation. Caren

Kaplan, Norma Alarcón, and Minoo Moallem, eds., pp. 1–16. Durham, NC: Duke University Press.

Kaplan, Caren, and Inderpal Grewal. 1999. Transnational Feminist Cultural Studies: Beyond the Marxism/Postructrialism/Feminism Divides. In Between Woman and Nation. Caren Kaplan, Norma Alarcón, and Minoo Moallem, eds., pp. 349–363. Durham, NC: Duke University Press.

Kauffman, Albert H., Nina Perales, and Leticia Saucedo (MALDEF). 1999. Plaintiffs' Post-Trial Brief in GI Forum et al. v. Texas Education Agency et al., No. Civ A, SA-97-CA1278-EP, 2000 WL 222268 (W.D. Tex. January 7, 2000).

Keller, Ellen Fox. 1992. Secrets of Life, Secrets of Death: Essays on Language, Gender, and Science. New York: Routledge.

Kelley, Robin D. G. 1997. Yo Mama's Dysfunktional! Fighting the Culture Wars in Urban America. Boston: Beacon Press.

———. 2002. Freedom Dreams: The Black Radical Imagination. Boston: Beacon Press.

Kennedy, Edward M. 2007. The Chairman's Report on the Conflicts of Interest Found in the Implementation of the Reading First Program at the Three Regional Technical Assistance Centers. U.S. Senate Health, Education, Labor, and Pensions Committee. http://kennedy.senate.gov/newsroom/press_release.cfm?id=3cc1e674-cb51-42c2-a4f9-90395a0dc291. Accessed January 22, 2008.

King, Toni C., Lenora Barnes-Wright, Nancy E. Gibson, Lakesia D. Johnson, Valerie Lee, Betty M. Lovelace, Sonya Turner, and Durene I. Wheeler. 2002. Andrea's Third Shift: The Invisible Work of African-American Women in Higher Education. In This Bridge We Call Home: Radical Visions for Transformation. Gloria E. Anzaldúa and Analouise Keating, eds., pp. 403–415. New York: Routledge.

Kluger, Richard. 1975. Simple Justice: The History of Brown v. Board of Education and Black America's Struggle for Equality. New York: Vintage Books.

Kolker, Claudia. 1999. Texas Offers Hard Lessons on School Accountability: Education: Cheating Alleged after Job Security Is Linked to Test Scores. Los Angeles Times. April 14. http://www.lexisnexis.com/universe. Accessed May 5, 2002.

Kozol, Jonathan. 1991. Savage Inequalities: Children in America's Schools. New York: Harper Perennial.

Kramer, Benjamin. 2002. Fear and Accountability in the Schools. http://interversity.org/lists/arn-l/archives/Sep2002_date/msg00993.html. Accessed September 29, 2002.

Kritzman, Lawrence. 1988. Foucault and the Politics of Experience. In Michel Foucault: Politics Philosophy Culture: Interviews and Other Writings. Lawrence Kritzman, ed., Alan Sheridan and others, trans., pp. ix–xxv. New York: Routledge.

Kuhn, Thomas. 1996 [1962]. The Structure of Scientific Revolutions. Chicago: University of Chicago Press.

Kuhr, Nancy. 1971. Segregated Public Schools in Texas, 1876–1940. Master's thesis, University of Texas at Austin.

Laclau, Ernesto, and Chantal Mouffe. 1985. Hegemony and Socialist Strategy: Towards a Radical Democratic Politics. Winston Moore and Paul Cammack, trans. London: Verso.

Latour, Bruno. 1987. Science in Action: How to Follow Scientists and Engineers through Society. Cambridge, MA: Harvard University Press.

Leacock, Eleanor, ed. 1971. The Culture of Poverty: A Critique. New York: Simon and Schuster.

Lemann, Nicholas. 1999. The Big Test: The Secret History of the American Meritocracy. New York: Farrar, Straus and Giroux.

Lewin, Tamar, and Jennifer Medina. 2003. To Cut Failure Rate, Schools Shed Students. New York Times. July 31. http://www.nytimes.com/2003/07/31/nyregion/31PUSH.html?th=?pagewanted=print&positio. Accessed August 3, 2003.

Lewis, Diane. 1973. Anthropology and Colonialism. Current Anthropology 14(5):581–591.

Lewis, Oscar. 1965. The Culture of Poverty. Scientific American 215:19–25.

Lipman, Pauline. 2004. High Stakes Education: Inequality, Globalization, and Urban School Reform. New York: RoutledgeFarmer.

Lipsitz, George. 1998. Possessive Investment in Whiteness: How White People Profit from Identity Politics. Philadelphia: Temple University Press.

Lorde, Audre. 1984. Sister Outsider. Trumansburg, NY: Crossing Press.

Los Angeles Times. 2003. Times' Exit Poll Results. Los Angeles Times. October 9: A26. http://a1022.g.akamai.net/f/1022/8158/5m/images.latimes.com/media/acrobat/2003-10/9730777.pdf. Accessed September 6, 2004.

Lowe, Lisa. 1996. Immigrant Acts: On Asian American Cultural Politics. Durham, NC: Duke University Press.

MacKenzie, Donald A. 1981. Statistics in Britain, 1865–1930: The Social Construction of Scientific Knowledge. Edinburgh: Edinburgh University Press.

MacKinnon, Catharine A. 1995 [1982]. Feminism, Marxism, Method, and the State: An Agenda for Theory. Signs 7(3):515–544. Reprinted in Feminist Legal Theory I: Foundations and Outlooks, Frances Olsen, ed., pp. 53–82. New York: New York University Press.

MacLeod, Jay. 1995. Ain't No Making It: Aspirations and Attainment in a Low-Income Neighborhood. Boulder, CO: Westview Press.

Maher, Bill. 2003. Leave No Child Behind Means Make 'Em Vanish. http://interversity.org/lists/arn-l/archives/Aug2003/msg00150.html. Accessed November 17, 2004.

Maher, Frinde. 2002. The Attack on Teacher Education and Teachers. Radical Teacher 64:5–8.

Maldonado, Julie Rae. 2003. Comment: TAKS' Takeover Makes School a Lot Easier. San Antonio Express-News. March 24. http://news.mysanantonio.com/story.cfm?xla=saen&xlb=130&xlc=968028&xld=130. Accessed June 20, 2003.

Mansbridge, Jane J. 1986. Why We Lost the ERA. Chicago: University of Chicago Press.

Marable, Manning. 1991. Race, Reform, and Rebellion: The Second Reconstruction in Black America, 1945–1990. 2nd Edition. Jackson: University Press of Mississippi.

Marcus, George E. 1998 [1994]. On Ideologies of Reflexivity in Contemporary Efforts to Remake the Human Science. In Ethnography through Thick and Thin. George Marcus, ed., 181–202. Princeton, NJ: Princeton University Press.

Marcus, George E., and Dick Cushman. 1982. Ethnographies as Texts. Annual Review of Anthropology 11:25–69.

Marcus, George E., and Michael Fischer. 1986. Anthropology as Cultural Critique: An Experimental Moment in the Human Sciences. Chicago: University of Chicago Press.

Margonis, Frank. 1992. The Cooptation of "At Risk": Paradoxes of Policy Criticism. Teachers College Record 94(2):343–364.

Marshall, James D. 1999. The Mode of Information and Education: Insights on Critical Theory from Michel Foucault. In Critical Theories in Education. T. S. Popkewitz and L. Fendler, eds. New York: Routledge.

Martin, Rosalee. 2001. Interview with Ruth Davis Sauls. May 16. Parallel and Crossover Lives: Texas before and after Desegregation, an Oral History Project of the Texas Council for the Humanities. http://www.public-humanities.org/crossoversite/NEW%20HTML/HTHTML%20plus%20Bios/Sauls.html. Accessed April 1, 2002.

Martinez, Michelle. 2002. Schools Rally Their Students to Take TAAS: Austin Officials Hope Incentives Boost Poor Attendance Records. Austin American-Statesman. February 18: B1.

———. 2003. As TAKS Debuts, a Student Will Pass: San Antonio Teen Protesting Emphasis on Standardized Test. Austin American-Statesman. February 25. http://www.austin360.com/statesman/editions/tuesday/metro_state_2.html. Accessed February 25, 2003.

Martinez, Michelle, and Erik Rodriguez. 2003. Many 10th-Graders on Way to Flunking, Test Data Show. Austin American-Statesman. June 5. http://www.statesman.com/metrostate/content/metro/schools/0605taks.html. Accessed July 30, 2003.

Marx, Karl. 1978 [1844]. Alienation and Social Classes. In The Marx-Engels Reader. 2nd Edition. Robert C. Tucker, ed. New York: W. W. Norton.

Massey, Douglas, and Nancy Denton. 1993. American Apartheid: Segregation and the Making of the Underclass. Cambridge, MA: Harvard University Press.

McArthur, Judith N. 1998. Creating the New Woman: The Rise of Southern Women's Progressive Culture in Texas, 1893–1918. Urbana: University of Illinois Press.

McClaurin, Irma. 2001. Theorizing a Black Feminist Self in Anthropology: Toward an Autoethnographic Approach. In Black Feminist Anthropology:

Theory, Politics, Praxis, and Poetics. Irma McClaurin, ed., pp. 49–76. New Brunswick, NJ: Rutgers University Press.

McDermott, Raymond P. 1997. Achieving School Failure 1972–1997. In Education and Cultural Process: Anthropological Approaches. G. D. Spindler, ed., pp. 110–135. Prospect Heights, IL: Waveland Press.

McDonald, Jim. 2002. Area Map for Austin, TX. http://www.jimmac.com/areamap.cfm. Accessed April 23, 2002.

McNay, Lois. 1992. Foucault and Feminism: Power, Gender, and the Self. Boston: Northeastern University Press.

———. 1994. Foucault: A Critical Introduction. Cambridge: Polity Press.

McNeil, Linda. 2000a. Contradictions of School Reform: Educational Costs of Standardized Testing. New York: Routledge.

———. 2000b. Sameness, Bureaucracy, and the Myth of Educational Equity: The TAAS System of Testing in Texas Public Schools. Hispanic Journal of Behavioral Sciences 22(4):508–523.

McNeil, Linda, and Angela Valenzuela. 2001. Harmful Impact of the TAAS System of Teaching in Texas: Beneath the Accountability Rhetoric. In Raising Standards or Raising Barriers? Inequality and High-Stakes Testing in Public Education. Gary Orfield and Mindy Kornhaber, eds., pp. 127–150. New York: Century Foundation Press.

Menchaca, Martha. 1997. Early Racist Discourses: The Roots of Deficit Thinking. In The Evolution of Deficit Thinking: Educational Thought and Practice. Richard Valencia, ed., pp. 13–40. Washington, DC: Falmer Press.

———. 2001. Recovering History, Constructing Race: The Indian, Black, and White Roots of Mexican Americans. Austin: University of Texas Press.

Metcalf, Stephen. 2001. Numbers Racket: W. and the Uses of Testing. New Republic 224(7):21–24.

———. 2002. Reading between the Lines. The Nation. January 28: 18–22.

Miles, Robert. 1993. Apropos the Idea of 'Race' . . . Again. In Race after Race Relations. R. Miles, ed. New York: Routledge.

Miller, Lamar P. 1974. Introduction. In The Testing of Black Students: A Symposium. Lamar P Miller, ed. Englewood Cliffs, NJ: Prentice-Hall.

Miller, Lamar P., ed. 1974. The Testing of Black Students: A Symposium. Englewood Cliffs, NJ: Prentice-Hall.

Miller, Peter, and Ted O'Leary. 1987. Accounting and the Construction of the Governable Person. Accounting, Organization, and Society 12(3):235–265.

Miranda, Debra. 2002. What's Wrong with a Little Fantasy? Storytelling from the (Still) Ivory Tower. In This Bridge We Call Home: Radical Visions for Transformation. Gloria E. Anzaldúa and Analouise Keating, eds., pp. 192–202. New York: Routledge.

Mohanram, Radhika. 1999. Black Body: Women, Colonialism, and Space. Minneapolis: University of Minnesota Press.

Mohanty, Chandra Talpade. 1992. Feminist Encounters: Locating the Politics of Experience. In Destabilizing Theory: Contemporary Feminist Debates.

Michèle Barrett and Anne Phillips, eds., pp. 74–92. Stanford, CA: Stanford University Press.

Montejano, David. 1986. Anglos and Mexicans in the Making of Texas, 1836–1986. Austin: University of Texas Press.

Moraga, Cherríe. 1983. Preface. In This Bridge Called My Back: Writings by Radical Women of Color. 2nd Edition. Cherríe Moraga and Gloria Anzaldúa, eds., pp. xiii–xix. New York: Kitchen Table, Women of Color Press.

Moraga, Cherríe, and Gloria Anzaldúa, eds. 1983. This Bridge Called My Back: Writings by Radical Women of Color. 2nd Edition. New York: Kitchen Table, Women of Color Press.

Morantz, Alison. 1996. Desegregation at Risk: Threat and Reaffirmation in Charlotte. In Dismantling Desegregation: The Quiet Reversal of Brown v. Board of Education. Gary Orfield and Susan Eaton, eds., 179–206. New York: The New Press.

Morrow, Raymond Allan, and Carlos Alberto Torres. 1995. Social Theory and Education: Critique of Theories of Social and Cultural Reproduction. Albany: State University of New York Press.

Moses, Robert P., and Charles E. Cobb. 2001. Radical Equations: Math Literacy and Civil Rights. Boston: Beacon Press.

Mouffe, Chantal. 1979. Hegemony and Ideology in Gramsci. In Gramsci and Marxist Theory. Chantal Mouffe, ed., pp. 168–204. London: Routledge and Kegan Paul.

Moynihan, Daniel P. 1965. The Negro Family: The Case for National Action. Washington, DC: Office of Planning and Research, U.S. Department of Labor.

Mulinari, Diana, and Kerstin Sandell. 1999. Exploring the Notion of Experience in Feminist Thought. Acta Sociologica 42(4):287–297.

Mulvenon, Sean, Charles E. Stegman, and Gary Ritter. 2005. Test-Anxiety: A Multifaceted Study on the Perceptions of Teachers, Principals, Counselors, Students, and Parents. International Journal of Testing 5(1):37–61.

Murphy, Dean E. 2003. Affirmative Action Foe's Latest Aim Complicates California Recall Vote. New York Times. August 3. http://www.lexisnexis.com/universe. Accessed August 8, 2003.

Nader, Laura. 1972. Up the Anthropologist—Perspectives Gained from Studying Up. In Reinventing Anthropology. Dell H. Hymes, ed., pp. 284–311. New York: Pantheon Books.

Nairn, Allan. 1980. The Reign of ETS: The Corporation That Makes Up Minds: Ralph Nader Report on the Educational Testing Service.

National Council of Teachers of Mathematics. 2000. Letter to Senator Wellstone Expresses Support for "Fairness and Accuracy in Student Testing Act." http://www.nctm.org/news/speaksout/wellstone.htm. Accessed April 9, 2003.

Newman, Gwen. 1987. The Select Committee on Public Education. Master's thesis. University of Texas, Austin.

Nichols, Sharon, and David C. Berliner. 2005. The Inevitable Corruption of Indicators and Educators through High-Stakes Testing. Tempe, AZ: Education Policy Studies Laboratory, Arizona State University. http://www.asu .edu/epsl/EPRU/documents/EPSL-0503-101.EPRU.pdf. Accessed March 22, 2005.

Nobles, Melissa. 2000. Shades of Citizenship: Race and the Census in Modern Politics. Stanford, CA: Stanford University Press.

Oakes, Jeannie. 1985. Keeping Track: How Schools Structure Inequality. New Haven, CT: Yale University Press.

———. 2003. Schools Find No Help in Carrots and Sticks: The Vaunted Policy Has Led to Numbers, Trickery, and Scandals, Not Better Education. August 8. http://www.latimes.com/news/printedition/opinion/la-oe-oake s8aug08,1,945484.story?coll=la-news-comment. Accessed August 19, 2003.

Olivo, Dora. 2003. Children's Stories—The Impact of High Stakes Testing. http://www.doraolivo.com/childrenstories.html. Accessed July 30, 2003.

Omi, Michael, and Howard Winant. 1994. Racial Formation in the United States: From the 1960s to the 1990s. 2nd Edition. New York: Routledge.

Orfield, Gary. 1996. Plessy Parallels: Back to Traditional Assumptions. In Dismantling Desegregation: The Quiet Reversal of Brown v. Board of Education. G. Orfield and S. Eaton, eds., 23–52. New York: The New Press.

Orfield, Gary, and Mindy Kornhaber, eds. 2001. Raising Standards or Raising Barriers? Inequality and High-Stakes Testing in Public Education. New York: Century Foundation Press.

Orwell, George. 1984 [1949]. 1984: A Novel. New York: Signet Classic.

Padilla, Amado M., ed. 2000. Special Issue (GI Forum et al. v. Texas Education Agency et al.). Hispanic Journal of Behavioral Sciences 22(4).

Palast, Greg. 2004. The New Educational Eugenics in George Bush's State of the Union. http://www.gregpalast.com/detail.cfm?artid=310.

Palmaffy, Tyce. 1998. The Gold Star State. Policy Review. March–April. 88(30):9.

Peabody, Zanto. 2003a. Nervous Kids, Schools Face TAKS This Week: Thousands Expected to Fail New Exam. Houston Chronicle. February 23. http://www.chron.com/cs/CDA/story.hts/front/1791684. Accessed February 25, 2003.

———. 2003b. Sharpstown Numbers Game Shows Flaw in School Reform. Houston Chronicle. July 5. http://www.chron.com/cs/CDA/story.hts/met ropolitan/1980843. Accessed July 8, 2003.

Peabody, Zanto, Julie Mason, and Alan Bernstein. 2003. Paige's Methods at HISD Reassessed; Acclaim for His Improvements Is Tempered by Criticism That Pressure Fostered Abuse. Houston Chronicle. August 3: Al. http://www.lexisnexis.com/universe. Accessed March 9, 2004.

Pearson. 2002a. Our History. http://www.pearson.com/aboutus/history.htm. Accessed July 13, 2002.

———. 2002b. Pearson Education. http://www.pearson.com/aboutus/pearson /index.htm. Accessed July 13, 2002.

Pepper, Margot. 2006. No Corporation Left Behind: How a Century of Illegitimate Testing Has Been Used to Justify Internal Colonialism. Monthly Review: An Independent Socialist Magazine 58(6):38–48.

Pérez, Laura Elisa. 1999. El Desorden, Nationalism, and Chicana/o Aesthetics. In Between Woman and Nation. Caren Kaplan, Norma Alarcón, and Minoo Moallem, eds., pp. 19–46. Durham, NC: Duke University Press.

Persuad, Randolph B., and Clarence Lusane. 2000. The New Economy, Globalization and the Impact on African Americans. Race and Class 42(1):21–34.

Peters, John D. 1997. Seeing Bifocally: Media, Place, and Culture. In Culture, Power, Place: Explorations in Critical Anthropology. Akhil Gupta and James Ferguson, eds., pp. 75–92. Durham, NC: Duke University Press.

Peterson, David, and Forrest Wilder. 2002. Test Tube Kids: Why Is the University of Texas Pushing a Charter School in East Austin? Texas Observer. December 20, 94(23):4. http://www.texasobserver.org/showArticle.asp?ArticleID=1213. Accessed January 10, 2003.

Popkewitz, Thomas S. 1999. A Social Epistemology of Educational Research. In Critical Theories in Education. T. S. Popkewitz and L. Fendler, eds. New York: Routledge.

———. 2000. The Denial of Change in Educational Change: Systems of Ideas in the Construction of National Policy and Evaluation. Educational Researcher 29(1):17–29.

Porter, Theodore. 1986. The Rise of Statistical Thinking, 1820–1900. Princeton, NJ: Princeton University Press.

———. 1995. Trust in Numbers: The Pursuit of Objectivity in Science and Public Life. Princeton, NJ: Princeton University Press.

———. 2002. Statistical Utopianism in an Age of Aristocratic Efficiency. Osiris (annual), pp. 210–227.

Procacci, Giovanna. 1991. Social Economy and the Government of Poverty. In The Foucault Effect: Studies in Governmentality. Graham Burchell, Colin Gordon, and Peter Miller, eds., pp. 151–168. Chicago: University of Chicago Press.

Public Agenda, Phi Delta Kappan / Gallup, Business Roundtable, American Association of School Administrators, Harris Interactive. 2000. National Surveys about High-Stakes Testing. http://www.ecs.org/clearinghouse/16/21/1621.htm. Accessed March 27, 2003.

Public Education Integrity Taskforce. 2001. A Report to Comptroller Carole Keeton Rylander. Austin: Texas Comptroller of Public Accounts. http://www.window.state.tx.us/tspr/peitf/index.htm. Accessed April 4, 2005.

Pugmire, Tim. 2002. Settlement Reached in Test Score Lawsuit. Minnesota Public Radio News. November 12. http://news.minnesota.publicradio.org/features/200211/25_pugmiret_testsettle/. Accessed November 17, 2004.

Pyle, Emily. 2005. Test Market: High-Stakes Tests Aren't Good for Students, Teachers, or Schools. So Who Are They Good For? Texas Observer. May

13. http://www.texasobserver.org/article.php?aid=1947. Accessed January 8, 2008.

Rabinow, Paul, ed. 1984. The Foucault Reader. New York: Pantheon.

Raffel, Jeffrey A. 1998. Historical Dictionary of School Segregation and Desegregation: The American Experience. Westport, CT: Greenwood Press.

Rather, Dan. 2004. The Texas Miracle; Texas Schools Cooking the Books? CBS. 60 Minutes II. January 7.

Reyes, Augustina. 2001. Alternative Education: The Criminalization of Student Behavior. Fordham Urban Law Journal 29:539–559.

Richards, Craig, Rima Shore, and Max Sawicky. 1996. Risky Business: Private Management of Public Schools. Washington, DC: Economic Policy Institute.

Roberts, Dorothy. 1997. Killing the Black Body: Race, Reproduction, and the Meaning of Liberty. New York: Vintage Books.

Robinson, Cedric. 2000 [1983]. Black Marxism: The Making of the Black Radical Tradition. Chapel Hill: University of North Carolina Press.

Robison, Clay, and R. G. Ratcliffe. 2003. Session Will Make Legislative History: GOP to Gain Full Control of Capitol. Houston Chronicle. January 12: A1. http://www.lexisnexis.com/universe. Accessed June 2, 2004.

Rodriguez, Daniel B., and Barry R. Weingast. 2003. The Positive Political Theory of Legislative History: New Perspectives on the 1964 Civil Rights Act and Its Interpretation. University of Pennsylvania Law Review 151(4):1417–1515.

Rosaldo, Renato. 1976. The Story of Tukbaw: "They Listen as He Orates." In The Biographical Process: Stories in the History and Psychology of Religion. Frank Reynolds and Donald Capps, eds., pp. 145, 147–48. The Hauge: Mouton.

Rosales, Rodolfo. 2000. The Illusion of Inclusion: The Untold Political Story of San Antonio. Austin: University of Texas Press.

Rose, Hilary, and Steven Rose, eds. 1976. The Political Economy of Science: Ideology of/in the Natural Sciences. New York: Holes and Meier; London: Macmillan.

Rothschild, Emma. 1995. Social Security and Laissez Faire in Eighteenth Century Political Economy. Population and Development Review 21(4):711(34).

Rouse, Joseph. 1992. What Are Cultural Studies of Scientific Knowledge? Configurations 1:1–22.

———. 1995. Questions of Identity: Personhood and Collectivity in Transnational Migration to the United States. Critique of Anthropology 15(4):351–380.

Rubin, Joe, writer and director. 2007. Nice Work If You Can Get It. Educational Broadcasting Corporation. PBS. August 10, 2007.

Russett, Cynthis Eagle. 1989. Sexual Science: The Victorian Construction of Womanhood. Cambridge, MA: Harvard University Press.

Sacks, Peter. 1999. Standardized Minds: The High Price of America's Testing Culture and What We Can Do to Change It. Cambridge: Perseus Publishing.

Said, Edward W. 1989. Representing the Colonized: Anthropology's Interlocutors. Critical Inquiry. 15(2):205–225.

Saldívar-Hull, Sonia. 1999. Introduction to the Second Edition. In Borderlands: La Frontera: The New Mestiza. 2nd Edition. Gloria Anzaldua, ed., pp. 1–15. San Francisco: Aunt Lute Books.

———. 2000. Feminism on the Border: Chicana Gender Politics and Literature. Berkeley: University of California Press.

Salinas, Cinthia S., and Michelle Reidel. 2007. The Cultural Politics of the Texas Educational Reform Agenda: Examining Who Gets What, When, and How. Anthropology and Education Quarterly 38(1):42–56.

Saltman, Kenneth J. 2000. Collateral Damage: Corporatizing Public Schools—A Threat to Democracy. Lanham: Rowman and Littlefield Publishers.

Sandoval, Chela. 2000. Methodology of the Oppressed. Vol. 18. Minneapolis: University of Minnesota Press.

San Miguel, Guadalupe, Jr. 1987. "Let All of Them Take Heed": Mexican Americans and the Campaign for Educational Equality in Texas, 1910–1981. Austin: University of Texas Press.

San Miguel, Guadalupe, Jr., and Richard Valencia. 1998. From the Treaty of Guadalupe Hidalgo to Hopwood: The Educational Struggle of Mexican Americans in the Southwest. Harvard Educational Review 68:353–412.

Saucedo, Leticia. 2000. The Legal Issues Surrounding the TAAS Case. Hispanic Journal of Behavioral Sciences 22(4):411–422.

Scheper-Hughes, Nancy. 1995. The Primacy of the Ethical: Positions for a Militant Anthropology. Current Anthropology 36(3):409–440.

Schmidt, George N. 2002. Teachers Say "No!" to CASE: 12 Curie H.S. Teachers to Refuse to Give CASE Tests. Substance (October). http://www.substancenews.com/Oct02/caseno.htm. Accessed November 17, 2004.

Schmidt, Sarah. 2002. Texas: Miracle or Mirage? http://interversity.org/lists/arn-l/archives/Nov2002/msg00598.html. Accessed November 21, 2002.

Scott, Joan. 1991. The Evidence of Experience. Critical Inquiry. 17(4):773–797.

Seltzer, William, and Margo Anderson. 2001. The Dark Side of Numbers: The Role of Population Data Systems in Human Rights Abuses. Social Research 68(2), 481(33).

Shabazz, Amilcar. 1999. Expert Report of Amilcar Shabazz. Plaintiff's Expert Witness Testimony (Exhibit P56) in GI Forum et al. v. Texas Education Agency et al., No. Civ A, SA-97-CA1278-EP, 2000 WL 222268 (W.D. Tex. January 7, 2000).

Shapiro, Martin M. 1998. Declaration of Martin M. Shapiro. Plaintiff's Expert Witness Testimony in GI Forum et al. v. Texas Education Agency et al., No. Civ A, SA-97-CA1278-EP, 2000 WL 222268 (W.D. Tex. January 7, 2000).

Shaw, Donna. 2000. The Move against High-Stakes Testing. Curriculum Administrator 36(7):38–42, 45.

Shewhart, Walter. 1986 [1939]. Statistical Method from the Viewpoint of Quality Control. New York: Dover Publications.

Silko, Leslie Marmon. 1992 [1991]. Almanac of the Dead: A Novel. New York: Penguin Books.

Silva, Denise Ferreira da. 2001. Towards a Critique of the Socio-logos of Justice: The Analytics of Raciality and the Production of Universality. Social Identities 7(3): 421–454.

Simon, Roger. 1991 [1982]. Gramsci's Political Thought: An Introduction. London: Lawrence and Wishart.

Skrla, Linda, James Scheurich, and Joseph Johnson. 2000. Equity-Driven Achievement-Focused School Districts: A Report on Systematic School Success in Four Texas School Districts Serving Diverse Populations. Austin: Charles A. Dana Center, University of Texas, Austin.

Smith, Barbara. 1998. Truth That Never Hurts: Writings on Race, Gender, and Freedom. New Brunswick, NJ: Rutgers University Press.

Spindler, George D., ed. 1997. Education and Cultural Process: Anthropological Approaches. Prospect Heights, IL: Waveland Press.

Spivak, Gayatri. 1988. Can the Subaltern Speak? In Marxism and the Interpretation of Culture. Cary Nelson and Lawrence Grossberg, eds., pp. 271–313. Urbana: University of Illinois Press.

Spivey, Donald. 1978. Schooling for the New Slavery: Black Industrial Education, 1868–1915. Westport, CT: Greenwood Press.

Stahl, Lesley. 2002. The Gender Gap: Boys Lagging. CBS. 60 Minutes. October 20.

Stepan, Nancy Leys, and Sander Gilman. 1993. Appropriating the Idioms of Science: The Rejection of Scientific Racism. In The Racial Economy of Science: Toward a Democratic Future. S. Harding, ed., pp. 170–193. Bloomington: Indiana University Press.

Stigler, Stephen M. 1986. The History of Statistics: The Measurement of Uncertainty before 1900. Cambridge, MA: Belknap Press of Harvard University Press.

Stocking, George, Jr. 1993. The Turn-of-the-Century Concept of Race. Modernism/modernity 1(1):4–16.

Stoler, Ann Laura. 1995. Race and the Education of Desire: Foucault's History of Sexuality and the Colonial Order of Things. Durham, NC: Duke University Press.

Stone-Mediatore, Shari. 1998. Chandra Mohanty and the Revaluing of "Experience." Hypatia 13(2):116–133.

Sturm, Susan, and Lani Guinier. 1996. The Future of Affirmative Action: Reclaiming the Innovative Ideal. California Law Review 84(4):953–1036. http://www.lexisnexis.com/universe. Accessed June 22, 2003.

Sudbury, Julia. 1998. "Other Kinds of Dreams": Black Women's Organizations and the Politics of Transformation. London: Routledge.

Suen, Hoi K. and Joseph L. French. 2003. A History of the Development of Psychological and Educational Testing. In Handbook of Psychological and Educational Assessment of Children: Intelligence, Aptitude, and Achievement. Cecil Reynolds and Randy Kamphaus, eds., pp. 3–23. New York: Guilford Press.

Sugrue, Thomas. 1996. The Origins of the Urban Crisis: Race and Inequality in Postwar Detroit. Princeton, NJ: Princeton University Press.

Suydam, Jim. 2002. State Education Chief Suggests Lower Passing Rates at First. Austin American-Statesman. November 9. http://www.lexisnexis.com/universe. November 19, 2002.

Takaki, Ronald. 1979. Iron Cages: Race and Culture in 19th-Century America. New York: Oxford University Press.

Tapper, Melbourne. 1999. In the Blood: Sickle Cell Anemia and the Politics of Race. Philadelphia: University of Pennsylvania Press.

Taylor, Frederick Winslow. 1967 [1947]. The Principles of Scientific Management. New York: W. W. Norton.

Taylor, Quintard. 1998. In Search of a Racial Frontier: African Americans in the American West, 1528–1990. New York: W. W. Norton.

Taylor, Steve. 2003. Things Get Hellish over Riddle's Remarks: Legislature: Caucus Defends Social Services after Lawmakers Criticism. Brownsville Herald. March 13. http://www.lexisnexis.com/universe. Accessed April 29, 2004.

Texas Education Agency (TEA). 2001a. 2001 Comprehensive Report. http://www.tea.state.tx.us/research/pdfs/2001comp/funds.pdf. Accessed March 1, 2003.

———. 2001b. 2001 District TAAS Participation Report: 2000 & 2001 TAAS Participation Profile for All Students (Grades 3–8, & 10): Austin ISD. http://www.tea.state.tx.us/perfreport/aeis/2001/part/district.srch.html. Accessed November 2008.

———. 2001c. 2001 Campus Participation Reports: 2000 & 2001 TAAS Participation Profile for All Students (Grades 3–8, & 10): Anderson HS; Austin HS; Bowie HS; Crockett; Johnson HS; Johnston HS; Lanier HS; McCallum HS; Reagan HS; Travis HS. http://www.tea.state.tx.us/ perfreport/aeis/2001/part/campus.srch.html. Accessed October 25, 2002.

———. 2002a. Texas Assessment of Knowledge and Skills (TAKS) Standard Setting: Summary of Projected Impact of Possible Standards—Estimate Numbers and Percentages of Students. http://www.tea.state.tx.us/student.assessment/taks/standards/attachment7.pdf. Accessed December 4, 2002.

———. 2002b. Texas School Districts: Austin ISD Data. wysiwyg://3/http://penick.tea.state.tx.us/SchoolDistrictLocator/ISD/austin.asp. Accessed April 21, 2002.

———. 2003a. TEA Contracts and Purchase Orders $100,000 or More. http://www.tea.state.tx.us/tea/FY02-03_100K_web.html. Accessed February 13, 2003.

———. 2003b. Texas Assessment of Knowledge and Skills: Met Standard and Commended Performance Results, All Students, Spring 2003, Grade 3

(English) Reading March Administration. http://www.tea.state.tx.us/stu dent.assessment/reporting/results/swresults/taks/2003/g3r_march.pdf. Accessed July 30, 2003.

———. 2003c. Texas Assessment of Knowledge and Skills: Met Standard and Commended Performance Results, All Students, Spring 2003, Grade 3 (English) Reading Retest April Administration. http://www.tea.state.tx.us/ student.assessment/reporting/results/swresults/taks/2003/g3r_april.pdf. Accessed July 30, 2003.

———. 2003d. Texas Assessment of Knowledge and Skills: Met Standard and Commended Performance Results, All Students, Spring 2003, Grade 3 (English) Reading Retest July Administration. http://www.tea.state.tx.us/ student.assessment/reporting/results/swresults/taks/2003/g3r_july.pdf. Accessed July 30, 2003.

———. 2003e. Texas Assessment of Knowledge and Skills: Met Standard and Commended Performance Results, All Students, Spring 2003, Grade 3 (Spanish) Reading March Administration. http://www.tea.state.tx.us/stu dent.assessment/reporting/results/swresults/taks/2003/g3rsp_march.pdf. Accessed July 30, 2003.

———. 2003f. Texas Assessment of Knowledge and Skills: Met Standard and Commended Performance Results, All Students, Spring 2003, Grade 3 (Spanish) Reading Retest April Administration. http://www.tea.state.tx.us/ student.assessment/reporting/results/swresults/taks/2003/g3rsp_april.pdf. Accessed July 30, 2003.

———. 2003g. Texas Assessment of Knowledge and Skills: Met Standard and Commended Performance Results, All Students, Spring 2003, Grade 3 (Spanish) Reading Retest July Administration. http://www.tea.state.tx.us/ student.assessment/reporting/results/swresults/taks/2003/g3rsp_july.pdf. Accessed July 30, 2003.

———. 2003h. Texas Assessment of Knowledge and Skills: Met Standard and Commended Performance Results, All Students, Spring 2003, Grade 10. http://www.tea.state.tx.us/student.assessment/reporting/results/swresults/ taks/2003/g10.pdf. Accessed July 30, 2003.

———. 2003i. Texas Assessment of Knowledge and Skills: Met Standard and Commended Performance Results, All Students, Spring 2003, Grade 11. http://www.tea.state.tx.us/student.assessment/reporting/results/swresults/ taks/2003/g11.pdf. Accessed July 30, 2003.

———. 2007. FY 2007 TEA Contracts and Purchase Orders $100,000 or More. http://www.tea.state.tx.us/tea/100K_contracts.html. Accessed April 19, 2007.

Texas Education Agency, Department of Accountability Reporting and Research. 2001. 2001 Accountability Manual: The 2001 Accountability Rating System for Texas Public Schools and School Districts and Blueprint for the 2002 through 2005 Accountability Systems. http://www.tea .state.tx.us/perfreport/account/2001/manual/. Accessed February 12, 2008.

———. 2002. 2002 Accountability Manual: The 2002 Accountability Rating System for Texas Public Schools and School Districts. http://www.tea.state.tx.us/perfreport/account/2002/manual/index.html. Accessed February 12, 2008.

Texas Education Agency, Division of Performance Reporting. 2003. Academic Excellence Indicator System: 2002–03 State Performance Report. http://www.tea.state.tx.us/perfreport/aeis/2003/state.html. Accessed November 17, 2004.

Texas Education Agency, Student Assessment Division. 2000. Texas Student Assessment Program Technical Digest for the Academic Year 1990–2000.

Texas NAACP. 1997. TAAS Resolution Commitment. http://www.texasnaacp.org/taasrc.htm. Accessed September 13, 2004.

Texas Observer. 2003. Kids Fail, Polluters Pass. February 28. 95(4):12. http://www.texasobserver.org/showArticle.asp?ArticleID=1272. Accessed November 17, 2004.

Texas Public Education Reform Foundation (TPERF). 2002a. Texans Say Education Is the Most Important Issue for the Legislature to Address in 2003. Paper presented at a legislative briefing. Austin, TX. March 19, 2003.

———. 2002b. Statewide Texas Education Survey. Paper presented at a legislative briefing. Austin, TX. March 19, 2003.

Texas State Teachers Association (TSTA). 2002. TSTA News Releases. http://www.tsta.org/news/Public%20Relations/sept_2002.shtml. Accessed March 27, 2003.

Thomas, William B. 1982. Black Intellectuals' Critique of Early Mental Testing: A Little-Known Saga of the 1920s. American Journal of Education 90: 258–292.

Torres, McNelly. 2003. Student Rebels at Taking Standardized Test. San Antonio Express-News. February 1:4B. http://www.lexisnexis.com/universe. Accessed November 17, 2004.

Townsend, Brenda. 2002. "Testing While Black": Standards-Based School Reform and African American Learners. Remedial and Special Education 23(4): 222–230.

Traweek, Sharon. 1993. An Introduction to Cultural and Social Studies of Sciences and Technologies. Culture, Medicine, and Psychiatry 17:3–25.

Trinh, T. Minh-ha. 1989. Woman, Native, Other: Writing Postcoloniality and Feminism. Bloomington: Indiana University Press.

Trouillot, Michel-Rolph. 1995. An Unthinkable History: The Haitian Revolution as a Non-event. In M.-R. Trouillot, Silencing the Past: Power and the Production of History. pp.70–107. Boston: Beacon Press.

———. 2001. The Anthropology of the State in the Age of Globalization: Close Encounters of the Deceptive Kind. Current Anthropology 42(1):125–138.

Trujillo, Armando. 1998. Chicano Empowerment and Bilingual Education: Movimiento Politics in Crystal City, TX. New York: Garland Publishing.

Urla, Jacqueline. 1993. Cultural Politics in an Age of Statistics: Numbers, Nations, and the Making of Basque Identity. American Ethnologist 20:818–43.

Valencia, Richard, ed. 1997. The Evolution of Deficit Thinking. Washington, DC: Falmer Press.

Valencia, R. R., and I. N. Guadarrama. 1996. High-Stakes Testing and Its Impact on Social and Ethnic Minority Students. In Multicultural Assessment: Clinical, Psychological and Educational Applications. Lisa Suzuki, Paul Meller, and Joseph Ponterotto, eds., pp. 561–610. San Francisco: Jossey-Bass.

Valencia, Richard, and Daniel G. Solórzano. 1997. Contemporary Deficit Thinking. In The Evolution of Deficit Thinking. Richard Valencia, ed., pp. 160–210. Washington, DC: Falmer Press.

Valencia, Richard, Angela Valenzuela, Kris Sloan, and Douglas E. Foley. 2001. At Odds: The Texas Accountability System—Let's Treat the Cause, Not the Symptoms: Equity and Accountability in Texas Revisited. Phi Delta Kappan 83(4):318–326.

Valenzuela, Angela. 1999. Subtractive Schooling: US-Mexican Youth and the Politics of Caring. Albany: State University of New York Press.

———. 2002. High-Stakes Testing and U.S.-Mexican Youth in Texas: The Case for Multiple Compensatory Criteria in Assessment. Harvard Journal of Hispanic Policy 14:97–116.

Vaughan, Megan. 1991. Curing Their Ills: Colonial Power and African Illness. Cambridge: Polity/Stanford University Press.

Velleman, Paul F. 2001. Statistical Graphics: Mapping the Pathways of Science. Annual Review of Psychology 52(1):305–335.

Veninga, James F. 1984. Texas: The End of Laissez Faire Education. http://www.humanities-interactive.org/texas/annexation/laissez_faire.htm. Accessed November 21, 2002.

Visweswaran, Kamala. 1994. Fictions of Feminist Ethnography. Minneapolis: University of Minnesota Press.

Walker, Alice. 1983. In Search of Our Mothers' Gardens: Womanist Prose. San Diego: Harcourt Brace & Company.

Walker, Bruce, Judy Ashcroft, Larry Carver, Patrick Davis, Lodis Rhodes, Gerald Torres, and Gary Lavergne. 2002. A Review of the Use of Standardized Test Scores in the Undergraduate Admissions Process at the University of Texas at Austin: A Report to President Larry Faulkner. http://www.utexas.edu/student/research/reports/admissions/taskforce.htm. Accessed April 8, 2003.

Walt, Kathy. 1998. Non-readers Shouldn't Go to 4th Grade: Poll: Majority Agree with Bush's Position. Houston Chronicle. March 9: A13. http://www.chron.com/cgi-bin/auth/story.mpl/content/chronicle/metropolitan/98/03/09/schools.2-0.html. Accessed March 27, 2003.

Ward, Cynthia. 1997. Toward Cantankerous Community: A Review of The Rooster's Egg: On the Persistence of Prejudice, by Patricia J. Williams.

William and Mary Journal of Women and the Law 3:249. http://www.lexis nexis.com/universe. Accessed April 7, 2004.

Ward, Kenric. 2003. Graduation Gaps, "Pushouts" and Prayer for Dearing. Press Journal (Vero Beach, FL). August 10. http://www.lexisnexis.com/ universe. Accessed March 9, 2004.

Washington Times. 2003. Standardizing Unfairness. Washington Times. August 6: A16.

Washington, Valora. 1979. Do Desegregation+Competency Testing=Equity +Quality? Educational Leadership 36(5):325–326.

Wasserman, Selma. 2001. Quantum Theory, the Uncertainty Principle, and the Alchemy of Standardized Testing. Phi Delta Kappan 83(1):28–40.

Wat, Eric C. 2003. High Stakes: Black and Latino Parents Are Demanding Better Schools and Fewer Tests. The Black Commentator 24. January 9 (reprint). http://www.blackcommentator.com/24/24_re_print.html. Accessed January 10, 2003.

Wells-Barnett, Ida B. 1970. Crusade for Justice: The Autobiography of Ida B. Wells. Alfreda M. Duster, ed. Chicago: University of Chicago Press.

———. 1991 [1895]. A Red Record: Tabulated Statistics and Alleged Causes of Lynchings in the United States, 1892–1893–1894. In Selected Works of Ida B. Wells-Barnett. Trudier Harris, ed., pp. 138–252. New York: Oxford University Press.

Wellstone, Paul D. 2000. High Stakes Test: A Harsh Agenda for America's Children. Remarks at Teacher's College, Columbia University, March 31. http://www.educationrevolution.org/paulwellstone.html. Accessed April 9, 2003.

Werner, Anna. 2003. Are Employees Encouraged to Lie about Dropouts? http://www.khou.com/news/defenders/investigate/khou030210_gs_defendersHISDdropouts.40a29. Accessed February 11, 2003.

White, Lee Wayne. 1974. Popular Education and the State Superintendent of Public Instruction in Texas, 1860–1899. PhD dissertation, University of Texas at Austin.

Whitford, Betty Lou, and Ken Jones. 2000. Accountability, Assessment, and Teacher Commitment: Lessons from Kentucky's Reform Efforts. Albany: State University of New York Press.

Williams, Raymond. 1977. Marxism and Literature. Oxford: Oxford University Press

Willis, Paul. 1981 [1977]. Learning to Labor: How Working Class Kids Get Working Class Jobs. New York: Columbia University Press.

Willis, William S. 1969. Skeletons in the Anthropological Closet. In Reinventing Anthropology. D. Hymes, ed., pp. 121–151. New York.

Wilson, Anna Victoria, and William E. Segall. 2001. Oh, Do I Remember! Experiences of Teachers during the Desegregation of Austin's Schools, 1964–1971. Albany: State University of New York Press.

Wilson, William J. 1987. The Truly Disadvantaged. Chicago: University of Chicago Press.

Winegarten, Ruthe. 1995. Black Texas Women: 150 Years of Trial and Tri-
    umph. Janet G. Humphrey and Frieda Werden, Consulting Editors. Aus-
    tin: University of Texas Press.
Wolfe, Margery. 1992. Thrice-Told Tale: Feminism, Postmodernism, and Eth-
    nographic Responsibility. Stanford, CA: Stanford University Press.
Wong, Kenneth and Anna Nicotera. 2004. *Brown v. Board of Education* and
    the Coleman Report: Social Science Research and the Debate on Educa-
    tional Equity. Peabody Journal of Education 79(2):122–135.
Woodward, Kathleen. 1999. Statistical Panic. Differences: A Journal of Femi-
    nist Cultural Studies 11(2):177–203.
Woolf, Stuart. 1989. Statistics and the Modern State. Comparative Studies in
    Society and History 31(3):588–604.
Wrigley, Terry. 2004. "School Effectiveness": The Problem of Reductionism.
    British Educational Research Journal 30(2):227–244.
Wyatt, Tommy. 1979. Rappin': Black America, How Soon We Forget. Villager
    7(30):1.

# Index

**Amanda Walker Johnson** is Assistant Professor of Anthropology at the University of Massachusetts Amherst.